CITIZEN CANINE

TEN ESSENTIAL SKILLS
EVERY WELL-MANNERED
DOG SHOULD KNOW

Mary R. Burch, PhD

AN OFFICIAL PUBLICATION OF THE AMERICAN KENNEL CLUB

Andrew DePrisco, Editorial Director
Amy Deputato, Senior Editor
Jamie Quirk, Editor
Jerome Callens, Art Director
Karen Julian, Publishing Coordinator

Photographs by Sheri Berliner, Mary Bloom, Mary Burch, Cioli & Hunnicutt/BowTie Studio, Isabelle Francais, James Leatherberry, and Robert Young.

A very special thanks to photographers Mary Bloom and James Leatherberry, who provided most of the photographs for this book. Their photos of the test in action brought the Canine Good Citizen Program to life.

Library of Congress Cataloging-in-Publication Data

Citizen canine / by the American Kennel Club.
    p. cm.
Includes index.
ISBN 978-1-59378-644-1
1. Dogs--Training. I. American Kennel Club.
SF431.C495 2009
636.7'0887--dc22

2009028847

ENVIRONMENTAL BENEFITS STATEMENT

AKC and Kennel Club Books saved the following resources by printing the pages of this book on chlorine free paper made with 10% post-consumer waste.

TREES	WATER	SOLID WASTE	GREENHOUSE GASES
6 FULLY GROWN	2,612 GALLONS	159 POUNDS	542 POUNDS

Calculations based on research by Environmental Defense and the Paper Task Force. Manufactured at Friesens Corporation

Kennel Club Books
A Division of BowTie, Inc.
40 Broad Street
Freehold, NJ 07728

Printed and bound in Canada
17 16 15 14 13 12 11 10   2 3 4 5 6 7 8 9 10

ACKNOWLEDGMENTS

Citizen Canine: Ten Essential Skills Every Well-Mannered Dog Should Know is the definitive guide to the American Kennel Club's Canine Good Citizen (CGC) Program. This book provides how-to tips for teaching each of the ten skills, and all of the techniques suggested are based on sound behavioral principles. The Special Applications chapter presents exciting, never-before-seen information from unique CGC programs that are considered national models. Additional information on the background of the CGC Program, the Responsible Dog Owner's Pledge, and what you can do with your dog before and after CGC makes this book relevant for every single person who owns a dog or cares about the well-being of the canines we love.

Mary R. Burch, PhD, is the Director of the American Kennel Club's Canine Good Citizen and AKC S.T.A.R. Puppy Programs. Dr. Burch is an award-winning dog writer and author of ten books, including *Volunteering with Your Pet, The Border Collie,* and *How Dogs Learn.* Dr. Burch has trained dogs to the advanced levels of obedience, and she is a Certified Applied Animal Behaviorist and a Board Certified Behavior Analyst (the human end of the leash). She is a frequent consultant in radio, television, and print media.

Dennis B. Sprung is the President and CEO of the American Kennel Club. He has been responsible for many other AKC books and publications, including *AKC Dog Care and Training.* Involved in the sport of dogs for more than forty years, Mr. Sprung has been a dog owner, exhibitor, breeder, judge, AKC Delegate, and president of an all-breed club. Mr. Sprung has traveled to dog events worldwide, and he routinely interacts with internationally recognized experts on timely dog-related topics.

We would like to recognize the following AKC staff members who reviewed information related to their subject-matter expertise:

Noreen Baxter	Mary Donnelly	Meghan Lyons	Robin Stansell
Laura Bullock	Michael Liosis	Heather McManus	Daphna Straus
Curt Curtis	Doug Ljundgren	Mari-Beth O'Neill	
Gina DiNardo	John Lyons	Tom Sharp	

We would like to especially thank Demond Hunt and Sharon Wilson for the extraordinary work they do for the AKC Canine Good Citizen and AKC S.T.A.R. Puppy Programs.

TABLE OF CONTENTS

THE NEED
FOR CANINE
GOOD CITIZENS

With 73 million dogs in America living in 69 million households, man's best friend is more popular than ever. Currently, an astounding $43 billion are spent every year on canine toys, supplies, treats, and training books, attesting to the fact that dog owners love their dogs and want what's best for them. But despite a proliferation of written guides and a steady stream of information about dogs in the popular media, there are some problems with dog ownership in our country. Why?

More and more people have taken on the responsibility of dog ownership, but, lacking time and understanding about their dog's needs, not all dog owners are raising well-behaved canine companions. Problems ranging from nuisance barking to attacks against children have many communities responding with restrictive laws and deep concern. "No Dogs Allowed" signs abound in privately owned businesses and residential areas. People with poorly trained dogs, those they come in contact with, and the dogs themselves are suffering.

he American Kennel Club Canine Good Citizen (CGC) Program is the answer to the pressing question of how to ensure that all dogs are well-behaved, welcome members of any community. Not just another training guide, this is the first and only book to provide a prescriptive approach and a detailed curriculum based on sound behavioral principles for obtaining the Canine Good Citizen award from the American Kennel Club (AKC). The AKC, the nation's leading authority on dogs in our country for more than 125 years, developed the Canine Good Citizen Program as the gold standard of training for every dog in America, regardless of age or breed. Whether you decide to earn the CGC certificate or not, this book will provide you with the foundation you need to be a responsible dog owner, and it will show you how to teach your dog the skills he needs to be a well-mannered pet.

Never before has there been such a critical need for the AKC Canine Good Citizen Program or for a simple-to-use, informative book that prepares dogs to earn the Canine Good Citizen award.

In the 1950s, families across America sat in front of their black-and-white televisions to watch Lassie, the nation's image of the ideal dog. This wonderful, beautiful Collie would instantly come when called, jump through a window on command, and instinctively find the little boy who was lost. Viewers were impressed with the concept of a well-trained dog, and during these *Leave It to Beaver* years dogs came to be thought of as family members.

However, by the 1980s, problems caused by irresponsible dog owners had dramatically changed and damaged the reputation of man's best friend. As a result of the graphic media coverage of several maulings and deaths caused by dogs, 1980s America found itself in the midst of what the popular press described as "pit bull hysteria." The coverage of pit bull attacks lent an unnecessary stigma to all larger, muscular dogs. Many emotionally charged articles and television spots neglected to mention that these horrible incidents were not the dogs' fault and that any bad feelings should be targeted at the dogs' owners. In the 1980s, an increasing number of state and local governments passed legislation that placed restrictions on dog ownership. Since the year 2000, these restrictions have continued to increase in a growing number of municipalities. For example, in some plac-

es, there are limits on the number of dogs per household as well as all-out bans on dogs in certain housing and recreational areas. Specific breeds have been outlawed from entire cities or counties, and, as a result, families have been forced to find other homes for their pets, sometimes being given only days to do so.

THE AKC CGC TEST is an evaluation of the basic skills that every dog should know. The ten test items are:

1 Accepting a friendly stranger

2 Sitting politely for petting

3 Appearance and grooming

4 Out for a walk

5 Walking through a crowd

6 *Sit* and *down* on command/ staying in place

7 Coming when called

8 Reaction to another dog

9 Reaction to distractions

10 Supervised separation

Long aware of the need to protect the rights of people who love their dogs, the AKC implemented the CGC Program in 1989 with the goal of promoting responsible dog ownership and recognizing dogs for good behavior both at home and in the community. Several versions of the evaluation were field-tested with hundreds of dogs before the CGC Program was implemented at the national level. In its current format, the CGC award shows a commitment to responsible dog ownership, and passing the ten-item CGC Test means that a dog is under basic instructional control, can respond to simple commands while on leash, and, most important, is reliable in the presence of people and other animals.

These are the skills that should be part of every dog's basic education. In addition to having owners teach their dogs basic good manners, the comprehensive AKC CGC Program also educates owners about the responsibilities of ownership so that they can enjoy their dogs to the fullest.

The AKC CGC Program is a noncompetitive program open to all dogs, purebreds and mixed breeds alike. The heart of the CGC Program is the AKC CGC Test, which assesses the ability of a dog to be a well-behaved member of the community. The CGC certificate that is earned by passing the test proves the owner's commitment to having a well-mannered dog.

There are an increasing number of benefits for those who have earned the CGC award. For example, in some locations, CGC dogs gain access to dog parks and hiking trails, and certain apartment buildings and condominiums require that dogs have their CGC certificates before their owners are permitted to move in with them. Several of this country's largest service and therapy-dog organizations require dogs to pass the CGC Test as a prerequisite for therapy-dog work.

Many 4-H groups have added CGC as the curriculum for beginning dog training. And as of 2009, forty states and the United States Senate have passed Canine Good Citizen resolutions, showing that our nation's legislators support the AKC CGC Program as a means of increasing responsible dog ownership and ensuring well-mannered dogs remain welcome in our communities.

This book will help you teach your dog each of the ten CGC skills. You'll learn the exercises, how to teach them, how to practice at home, and special considerations for teaching each skill. Scenarios illustrate the importance of each of the CGC test items, and behavioral concepts are explained so that you understand the reasoning behind the recommendations.

There are many training philosophies and effective methods for training dogs. In this book, we describe an approach based on positive reinforcement. In "Finding CGC Training and Testing Near You," you'll learn how to find the trainer who best meets the needs of you and your dog.

The shaded sections that begin each chapter are the actual test items as described in the *AKC Canine Good Citizen Evaluator Guide*.

▲A well-trained dog will show good manners when someone approaches and speaks to the handler.

CGC TEST ITEM 1 ACCEPTING A FRIENDLY STRANGER

This test demonstrates that the dog will allow a friendly stranger to approach him and speak to the handler in a natural, everyday situation.

The Evaluator walks up to the dog and handler and greets the handler in a friendly manner, ignoring the dog. The test begins with the dog seated at the handler's side.

The Evaluator and handler shake hands and exchange pleasantries (e.g., "Hello, it's good to see you again," as they shake hands). In this test, the Evaluator does not interact with the dog.

- The dog must show no sign of resentment, aggression, or shyness.
- The dog may not jump on or rush to the Evaluator to initiate contact. The dog may not lunge forward to greet the Evaluator.
- The dog should be under control throughout the exercise. If the handler must use excessive corrections (e.g., trying to hold the dog to prevent jumping) to control the dog, the dog should not pass the exercise.

W e've all met them when we're out in public—those happy, friendly, exuberant dogs who jump on us to say hello. We approach to greet the owner of such a dog, and within seconds we're being pounced on and receiving a heartfelt, slurpy, wet kiss from a spirited, furry bundle of joy. For those of us who love dogs, there are times when delightful canine kisses are welcome and we're happy to receive them. But sometimes, such as when we're enjoying a quiet walk or wearing business clothes, being jumped on by a frisky dog without an invitation may not be a good thing.

But never mind the business clothes. Some people are flat-out afraid of dogs. When an overzealous 60-pound canine-greeting-committee-of-one lunges and appears to be out of control, these individuals find themselves feeling fearful and uncomfortable even though the dog is offering a well-intended, convivial greeting. In nursing homes and other therapy settings, dogs who give greetings that are so enthusiastic that a person can be knocked down or scratched are not suitable as canine "therapists" until further training has been provided.

Is it ever acceptable for a dog to jump up on a person to say hello, jump into someone's lap, or rush up to someone in excitement? It might be, but the key here is whether or not the dog has been invited to initiate physical contact with the "friendly stranger." Remember that being a responsible dog owner means that your dog never infringes on the rights of another person. Even a friendly dog should not jump up on a person you meet on the street or into someone's lap without an invitation.

▶ **In CGC Test Item 1, Accepting a Friendly Stranger, the Evaluator interacts with the handler. Interacting with the dog comes in later exercises.**

When you and your dog meet someone in public, being overly excited to see the person is not the only problematic thing that a dog can do. Some dogs are at the opposite end of affability. These are the extremely shy dogs that may hide behind their owners when a stranger approaches, pull away from an unfamiliar person, or in some cases urinate inappropriately.

Meeting a friendly stranger in a calm, collected manner is a skill that every dog needs in order to be well regarded by people other than his owner. Meeting new people falls into the category of socialization. *Socialization means learning to interact with others in a manner that is acceptable.* Dogs need to be socialized to deal with people outside of their families as well as with other dogs. Socializing your dog is one of the most important things you can do as a responsible owner. Socialization activities can begin when the dog is a puppy and should continue throughout his life.

The "friendly stranger" in the AKC CGC Test is someone who simulates a person you might meet when you and your dog are out for a walk. In this test item, when the Evaluator approaches, you will say hello, shake hands, and have a brief interaction. The friendly stranger in a CGC Test is a person who does not live in the dog's household, is not an instructor who has been handling the dog every week in class, and is not a canine professional or relative who knows the dog very well.

▲ Small dogs benefit from Canine Good Citizen training. Without socialization, small dogs can develop a fear of new people and situations.

In this segment of the test, the point of the exercise is for the dog to behave acceptably when his owner meets and interacts briefly with a stranger. This exercise does not involve the stranger's talking to or petting the dog; this will happen in subsequent exercises.

Why Socialization Is Important

Adequate socialization is the key to owning a dog that is happy, well adjusted, and eager to meet new people. Dogs that are well socialized are friendly and biddable (easily controlled). They create the impression to others that they are safe animals with reliable, predictable behavior. Dogs that are good citizens demonstrate impeccable canine manners. These are dogs that accept friendly strangers and are welcome members of the community.

In addition to being well mannered and well liked, there is another important reason for every dog to have CGC skills. These days, dog owners are losing their rights because some owners are not responsible. Breed-specific legislation (BSL) has been proposed or passed in a number of states. BSL is legislation that targets certain breeds. When a law is proposed that says no more dogs of a specific breed can live in a particular city, this is an example of BSL. In BSL, a breed is targeted as a whole, with no regard for the good behavior or advanced training of individual dogs within the breed. This type of legislation restricts the rights of dog owners and, in most cases, targets specific medium to large breeds. Because the perception of many people is that large dogs can be dangerous, it is critical that dog owners teach their dogs to meet people in a controlled manner. It is the deed that matters, not the breed.

Small dogs also need socialization. Socializing small dogs teaches them useful skills, such as how to walk on leash and how to interact with people and other animals. The adequate socialization of toy breeds results in dogs that are confident and unafraid of the world around them.

Getting to Know You: When Does Socialization Begin?

Socialization means interacting with (or socializing with) others. Socialization is also a broader concept that involves exposing dogs to people, places, situations, sounds, other dogs, and other species that may be in the dog's life, such as cats, birds, or horses. Properly socializing your dog means providing continuing exposure to the world so that your dog becomes self-assured and unafraid of new experiences.

In a newborn litter, the very first socialization a puppy will receive will be from his dam (mother) and littermates. As a matter of fact, there is actually a period of time when the puppy is still in his litter that is referred to as the *socialization period*.

In the first two weeks of life, puppies spend about 90 percent of their time sleeping. In these early days, before they even open their eyes, sweet little neonatal puppies will turn to Mom and littermates to keep warm. In a normal litter, the third week of life is marked by the puppies' opening their eyes, tottering around on legs that are unsteady, and beginning to interact with their littermates by chewing on their ears and crawling over them.

When the puppies are three to twelve weeks old, the socialization period is taking place. This is when puppies begin to develop social relationships with the people and other dogs (their dam and littermates) in their lives. When puppies have no exposure to human contact during the socialization period, it will be difficult for them to adjust to people as they get older. They become dogs that may have a difficult time bonding with humans and they may be difficult to train. It is absolutely possible to train dogs that had a bad start in life, but there may be some additional challenges along the way.

Similarly, if puppies are for some reason separated from the litter at a very young age, it may be hard for them when they get older to develop appropriate relationships with other dogs. These puppies may grow up to be either extremely fearful of other dogs or pushy and dominant because they've never been taught to relate to members of their own species.

One of the most important lessons a puppy learns from his dam and siblings is *bite inhibition*. Bite inhibition is when a dog intentionally controls the intensity of a bite. In the litter, when a puppy is nursing, if he bites the dam too hard, she will nip him or stand up and walk away, teaching a valuable lesson by leaving—and taking breakfast with her. The puppy soon learns that he needs to control himself and that biting hard is not OK.

When puppies in a litter are playing their rough-and-tumble games, sometimes a puppy will get carried away and bite a sibling just a little too hard. The sibling might jump up and yelp. He may leave the game or may growl, snap, or bark as if to say, "Don't do that! That hurts!" The puppy learns that if he wants the fun game with his littermate to continue, he cannot bite too hard.

Responsible breeders start providing socialization activities for puppies as young as two weeks old. Breeders will hold and massage puppies and provide other gentle stimulation, such as playing music and introducing new sounds. As the pups get a little older, friends are invited to visit and hold the puppies so that, from the time they are very young, the puppies are accustomed to meeting people. By the time a puppy comes to your home, a responsible breeder will have taken that puppy for rides in the car and on trips to the veterinarian's office. The puppy will have been exposed to a crate, and a house-training schedule will have been implemented.

Socialization at Home

So you've adopted a puppy or an older dog and you've brought him home. Now what? If you got a rescue dog, a dog from a shelter, or a dog that had a rough start in life, your dog needs socialization at home and in the community. If he came from a responsible breeder who did everything right until the day you took the dog home, your dog still needs socialization at home and in the community. Socialization is not something that should be addressed for a short time and then stopped. If you are a responsible owner, socializing your dog will be an ongoing activity that occurs as a natural part of everyday living.

To make sure that dogs continue to have good relationships with people and other animals, the first step you should take is to build a bond with your new companion through play and activities. Daily puppy playtime for dogs of all ages has tremendous value. In puppy playtime, you continue the activities of the litter. Structured daily play will be an activity that your dog will look forward to throughout his life.

Is Your Dog Well Socialized?

Some dogs are mellow. Their behavior and temperament are such that from the time they were puppies, they were calm when meeting new people. Some owners who attend CGC classes are lucky in that, on the very first night, before any instruction at all, their dogs can naturally pass the Accepting a Friendly Stranger CGC test item. If you happen to be an owner with an extremely mellow dog that meets new people in a cool, collected way, you can focus on teaching other new skills. Remember, though, that socialization should be an ongoing part of every dog's education, and your courteous canine will always benefit from a chance to meet new people.

SAMPLE PUPPY PLAYTIME GAMES
(FOR DOGS AND PEOPLE OF ALL AGES)

- Sit on the floor and cuddle or hug your dog.
- Give your dog a massage.
- Play games with your dog, using his favorite toys.
- Touch your dog's feet and ears in between pets and massage.
- Throw a toy and encourage your dog to retrieve ("Get it!").

When dogs have a problem with meeting new people, it usually involves one of two situations: either the dog is overexuberant or the dog is extremely shy. Both of these problems can be addressed with training and exposure to new people. Before starting CGC training, you can check to see if your dog needs training on accepting a stranger. Take your dog (or puppy) for a walk in your neighborhood or at a local park. When someone approaches, allow the person to come over and pet the dog. What does your dog do when an unfamiliar person approaches and speaks to you? If your dog stands calmly and is under control while being petted, you're one step ahead of the game.

Does the dog try to jump on the stranger, pull away, hide behind you, or lunge at the stranger in excitement? If you see any of these behaviors, you'll need to do some training. Accepting a friendly stranger will allow your dog and you to confidently meet anyone in public and have a pleasant and enjoyable experience.

▼ In the Accepting a Friendly Stranger CGC test item, the dog will begin the exercise by sitting as the "stranger" approaches.
◄ The dog may remain sitting, but it is natural for dogs who are beginning their training to stand when someone approaches. This is acceptable in the CGC Test.

Different Personalities

Exuberant Dogs

The exuberant dog is one that has a very high activity level. This is the extremely ener-getic, high-spirited dog. This type of buoyant, effervescent dog is a joy to own after he has learned some manners. Before learning CGC manners, he may bounce and spin, pulling his owner toward any unfamiliar person who is approaching. Exuberant dogs can be easily overstimulated; however, one trick to working with these dogs is to very systematically expose them to new people, situations, and other animals.

For the CGC Test, you're going to teach your dog to sit (see Test Item 2) while the "friendly stranger" approaches and shakes your hand. For dogs that need work on socialization, in addition to teaching skills such as *sit* at home or in a class, you'll want to take your dog on regular "field trips" in the community. These outings will give you and your dog plenty of opportunities to meet new people.

Shy Dogs

When it comes to accepting a friendly stranger, shy dogs may need some training and experience in order to pass this CGC test item. As with dogs that are exuberant, shaping behaviors slowly works well with shy dogs. Shy dogs can be gradually de-sensitized to new people who approach and greet their owners. When working with a dog that is shy or fearful, it is important that you don't give the dog a lot of attention for being shy. Each time an unfamiliar person approaches to say hello, if you coddle and give a great deal of attention to the trembling dog by saying, "There, there, you're all right," you'll soon have a dog that is fearful with everyone.

Small Dogs

There's an unfortunate trend for movie stars and celebrities to carry toy breeds every-where they go. Some celebrities dress their dogs in clothes that match their own outfits. Toy breeds (along with other small breeds and small mixed-breed dogs) aren't fashion accessories. Toy breeds aren't babies. Toy breeds don't need lives in which their feet are never permitted to touch the ground. All dogs, including those who are pint-sized, deserve to have the training and socialization provided by the AKC CGC Program.

If you meet or see on television a toy-breed dog that appears to quiver and shake when a new person approaches, chances are you're looking at a dog that has not been trained or adequately socialized. Signs of distress in a small dog will include a submissive lifting of the paw, trembling, or attempting to pull away from the person who is greeting his owner. If you've ever seen this happen, and this is your impression of small dogs, don't let them fool you.

The toy breeds may be small in size, but when well trained and properly socialized, they are confident dogs with huge personalities. All you have to do is attend AKC events to see well-socialized small dogs in action, succeeding at obedience, excelling in agility, and doing well in the fun sport of AKC Rally. Every weekend, in CGC tests across the country, toy breeds pass fair and square, holding their own among the larger breeds that are typically known to do well in training activities.

And don't forget the wonderful socialization opportunities provided to small dogs that participate in conformation. Conformation shows are bustling, crowded events. While toy breeds entered in conformation may be carried by their handlers to the ring to keep their coats clean for showing, these are dogs that will confidently strut on a leash (just watch them in the ring) in the very distracting setting of a dog show. They accept many friendly strangersin the form of judges.

What about toy breeds and smaller dogs that come from shelters and do not participate in conformation? The most likely shelter dogs to get adopted are small dogs and puppies. Shelters may wish to be particularly selective about toy-breed and small-dog adoptions, selecting homes that will provide training and socialization opportunities for these remarkable little dogs.

Baby Steps: Using Systematic Desensitization to Teach New Behaviors

The behavioral procedure in which you systematically expose a dog to new situations is called *systematic desensitization*. Systematic desensitization involves using a hierarchy that ranges from the least to the most problematic situations. For example, if your dog is afraid of wheelchairs, you could bring him into a room in which a wheelchair is sitting in the corner. Eventually, you could move the dog closer to the wheelchair. Then, you could have the dog walk close to the unmoving wheelchair and, finally, have the chair wheeled toward your dog.

To use systematic desensitization to teach acceptance of a friendly stranger, you can manipulate several of the behavior's components (including the distance your dog is from the new person, meeting a familiar versus an unfamiliar person, the length of time a person interacts with you, and meeting a person who is low-key versus one who is very animated). In all CGC exercises and training, the dog is on a leash.

Above and Beyond Accepting a Friendly Stranger

When your dog can perform all of the exercises mentioned on the next two pages (meaning that he sits calmly while you are greeted by an unfamiliar person), you can practice exercises that are more difficult. CGC Test Items 2, 3, 4, 5, 8, and 9 expand on the Accepting a Friendly Stranger test item by having the dog tolerate petting and handling, walking on a leash and through a crowd of people, and reacting appropriately in the presence of other dogs and distractions. Once your dog has mastered accepting a friendly stranger, you're on your way to earning the AKC CGC award.

PREPARING FOR CGC

You can begin training in the comfort of your own living room or backyard, but a dog with CGC skills is one that is well socialized and has the manners for community living, so you'll eventually want to do some training in public settings. You can "graduate" from the living room to the street in front of your house, then to walking around the block, then to going to a nearby park, and eventually to training in active areas such as a dog club, a public park, or a pet-supply store.

Using this book, you can prepare for the CGC Test on your own, but attending a CGC or basic training class is always an excellent idea. In classes with other dogs and people, you have access to assistance and additional training tips as well as to helpers (who can be your friendly strangers) and distraction dogs. In cases where you have a dog that is afraid of men or children, attending a class will provide your dog with opportunities to interact with them. If you decide to attend a training class, ideally you should find one designed specifically for teaching AKC CGC skills. However, if such a class is not available in your area, a basic obedience training class can teach many of the elements of CGC. Be sure to tell the instructor of a basic class that passing the AKC CGC Test is your goal.

1 Take your dog for a walk in a local park, at a pet-supply store, or somewhere else where you will encounter other people. Have your dog sit at your left side as a person walks by, about 15 feet away. Can your dog do this without becoming overly excited?

EXERCISES
FOR ACCEPTING A FRIENDLY STRANGER: PLACES TO GO & PEOPLE TO MEET

2 If the dog will sit at your side while someone passes 15 feet away from you, have the dog sit at your side while someone passes 10 feet away. If the dog is excitable and jumps out of the *sit* or attempts to pull you toward the person, increase the distance. You can also practice sitting by giving your dog reminders, such as "Sit . . . sit, good dog," and rewarding with food if you are using food rewards.

3 When the dog will sit at your side as someone passes 10 feet away, you're ready to repeat these steps with someone 5 feet away.

4 When your dog will sit and watch a person pass at a distance of 5 feet away, do the exercise again. This time, speak to the person, saying something brief, such as "Nice day out here, isn't it?" or "Isn't this a great place to bring dogs?" Watch how your dog responds. If he behaves acceptably when you speak to someone who is 5 feet away, you're ready for the next step.

5 At this point, you may need a helper. You can ask a friend, neighbor, or someone in your training class to help you with this. Instruct the helper to stand about 15 feet away from you and your dog and wait for you to signal that he should approach. With your dog at your left side, get the dog to sit and then give the signal for your helper to approach. The helper should say something like, "Hi, how are you?" and reach out to shake your hand. In this exercise, the helper does not speak to or touch the dog. You answer, and the helper walks away.

If the dog tries to jump on the person, you should prompt the dog to sit and reward the sitting behavior. For some dogs, this exercise could require several days of practice in which the helper begins at 15 feet away and then stops at 5 feet away to verbally greet you and your dog. If a shy dog tries to hide behind you during this exercise, do not pick the dog up and hold him in your arms.

6 Continue to practice this exercise. Vary the helpers or unfamiliar people who approach to greet you. Make sure that your dog experiences you being greeted by an adult male, an adult female, and a child.

7 In addition to varying the people who will approach and act as friendly strangers (i.e., male, female, younger, older), you should have your helpers vary the style in which they interact with you. Initially, a helper can greet you with very flat affect. A bored-sounding, quiet voice will not frighten a dog that is wary of strangers. As your dog successfully meets people and shows the ability to be under control and unafraid, you can have the helper approach with greetings that are increasingly animated. An excited-sounding friendly stranger can rush up and say in a louder voice, "HEY, HOW YA DOIN'?" The ability to respond to people who behave like this is required for a dog that is steady in the community. This skill is also a requirement for therapy dogs, who may encounter a variety of people in therapy settings who speak loudly or move quickly.

▲ **It is always a pleasure to greet a dog who is friendly and under good control.**

8 As your dog becomes steady when an unfamiliar person approaches and briefly exchanges pleasantries with you (e.g., "Hi, how are you? Nice to see you."), extend the length of time from a brief verbal exchange to a conversation.

9 Remember that socialization means exposure to new things as well as to new people. When you're on walks or outings, give your dog a chance to walk on different surfaces, such as grass, concrete, and slick floors. Encourage your dog to jump over low obstacles on a trail and to walk with you on a sidewalk (on leash, of course) near busy traffic.

10 In the preceding exercises, you can have the stranger give your dog a treat. This will help your dog learn that good things come from interacting nicely with other people. 🐾

▲ So that dogs remain well-respected members of our communities, every dog should be calm and non-threatening when meeting people.

CGC TEST ITEM 2 — SITTING POLITELY FOR PETTING

This test demonstrates that the dog will allow a friendly stranger to touch him while he is out with his handler. With the dog sitting at the handler's side (either side is permissible) to begin the test, the Evaluator approaches and asks, "May I pet your dog?" The Evaluator then pets the dog on the head and body. The handler may talk to his or her dog throughout the exercise.

After petting the dog, the Evaluator may circle the dog, or simply back away to begin the next test.

- The dog must show no signs of shyness or resentment.
- As the Evaluator begins to pet the dog, the dog may stand to receive petting.
- The dog may not struggle and pull away to avoid petting.
- The dog may move slightly forward to receive petting, but should not lunge at the Evaluator or rush or jump forward.
- The dog may appear to be happy about the contact with the Evaluator and may have some body movements.
- The dog should appear to be under control throughout the exercise.

I t's a crisp, clear fall day, and there's no better way to celebrate one of nature's most perfect gifts than taking your dog to a local park for a peaceful, long walk on the trails. Off you go, just you and your new dog. The exhilaration that comes from an experience like this is the reason that many people decide to add four-legged friends to their households. You're relishing the cool breeze, and your dog is having great fun on his end of the leash, sniffing the trail and enjoying the scenery. Within minutes, people begin passing you on the trail.

With the CGC award as a goal, you've been working on teaching your dog how to accept friendly strangers (CGC Test Item 1), so when strangers pass and say hello, your dog behaves beautifully. Sooner or later, though, you're going to learn a secret about dogs. The secret is that dogs and puppies are proven people magnets, and the dog lovers in this world are plentiful. When dog lovers see a dog, they want to touch, hug, ask questions about, and interact with this wonderful canine creature.

For the dog that is just beginning CGC training, strangers passing by, saying hello, and commenting on the gorgeous weather is one thing. However, having an enthusiastic dog lover stop to pet, embrace, and make a fuss over your dog is another story. With some untrained dogs (as well as those who are just beginning training), once the petting from a stranger begins, they turn into wiggling, spinning, jumping, giddy bundles of silliness. Some dogs may roll over when the petting begins, and a very active dog may jump on the unsuspecting person. These behaviors can be signs of an enthusiastic or excited dog; the dog that rolls over to expose his belly may be submissive or shy. Training is needed to correct any of these less-than-perfect greeting behaviors, and Item 2 (Sitting Politely for Petting) of the CGC Test is precisely where this training is evaluated.

Many dogs lose control when they are introduced to humans they've never met; these dogs need CGC training. In contrast, after some wiggling and wagging of happy tails, some canines have the impressive ability to use their most impeccable manners when greeting people for the first time. They'll sit quietly and tolerate petting, making the humans who meet them feel comfortable and appreciated. In animal-assisted therapy settings, these are the well-respected dogs that are considered to be reliable and safe.

Perhaps because of a lack of experience around people or limited exposure to humans early in life, some dogs may not respond well to petting. Such a dog might look away, appearing aloof and disinterested in the eager person who is trying his

▼ **The first step in the Sitting Politely for Petting test item is to get your dog into the sitting position.**

◀ **When the dog is sitting, the Evaluator will approach and pet the dog.**

hardest to make a new canine friend. The not-so-social, disinterested dog may actually move away from a person who attempts to pet him.

If you have a dog or puppy like this, don't despair. Daily playtime with an owner, paired with training and socialization, can be effective components of a program designed to teach your dog to be more socially oriented. When your dog can consistently perform CGC Test Item 2, you'll have a dog that can meet new people in public and will greet visitors to your home in a way that makes every guest feel welcomed—by you and your dog.

Teaching Dogs to Sit Politely for Petting

With practice and frequent exposure, the dog has already learned CGC Test Item 1: Accepting a Friendly Stranger. This exercise required that the dog stay composed and collected while an unfamiliar person approached and talked to you, the dog's owner.

In this next exercise, your canine companion will learn to sit at your side while an unfamiliar person approaches, speaks to you, reaches out, and pets the dog. By having an unfamiliar person pet your dog while the dog remains under control, we're upping the ante and getting to the heart of what Canine Good Citizen training is all about. CGC dogs make people feel comfortable.

Sitting politely for petting is a skill that consists of three primary components: (1) sitting on command, (2) tolerating petting, and (3) sitting while being petted by someone other than the owner. Earlier in this book, we talked about different training philosophies and methods. For the skills on the CGC Test, we provide you with methods and training tips. Remember that an experienced instructor can help you choose the training methods that you feel will be best for you and your dog.

Why Is *Sit* So Important?

Teaching your dog to sit on command is one of the easiest things to teach, yet it is one of the most important skills your dog will ever learn. There may be a time when you teach your dog an advanced skill, such as weaving through poles on an agility course, that is completely new to the dog and something that dogs do not do naturally. However, your dog already knows how to sit. Your job will be to teach the dog to sit on command. In behavioral terms, we say that you are gaining *stimulus control* with regard to the dog's sitting. A behavior is said to be under stimulus control when it occurs as a result of a stimulus that is presented. So, if you say "Sit," and the dog sits, sitting is under stimulus control with regard to your verbal instructions. If you have to say "Sit" four times and physically assist the dog to sit, the verbal cue *sit* is not under good stimulus control.

Sitting on command is one of the most critical building blocks for training any dog; a reliable *sit* is a part of the foundation upon which the rest of your dog's training will be built. In the extreme sense, being able to sit on command is a skill that could save your dog's life. If for some reason your dog was off leash across the street and a car was coming, calling the dog to you would be a bad choice. However, knowing that the dog will sit on command, you could say "Jake, SIT!" in a loud voice to get the dog into a safe, stationary position.

There are two primary uses for the *sit*. The first is as a skill that can be used in daily activities and dog events. For example, if someone comes to visit, you can instruct your dog to sit while greeting the visitor. At times when your hands are full or you need the dog to be still, you can instruct a trained dog to sit. Here's an example of using the *sit* command in this fashion: you're taking your dog on a therapy visit and when you get out of your car, you need to gather your computer case, purse, and some supplies. You could get the dog out first and put him in a *sit-stay* (we'll be learning the *stay* later on) while you collect your work supplies.

In AKC obedience and Rally competition, dogs are required to do automatic *sits* as a part of heeling patterns. In agility, the fast-moving sport in which dogs complete an obstacle course, many handlers choose to leave their dogs in a *sit* at the start line. There is also an obstacle called the "pause table" in agility on which the judge sometimes asks the handler to make the dog sit.

The second use for the *sit* on command is to use it as a behavior-control technique. As mentioned previously, if a dog is extremely excitable around new people, you can teach your dog to sit while greeting people to prevent him from jumping up. This strategy uses the behavioral technique called DRI, or *differential reinforcement of incompatible behaviors*. DRI means that you will select a behavior to reward (in this case, the *sit*) that is incompatible with the behavior you are trying to eliminate (jumping up on people).

Teaching Your Dog to Sit on Command

In CGC Test Item 2 (Sitting Politely for Petting), you are going to string together three behaviors: sitting on command, tolerating petting, and sitting while being petted by someone other than you. Two methods for teaching the *sit* on command are provided here.

The first method involves using food to guide the dog to sit. When food is used to guide the dog into position, trainers sometimes refer to this as using food as a *lure*. Using food to guide the dog means that the food is moved around by the trainer and the dog moves into position in order to get to the food. This is different from using food as a *reinforcer* or *reward*, which means that the dog gets the food after performing the behavior.

The second method of teaching the *sit* on command involves giving the dog physical guidance (or physical *prompts*) to get him into position. Physical guidance means the trainer actually touches the dog and moves him into position.

METHOD 1: Using Food to Guide the Dog to Sit

1 Get yourself ready. Choose a time when you have about twenty uninterrupted minutes that you can devote to a training session. Your dog will be on a leash and collar. You've already selected your food (or toy) reinforcers based on the reinforcer sampling you did before starting training. (Reinforcer sampling is the procedure in which a trainer allows a dog to come into contact with potential reinforcers to determine which reinforcers are likely to be most effective. Basically, reinforcer sampling involves trying a variety of treats, toys, and other consequences to find out what the dog likes best and would work for in training.) If food is your reinforcer, get your treat bag or put a few pieces of food in your pocket.

In some cases, dogs are more motivated by toys than they are by food. If this is the case for your dog, you can use a toy to guide the dog into position in the following exercises. Where we suggest you reward the dog with food, you'll give the dog the toy to hold for a few seconds if you're using a toy or ball.

We suggest that at the beginning of each training session you cheerfully say something to your dog to let him know that this is time for training. You can say something like, "Let's work!" to let the dog know what is happening.

Your dog will soon learn to recognize training time.

Be sure to bring along a ball, a toy, or something else that your dog has fun with. When "work" is over, play and fun with you should be the reward.

2 Stand in front of the dog. Your toes will be about 1 foot away from the dog's front paws, and the dog will be standing. Hold a piece of food in your hand as you stand in front of the dog. Let the dog see the food.

3 Move the food so you are holding it slightly (about 2 to 4 inches) higher than the dog's head and in front of his eyes (about 6 inches away).

4 Now, holding the food, move your hand (now slightly higher than the dog's head) toward the back of the dog's head. Your hand should be moving parallel to the floor. This motion will cause the dog to look up so that he can visually follow the food. Looking up and tipping his head back will result in the dog's rocking back into a *sit* without your touching him.

Remember, when you hold the food above the dog's head, it should be only about 2 to 4 inches above the dog. If you hold the food too high, there is a good chance that you'll accidentally teach him to jump for the food. If the food is held too low, the dog is likely to simply reach out and take the food without sitting.

Give the verbal instruction *sit* in a calm, unemotional, flat but firm, non-shrieking, normal voice. Avoid "up-speech" when you give your dog a command. Up-speech is when statements are expressed as questions, as in "Sit?" This indicates to a dog that you are not in charge and are not sure of yourself.

The timing of when you say "Sit" is extremely important. If you say "Sit" before the dog knows what is happening and before you are in position, he will ignore you, and then you will have taught your dog that your instructions and *you* can be ignored. Say "Sit" just as you move the food back over the dog's head, his back legs start to bend, and he is moving into the *sit* position.

As soon as the dog is in a *sit* position (rear end on the floor), say "Good boy!" (or whatever praise words you choose to use). Give the dog the food as a reward at the same time as you're saying "Good boy!" Thus, he sits, and as soon as he does, you praise him and give him the food.

Initially, your dog can sit momentarily (for a second or two) and then, after praising and giving the reward, you can say "OK!" (or whatever command you want to use to release the dog), taking a step away to have the dog stand up.

As your dog gets more proficient with sitting on command, things will happen faster and you'll be able to eliminate some of these steps. You will be able to stand in front of the dog, holding the food as in Step 3, and the dog will quickly sit when you say "Sit." When this happens, give the dog the food and praise; you won't need to do Step 4.

▲ **Using food as a lure is a technique that gets fast results when teaching behaviors such as *sit* and *down*.**

As a final step in teaching the *sit* on command with you in front of the dog, hold the food in your hand at your side as you say "Sit," and the dog will sit without being guided by the food. Reward and praise the dog.

What Comes After the Dog Sits with Owner in Front

When your dog reliably sits on command when you are standing in front of him, you can add some new skills.

■ Stand with your dog beside you (on leash). Have the dog sit on command at your side. When a dog competes in obedience events, he is required to sit and heel on the handler's left side. In the CGC Test, a dog may sit on either side—this is the handler's choice. Requiring that dogs work on the left side in formal obedience is a decades-old tradition that originally came from hunting. Most people are right-handed and would carry their rifles with their right hands; therefore, they would work their dogs on the left side. In competition events, the left side is used so that every competitor experiences the same heeling patterns and exercises. We suggest that if you plan on doing any other training activities with your dog, have the dog heel and sit on your left side to avoid confusion later on.

■ Start walking with your dog, stop, and instruct the dog to sit. If you need to revert to using food to guide the dog, you can do this, but phase out the food as soon as possible.

■ In your house or another location where the dog is 100 percent reliable when off leash, practice having the dog sit on command when you are several feet away.

■ After your dog sits with no help from you, begin extending the length of time for which the dog is required to sit (e.g., five seconds, then ten, twenty, thirty, etc.). For formal competition obedience, to earn the first title (Novice A), a dog is required to sit for one minute while his handler stands on the other side of the ring.

Using Physical Prompts to Teach New Skills

Physical prompting, or the use of physical prompts, is when a trainer puts his hands on the dog and guides the dog into position. For example, in using physical prompting to teach a dog to stand with his front paws on the edge of a bed, the trainer would say "Paws up" as he lifted up the dog's front end and guided the dog into position. When teaching sports to humans, instructors will often use physical prompting to teach skills such as how to hold a tennis racket or where to place one's shoulders when playing golf.

Remember that dog training has seen some dramatic changes since the late 1980s, and there is a trend toward positive, motivational training. Many obedience instructors and pet-dog trainers do not like the idea of physically placing dogs into position while teaching new skills. These trainers believe that using food or toys to guide dogs into place is the best technique for teaching new skills.

If you decide to use physical prompting to teach a skill, make sure that you know the dog well, you have handled him a lot, you don't use excessive force, and you feel confident that the dog won't mind being touched and physically moved.

Why Use Physical Prompts to Teach New Skills?

There are some trainers who prefer to physically prompt dogs that are being taught new skills. This technique has been around for decades, and many trainers feel comfortable using the techniques that they know best. Hopefully, these trainers will also choose to learn new methods and will select the best method for any given dog.

Guiding the dog into position can be a particularly useful technique for dogs that are not responsive to food or toys. Many shelter dogs could not care less about taking food from someone during a training session. Dogs that have been severely abused or neglected and dogs that are not well socialized can also fall into this category. When presented with food during a training session, these aloof dogs stand with blank looks on their faces as if to say, "I have no interest in your silly treats."

There are also individual dogs within some breeds that are not very responsive to food and toys used as lures or reinforcers. Chow Chows and Shar-Pei come to mind as examples of breeds that may be unimpressed with training treats and toys. Retired racing Greyhounds sometimes refuse to accept food during training, as do individual dogs of several other breeds. Remember, if you decide to use physical prompting, be sure that you know the dog well and that he has a history of tolerating touch.

METHOD 2: Using Physical Prompts to Teach *Sit*

Follow the suggestions outlined in the first step of Method 1. Get yourself ready, make sure you have about twenty minutes for training, and get your dog's leash and collar. You can use food as a reward with this method, although this technique is often selected for dogs that don't accept food.

With this method, you won't be in front of the dog; you'll be on one side so that you can get your hands on the dog. Choose the side on which you want the dog to work. Remember, if you want to do any formal training beyond CGC, you'll want to teach your dog to work on your left side. If you are right-handed, you may find it easier to physically prompt the dog if he is on your left side. If you are left-handed and find it awkward to use physical prompting with the dog on your left side, you can teach the skill with the dog sitting on your right side and then move the dog to your left side once he knows the skill.

Stand with your dog (on leash) at your left side. Hold the leash in your right hand. (Reverse these directions if you wish to train with the dog on the right).

With one coordinated, graceful motion in which you do several things at once, pull up (straight up toward the ceiling) gently on the leash with your right hand as you bend over or squat beside the dog, put your left arm/hand behind the dog's legs, and, with a scooping motion, help the dog into a *sit*. As the dog's rear end is being lowered into the *sit* position, say "Sit."

For some dogs, variations on this technique might work a little better. For example, for very calm dogs that do not spin and throw their heads around (so that you need to use the leash for control), you can place your right hand on the dog's chest as you guide his rear end into a *sit* as you say "Sit."

You might see a beginning trainer doing what comes naturally as he tries to teach the *sit*. The trainer wants the dog's rear end to go down, so he begins pushing on the rear end. Do not do this. While you may get to the point where you lightly pat the dog as a reminder to sit, pushing down in a forceful manner could cause harm to the dog's hips and legs. This is especially dangerous for puppies.

The instant that the dog is in the *sit* position, enthusiastically say "Good sit!" You want to get in the habit of praising your dog as he is learning new skills. For a dog that is not very responsive to social praise, you can tone down the enthusiasm but continue to praise as an indicator to the dog that he performed the skill correctly.

8 When you get the dog to the point that with your help (i.e., by pulling up on the leash or by placing your hand on his chest, tucking his legs, and assisting him in sitting) he sits quickly, you can begin to phase out your assistance. Give a very light tug on the leash and very lightly touch the backs of his legs as a prompt. Praise when he sits. Gradually phase out the prompts until your dog can sit without you touching him and when you simply say "Sit."

9 Now that your dog will sit on command, you're ready to move around and put some time in between the *sit* commands. Instruct the dog to sit, then just step off to the side and have the dog get out of the sitting position and come with you on leash. If your dog likes petting or patting, you can give him a pat and say "Good boy, let's go" to indicate that you are taking a short break. Remember that the suggested length of the training session is about twenty minutes, but this is not intended to be twenty minutes of one sit right after the other. You might do five *sit* attempts and then give the dog a short break during which you keep him on leash and walk around in a small

area, pet him, and then announce, "OK, let's work." Repeat this sequence a few times over the course of a twenty-minute session.

10 After the dog can sit on your left side when given the verbal cue *sit*, practice the skill with you on the right side, while standing in front of your dog, and while standing several feet away from your dog.

Tolerating Petting

Your dog has learned to sit. You've also been practicing meeting strangers, and in your daily puppy playtime (for puppies and adult dogs), you've been handling your dog a lot. Sitting on the floor with puppies and smaller dogs and playing games such as, "Tickle, tickle, I've got you now, you rascal," along with hugging, cuddling, and playing with toys have resulted in a lot of fun, but these games do far more than simply provide you and your dog with a good time. They also build a bond and get your dog accustomed to being handled.

The next step is to ask other people to pet your dog. When the dog tolerates petting and has learned to sit on command, it's time to combine the two skills. Ask a friend to help you. Have your dog sit at your side (on leash). Initially, the person can approach, say hello to you and the dog, briefly pet the dog, and then back up. Over time, the duration of petting can be increased until your dog will sit at your side and tolerate a minute or so of petting.

▼ **In the Canine Good Citizen Test, Items 1 and 2 flow together. The Evaluator will shake your hand (Test Item 1—Accepting a Friendly Stranger) and then will likely immediately begin Test Item 2 by asking for your permission to pet your dog.**

◀ **After greeting you, the Evaluator will pet your dog. This sequence of actions is how things usually happen when you are out with your dog in public—people will first speak to you and then ask to pet your dog.**

As a responsible dog owner, you have assumed the responsibility of keeping your dog safe and making him feel comfortable and unafraid when out in the world. However, sometimes people, even those who really love dogs, don't have a clue about how to approach them. You may have gone to a park with your dog and experienced what happens when a group of excited, wound-up children notices that there is a dog nearby: "Oooh, look at the dog!" shouts one, setting off squeals and loud exclamations. "Hey, doggy! Look at the pretty dog!" Here they come, running at you and your dog, and you aren't sure which one of you is more likely to have an anxiety attack over this. As a responsible owner, this would be a good time for you to say, "Don't run—that scares him—but you can walk up quietly if you'd like to pet my dog."

Sometime, somewhere, somehow, people (children and adults alike) got the strange idea that dogs like to have unfamiliar hands quickly approach to give them hard, quick, repeated pats on the head. Where did this come from? While some dogs can tolerate this, others don't like it one bit (can you blame

▲ Before you attempt to pet a dog, it's a good idea to extend your hand to allow the dog to meet you.

them?). A dog may be fearful of petting that comes in the form of a hand coming over his head and eyes. As a responsible owner, you should feel free to educate people before they start petting your dog by saying, "Please pet him under the chin," or "He prefers that you scratch his chest." Some breeds are particularly sensitive about "aggressive petters." Some larger breeds don't respond well to "head patters." A number of breeds (and individual dogs within breeds) often don't welcome hands coming over the tops of their heads so that they can't see what is coming.

We hear it all the time at the American Kennel Club: "I have a retired racing Greyhound, and everyone knows Greyhounds can't sit. My dog needs an exception on the CGC Test."

WITH TRAINING, SIT HAPPENS

With training, all dogs, and that includes Greyhounds, can learn to sit. Sitting may not be the preferred position for these regal hounds, but they can certainly learn to sit for the few moments required in the CGC Test.

Greyhounds can be taught to sit using Method 2, discussed earlier in this chapter. With your right hand on the dog's chest and your left sliding down his legs to tuck the dog into position, the "standing room only" Greyhound can be put into a *sit* position.

Many trainers who work with Greyhounds (and other large dogs) use food to guide the dogs into a *sit* (Method 1). However, instead of starting with the dog standing, many Greyhound trainers suggest using the food to guide the dog into the *down* position (see CGC Test Item 6: *Sit* and *Down* on Command/Staying in Place).

Once the dog is in the *down* position, food can be used to lure him up into a *sit* position.

▲ This group of rescued retired racing Greyhounds were all taught to sit by Cynda Crawford, PhD, DVM. Dr. Crawford trained the dogs so they could work as therapy dogs and compete in obedience when they were adopted.

Teaching Puppies to Sit for Petting

When it's time to teach sitting politely for petting, active puppies can present a challenge to trainers in the form of wiggling, wiggling, and more wiggling. There is a lot of joy associated with puppyhood. The tendency for puppies to act excited when meeting people is developmental and should not be viewed as a problem.

When teaching a puppy to sit politely for petting, set small, manageable goals; move forward very slowly; and plan training and activities that are fun and reinforcing. Don't try to get your puppy enrolled in college before he's had time for preschool.

▲ **Dogs that are trained to sit politely for petting are a pleasure to meet.**

What Comes Next?

After you combine sitting on command, tolerating petting, and sitting politely for petting, expand your dog's social skills by adding variations on these exercises:

- In formal obedience and conformation, your dog will stand for an examination by a judge. You can have a helper approach and pet your dog. In Novice A obedience, the first exercise that the dog will have to perform involves the judge walking up to the dog and touching his head, shoulders, and back (near the tail). Give this a try and see if your dog can do it.

- The ultimate version of this skill is to have your dog sit to meet people at home rather than in a practice setting such as a training class or at the park. For very active dogs, this could take a year or more of practice.

- Give your dog the chance to sit for petting at places such as the veterinarian's office, the pet-supply store, and other dog-friendly locations in the community. 🐾

▲ A well-groomed dog will surely be an attention-getter. CGC Test Item 3, Appearance and Grooming, shows that a dog will welcome being groomed by a person other than his owner.

CGC TEST ITEM 3 APPEARANCE AND GROOMING

This practical test demonstrates that the dog will welcome being groomed and examined and will permit a stranger, such as a veterinarian, groomer, or friend of the owner, to do so. This test also demonstrates the owner's care, concern, and sense of responsibility.

The Evaluator inspects the dog to determine if he is clean and groomed. The dog must appear to be in healthy condition (i.e., proper weight, clean, healthy, and alert). The handler should supply the comb or brush commonly used on the dog. The Evaluator softly combs or brushes the dog and, in a natural manner, lightly examines the ears and gently picks up each front foot.

■ It is not necessary for the dog to hold a specific position during the examination, and the handler may talk to the dog, praise him, and give encouragement throughout.

- The Evaluator may give the handler specific instructions for handling the dog in a manner that ensures safety. For example, when the feet are to be handled, the Evaluator may request that the handler lift each leg. The Evaluator may request that the handler steady the dog's head for checking the ears.

- Another technique the Evaluator may use is to hold the dog's head away with one hand and use the other hand to lift the foot.

- While the handler may be asked to steady the dog's head, lift a leg, etc., any dog requiring restraining so he can be examined should not pass the test. The key question for this test is, "Could a veterinarian or groomer easily examine the dog?"

- Some dogs will wiggle or squirm when they are excited. Some squirming is acceptable; however, this should not be so excessive that the dog cannot be brushed.

- The dog should not struggle (pull away with intensity) to avoid the brushing.

There's nothing that will turn heads quite like a clean, healthy, nicely groomed dog that has been well cared for. This is a dog with the good muscle tone that is acquired by regular exercise. This dog is maintained at a proper weight for his age and breed. This canine show-stopper is a happy-looking dog with a coat that shines and eyes that sparkle.

In CGC Test Item 3, Appearance and Grooming, the Evaluator will brush your dog and touch his feet and ears. In the real world, you'll want to expand these CGC skills into the full range of functional grooming activities. This chapter will show you how.

Appearance: Healthy and Happy, With a Sparkle in His Eye

Let's talk about appearance first. When we say "appearance" in CGC, we're not talking about being pretty or handsome or having attractive markings. We're referring to the overall good appearance that results when a dog is healthy.

Appearance as addressed in the CGC Test means that dogs are not seriously underweight or overweight. Underweight dogs could be in need of more food or a different diet, they could have some form of parasites, or they could have health problems that need medical attention. If your dog is significantly underweight, as a responsible owner, you should address the problem with your veterinarian. Being overweight can also prevent dogs from being as healthy as possible. A dog that is extremely overweight may be getting too much food, the wrong kind of food, or too little exercise, or there could be a medical problem that needs treatment. If you love your dog so much that you can't say no when it comes to food, you could be unintentionally hurting his health.

Also related to general appearance is your dog's skin and coat. The skin and coat are good visual indicators of a dog's health. The skin should not be dry or flaking, nor should it be excessively oily. The skin should be free from sores, rashes, and inflammation. An inspection of the coat of a healthy dog will reveal that there are no parasites, such as fleas or ticks. A healthy dog's coat is not dull or dry. A healthy coat has a shine to it and is not overly oily. Additionally, the dog's eyes are clear, and there is no discharge coming from his eyes or nose.

So You're Not a Groomer: Where to Go for Help

Grooming is the key to maintaining a healthy appearance. If this is your first dog, you may need some help learning the fundamentals of grooming. If you're one of those people who can figure out how to brush your dog's coat because you've brushed your own hair but your skills stop there, don't worry. Grooming your dog is something that will bring you a great deal of satisfaction, and you can learn basic grooming skills from experienced dog owners.

A great place to learn how to keep your dog looking his best is your local AKC-affiliated club. The AKC has nearly 5,000 clubs across the United States, and in these clubs you'll find new friends who are eager to share their knowledge and experience. If you have a breed such as the Poodle that requires a great deal of specialized grooming, you can join a specialty club. Specialty clubs are for one breed only, so in this type of club you'll find a whole group of people who own your breed.

If the time in your life isn't right to join a club, attend meetings, and participate in activities, another option is to simply contact the club to get the name of a club member who might be willing to meet with you once or twice to teach you how to groom your dog. Most dog lovers are thrilled to have an opportunity to help someone learn to give his dog better care. To find AKC clubs near you, go to www.akc.org and click on "Clubs."

Preparation Exercises for Appearance and Grooming

Remember the exercises and games we recommended for teaching your puppy or new dog to tolerate petting? The daily handling, petting, and massaging of your dog during your puppy playtime sessions lay the groundwork for teaching a dog to tolerate grooming.

Brushing and Combing Your Dog

One of the easiest grooming exercises you will do is brushing your dog. Brushing stimulates the release and distribution of oil in the coat to give it a shine. Brushing is also important because it removes dirt from the dog's coat.

With a puppy or newly acquired adult dog, begin by making sure that the dog is comfortable when shown the brush. You can put the brush on the floor and let the dog sniff it. Next, start

▲ If you brush your dog regularly, he will in turn accept being brushed by others.

brushing. Many dogs instantly love being brushed and will drop to the floor and roll over as if to say, "Right here on my tummy, please." If you have a dog that is afraid of the brush, start with short sessions. Begin by touching the dog with the brush, then adding a stroke or two, and eventually brushing one whole area.

◀ From the time your dog is a puppy, handling his feet will prepare him for the necessary foot- and nail-care tasks. Trimming the hair on the feet and maintaining nails at the proper length will keep your dog's feet healthy.

Depending on the type of coat your dog has, you may need a special kind of brush. There are brushing mitts that are worn like gloves and work very well with flat-coated dogs. The following section on brushing and combing describes other special grooming tools such as slickers, rakes, and stripping knives.

Desensitizing Your Dog to Equipment

Most dogs love the tactile stimulation that comes with brushing and grooming; with these dogs, you can jump right in with brushing, bathing, and other beauty routines. But some dogs, especially those who were not exposed to grooming as puppies, have a problem with being groomed and are afraid of the equipment. Desensitization is the best procedure for dealing with a grooming problem, such as fear of equipment or resistance to having a particular body part touched.

You've probably heard the saying "one step at a time." That's the idea behind systematic desensitization, which is a procedure that involves slowly introducing your dog to something new by first presenting a stimulus that is less of a problem than your ultimate goal. For example, let's say that your dog is very fearful of being brushed. You get out the brush and immediately attempt to brush his face, but you can't because the dog has started to spin, back up, and pull away. You have visions of your dog plastered to the ceiling like a cartoon character. To try desensitization, you would do the following:

▲ Taking the time to desensitize your dog to grooming items will reduce the risk of fearful reactions to brushes, nail grinders, hair dryers, and other equipment.

1 Select the brush you will use. Put it on the floor beside the dog, then pick up the brush and let the dog smell it.

2 When the dog is comfortable with the brush, don't start with his face or feet or other sensitive areas of the body. Show the dog the brush, lightly touch it to his hindquarters, and slowly begin to brush.

3 When you can brush the dog's back end (including the upper parts of the legs and his back near his tail), try brushing the dog's back until you can start at the neck and brush to the tail.

4 After you can brush your dog's back, move on to the chest.

5 Next, you're ready for the head, the face, and finally the feet.

Handling the Feet

In your daily quality-time sessions in which you sit on the floor with your pup or dog for games, hugging, and petting, you should be handling his feet. If you haven't started this already, begin by simply touching each foot, progressing to the point at which you can handle each foot for several seconds, look between the toes, and touch each nail. This will lead up to trimming the feet and caring for the nails. Not only is handling the feet good preparation for nail cutting but it also gives you a chance to make sure that your dog has not picked up a thorn or developed any sores between the pads of his feet.

If your dog has sensitive feet, you can do a desensitization program that focuses on the feet. Can you touch your dog's feet without the brush or clippers? In an ideal world, puppies are given plenty of handling from the time they are born. A part of that handling includes touching the feet and toes so that the puppies are ready for routine grooming and care.

1 If your dog's feet are sensitive, start by handling the upper leg, near the shoulder. Pet, brush, or massage the area.

2 Slowly (this may take a few sessions) move your hand down the dog's leg. Can you touch or brush the leg halfway between the shoulder and foot? When you can do this, continue to pet, massage, or brush closer to the foot.

3 For dogs that have a major problem with having their feet touched, treats can be used during desensitization to make sessions more rewarding.

4 Finally, holding the dog in a safe, secure position can prevent an accident with the clippers or grinder, and it can help calm the dog.

▲ Holding the dog in a secure position can help calm the dog as you clip his nails. Another good technique for pet dog owners is to have the dog lie on his side for nail care.

Bathing

Grooming should begin with a clean coat, which means you'll need to give your dog a bath using the proper equipment. This includes a nonslip surface, warm water, a leash and collar until your dog has a very reliable *stay*, treats for shaping good behavior, and a no-sting dog shampoo.

Take some time to study the different shampoos available for dogs. There are specialty shampoos for cleaning tear stains from the faces of white dogs, hypoallergenic shampoos, shampoos designed to make white fur brighter and dark coats darker, shampoos for curly coats, shampoos for wiry coats, shampoos for various skin problems, flea- and tick-repellent shampoos, shampoos that make your dog smell nice, and on and on.

Depending on your dog's coat type, a good conditioner can help reduce mats and "frizzies," thereby ensuring that your dog will always have a good hair day, even if you don't. Towels and hair dryers (there are dryers designed for dogs, but those made for humans will work just fine) will dry the coat. And one more thing—until you and your dog have the hang of the bathing routine, you may want to wear waterproof clothes!

▲ Elevating small dogs on a grooming table (not pictured) can save a groomer's or Evaluator's back. You can see from the Evaluator's position that testing small dogs all day would cause a backache or knee problems.

Small dogs can be bathed in a laundry sink, a kitchen sink, or a small tub, thereby saving the back of the dog washer. Medium-sized and large dogs can be bathed in a bathtub or, when the temperature is suitable, outside with the garden hose.

So it's time for a bath. Now what?

■ If you have a long-coated dog, make sure that there are no mats or tangles in his coat before bathing. Always give the dog a thorough brushing before starting the bath. Then, using warm water, thoroughly wet the dog.

■ Which end is up? When wetting and shampooing a dog, some people will tell you to start with the head and work toward the back. Others will tell you to start at the back and work toward the head. Either way will get the dog clean. If you live in an area where your dog may get the occasional flea, start at the head. You don't want to start at the rear end of the dog because the fleas will scurry to hide in the dog's ears. If you have a timid dog that does not like getting his head and face wet, start at the rear and work forward. This way, you'll save the worst for last, and bath time will be over after a quick wash of the face and head.

■ When the dog is wet, begin applying the shampoo and massaging it into a good, soapy lather. Go over every area of the dog, making sure to work the shampoo into the coat. Don't get shampoo in the dog's eyes or ears. If you need to, you can put a cotton ball in each ear to keep the water out.

■ When your dog is clean, rinse until there is no more soap in the water. If you've chosen to use a conditioner, follow the instructions on the bottle and apply it before you dry the dog.

■ Most dogs will attempt to shake the water out of their coats after a bath. This gives you a good head start on drying the dog, and you can follow this by towel-drying the dog to get much of the remaining water out of the coat.

■ For dogs that have thicker fur or longer coats, a handheld hair dryer can be used to blow-dry the coat. With fearful dogs, you might need to use desensitization to get them accustomed to the noise of the hair dryer. Pay close attention to the temperature when using a hair dryer to prevent damaging the coat or, worse, accidentally burning your dog. Some commercial dryers designed for dogs produce a lot of heat. These should always be used with close supervision—never put the dog in a crate under the dryer and leave the area. Particularly for brachycephalic (flat-faced) breeds, such as Bulldogs, Pugs, and Pekingese, this lapse in judgment can result in a disaster.

▲ **Owners will bring their dogs' own brushes or combs to the CGC Test. Long-coated dogs will usually be groomed with a brush, while owners might bring grooming mitts for flat-coated dogs.**

Cleaning the Ears

In the Appearance and Grooming test, the Evaluator lightly examines the dog's ears. Touching and handling the ears is the first step in the chain of grooming tasks that will prevent your dog from getting ear infections or parasites in the ears. A few simple tips will help you keep your dog's ears clean, dry, and free of infections or mites.

1 After you can touch and handle your dog's ears, move on to a more thorough exam. Start with one ear. Hold the ear in your hand, looking at and feeling the outside of it. Do you see any bumps, scratches, or other problems?

2 Next, check inside the ears. If the ears are dirty, use a clean cloth, cotton ball, or cotton swab to clean them. You can moisten the cloth or swab with ear wash (available at a pet-supply store or from your vet) or a little water and then remove the dirt or wax. If the ear has a lot of dirt or wax, you can use alcohol or mineral oil.

3 If you use a cotton swab, be extremely careful to not put the swab into the ear canal. If you have any questions about your ear-cleaning technique, your vet, a vet tech, or an experienced groomer can give you a quick lesson.

4 If there is any foul odor coming from your dog's ears or you've noticed your dog shaking his head, it could be mites or an infection, and you should have your veterinarian check the ears as soon as possible.

5 Dogs with heavier coats may have a lot of hair growing inside their ears. If the opening to the ear canal is blocked with hair, some of the hair needs to be trimmed. Be extremely careful when trimming hair in or around the ears because there are many small folds that you can accidentally cut. A good safety technique for beginning groomers is to hold the hair between the thumb and index finger and cut the hair that protrudes from the tops of the fingers.

Groomers often pluck the hair out of dogs' ears using forceps. Before you try this for the first time, make sure you have someone demonstrate how to do it. Clippers are also used on the insides of the ears of dogs, such as spaniels, with long ears. Clippers should be used with care, and it is a good idea to have someone teach you how to use them.

More About Brushing and Combing

In the Appearance and Grooming CGC test item, the Evaluator will softly brush or comb the dog. You'll bring your own brush, comb, or grooming mitt to the test; ideally, you will have selected your tool based on your dog's coat type. There are various tools of the trade for brushing or combing your dog. Most common include a pin brush, bristle brush, comb, and rake.

Typically, brushes with pins are used on dogs with medium to long coats. The pins pull through the coat, separating it, cleaning out dirt, and eliminating small tangles.

Bristle brushes can be used on shorter coats and on faces. They can also be used as the last step in brushing to make a dog "picture perfect" by smoothing out the surface of the coat. Back in the day, young girls were told to brush their hair for at least 100 strokes a day to keep it looking healthy and shiny. The bristle brush is that 100-strokes-a-day brush that can be used to keep your dog's coat looking good. Your dog will love it if you sit on the floor with him while watching your favorite TV show and give him a good brushing with a bristle brush.

Combs are good for grooming dogs with short hair or very fine hair. You don't want to drag a comb through a long, heavy coat. Combs are good for straightening and arranging short hair and removing debris. In areas where there are fleas, special flea combs can be used to remove these pests from the dog. The teeth of a flea comb are very close together so that something as small as a flea can be easily removed.

A grooming rake looks like a very small version of your basic garden rake, with

a handle and a row of teeth. A rake is an excellent tool for pulling out dead undercoat. Used on a breed such as the Siberian Husky that has a heavy undercoat, a rake can painlessly pull out enough undercoat to knit a sweater with! With the undercoat removed, the dog's coat can breathe and, as an added benefit, you'll have much less shed hair to vacuum up. A rake can also be used to split up tangles and mats in the coat.

◀ **Routine ear care can prevent your dog from getting infections or parasites in the ears.**

Other grooming tools include rubber brushes, grooming mitts (as mentioned earlier, gloves with texturized palms, usually used on flat coats), curry brushes (oval-shaped rings of metal or rubber attached to a handle), and slicker brushes (very fine soft metal teeth mounted in soft rubber on a handle). These tools are all used to neaten a dog's appearance, loosen mats, and remove unwanted hair.

To brush your dog, begin with a section at a time. For example, start with one back leg and gradually move to the second back leg, the belly, and so on. If the dog has a long or thick coat, don't simply run the brush over the top of the coat. Doing this may make the top of the coat look nice, but you will cover up tangles underneath. Work in sections of a few inches each, holding up the hair and and carefully brushing each section.

If you find a tangle, don't just force the brush through the tangle. Hold the tangle by placing your fingers between the tangle and the dog's body. This method prevents the painful pulling of hair that quickly creates a dog that no longer tolerates brushing.

Using the proper equipment for your dog's coat along with techniques that make grooming a pleasant experience will ensure that you don't accidentally create grooming-related behavior problems.

Time for a Haircut

If you have a flat-coated, "wash-and-wear" dog, such as a German Shorthaired Pointer or a Doberman Pinscher, you won't have many hairstyle choices to make. If you have a dog with a fuller or longer coat, you will have some grooming options to think about. Is your dog a purebred Poodle, and do you want him to be clipped in one of the standard cuts for the breed? If so, you can either refer to a book that shows you how to do Poodle clips, learn from another Poodle owner, or have a professional groomer clip your dog's hair for you. A shaggy terrier mix from the shelter can become the world's most adorable dog when clipped with a schnauzer cut.

Think about your lifestyle and which haircut will be best for your dog. An Old English Sheepdog has hair over his eyes in the conformation ring, but you may want to cut this hair (or, at the minimum, use barrettes) if your dog is competing in agility. In the show ring, your English Springer Spaniel looks great with a full coat and belly hair that goes nearly to the floor, but a shorter cut may be better for a family pet that has retired from competition and enjoys a daily swim in the pool.

The most common tools you'll need for giving your dog a stylish canine haircut include scissors, thinning shears, and, with some breeds, electric clippers. If you choose to use clippers, make sure you get some training from an experienced person so that you'll know which blade is best for your dog.

Foot and Nail Care

As with humans, dogs need proper care of their feet and nails. The feet of heavily coated breeds should appear neat. This is for more than cosmetic reasons. When the hair between the footpads is trimmed, air can circulate better, and the dog is less likely to get infections.

Professional groomers use clippers to trim between a dog's toes. However, this takes skill and practice. If you have a well-trained dog that will hold still while you groom his feet, you can use scissors to clip the hair on the bottom of the feet and between the toes.

As for the nails, it is surprising how many experienced dog trainers have trouble clipping their dogs' nails. Rather than dealing with a dog that goes berserk when he sees the nail clippers, some owners will have the dog's nails clipped by a groomer or veterinarian throughout the dog's entire life. Training your dog to accept nail care early in his life not only makes your life easier but could also save you a lot of money.

If you have trouble clipping your dog's nails, don't despair. This is a skill you can learn. The first step is to make sure that you can handle the dog's feet. Positive motivational procedures combined with desensitization are the trick to being able to handle ticklish paws.

Nail clippers come in several varieties; the most well-known types are the scissor-style clippers and the guillotine clippers. For a little more money, there are safety clippers that actually have a lighted sensor that tells you when you are getting too close to the inner part of the nail, called the *quick*, which contains sensitive nerves and blood vessels. To prevent cutting the quick when using clippers, be conservative and take off only small pieces at a time.

A grinder is another helpful tool for shortening your dog's nails. The grinder is a handheld tool with a grinding bit that is covered with a sandpaper-like surface. If you are disciplined about maintaining your dog's nails regularly, the grinder may be all that you need, and you can avoid having to use clippers. However, the grinder heats up, so don't risk burning your dog by using a grinder on overly long nails. Nail clipping is another task for which we recommend some hands-on training from a knowledgeable person.

Selecting a Groomer

You might have a breed with a coat that depends on advanced grooming skills to look its absolute best. Or you might decide that dog grooming is not on your lengthy list of talents. Or you might be very busy, and you'd like to have someone else groom your dog. Good news! There are professional groomers who are ready and waiting to provide this service to you. You can find a groomer in the yellow pages of your phone book, through recommendations from dog-owning friends or your veterinarian, or at a local pet-supply store.

The nature of grooming is such that if your dog has a bad experience with a groomer or grooming equipment, it can result in his being very fearful for a long time. For this reason, when you are selecting a groomer, ask about the person's training and skills. If you have a breed that requires a particular style or clip, find out if the groomer has ever worked on your breed.

It's a good idea to ask if the groomer would be willing to let you observe from a distance as he grooms a dog. The groomers at many pet-supply superstores work behind large windows so that customers can observe.

Take a close look at your dog after his first visit to a new groomer. Are you happy with the results? What was the quality of the bath and cut? Also pay attention to how your dog responds to the groomer. A dog should not be traumatized when he visits the groomer. When you observe, you should not see anyone hitting, striking, or being rough with dogs that squirm and act fearful.

◀ **The CGC test items are functional skills that are important for everyday living. Teaching your dog to accept grooming also prepares him for being examined by a veterinarian.**

More than Just a Test Item

Your dog's appearance and grooming will be important throughout the life of your dog, not just for the CGC Test. Grooming goes far beyond making your dog look nice—it plays an important role in keeping your dog's skin, coat, eyes, ears, and feet healthy and problem-free.

Beginning when your dog is a puppy, practicing specifically for the CGC Test will help desensitize him to grooming equipment and routines. As you work with your dog, think of the functional aspect of this test item, which was intended to produce a dog that accepts grooming and routine veterinary checkups without conflict.

Working on additional items toward this goal is a good idea. For example, even though it is not on the CGC Test, you should also check your dog's mouth, much like a veterinarian would do. Regular brushing with special toothpaste made for dogs will keep the teeth clean and prevent gum disease.

Remember, exposing a puppy to grooming tasks early in his life will result in a dog that looks forward to grooming. With a dog that

▲ **When preparing your dog for the Appearance and Grooming test item, he will learn the important life lesson that he can trust you and other people to handle him with care.**

is getting a late start, sound behavioral procedures such as desensitization and positive reinforcement can be used to teach the dog to tolerate grooming.

Finally, tactile stimulation, also known as touch, can be a very powerful reinforcer for both humans and animals. With regular practice, your dog will soon welcome grooming time with you. Passing Test Item 3 of the AKC Canine Good Citizen Test demonstrates that your dog is compliant, under control, and well cared for. 🐾

▲ Daily walks offer significant benefits for owners, dogs, and their relationship with each other. Dogs should be under control when taking a walk both in the CGC Test and in their neighborhoods.

OUT FOR A WALK (WALKING ON A LOOSE LEASH)

This test demonstrates that the handler is in control of the dog. The dog may be on either side of the handler, whichever the handler prefers. (Note: The left-side position is required in AKC obedience competitions.)

The Evaluator may use a preplanned course or may direct the handler by calling out instructions (e.g., "right turn"). Whichever format is used, there must be a right turn, left turn, and about turn, with at least one stop in between and one at the end.

The handler may talk to the dog throughout the "walk" to encourage him and may give praise. The handler may also give the dog a command to sit at the stop, if desired.

- The dog's position should leave no doubt that the dog is attentive to the handler and is responding to the handler's movements and changes of direction.
- The dog need not be perfectly aligned with the handler and need not sit at the stops.

- The dog should not be constantly straining at the leash so that the leash is pulled tight. The Evaluator may instruct the handler to loosen (put more slack in) the leash. An occasional tight leash may be permitted.
- Excessive sniffing of the floor or ground, such that the dog will not walk along with the owner, should result in the dog not passing the test.
- If the dog is totally inattentive to the handler (e.g., does not change directions), he should not be passed.

A soon as the decision has been made to get a dog, one of the very first visions a person has is of taking his wonderful new dog for a walk. Full of great anticipation and excitement, he imagines exactly how it will go. With the perfect puppy on a thoughtfully selected, attractive new leash, he'll walk down the sidewalk with pride. Everyone will stop to pet the dog and compliment the owner, the sun will be shining, the birds will be singing, and there will be music playing in the background.

Sometimes, though, it doesn't turn out like this. Instead, like an escapee from the Iditarod, the excited, active, strong dog pulls on the leash with great force, dragging the owner down the street. However, don't for one minute think that large and mid-sized dogs are the only culprits when it comes to wrecking a walk. Small dogs that pull also make walking them unpleasant. Because of their speed and small size, they can wrap the leash around their owners' legs before you can say "training." After coming home from several walks with leash marks deeply embedded in your fingers and the palms of both hands from a large dog's pulling, or a serious case of embarrassment over a total inability to control a 6-pound ball of fur, you may make the permanent decision that your dog can get all of the exercise he needs in the backyard. When this happens, both you and the dog lose.

Item 4 of the AKC Canine Good Citizen Test is Out for a Walk (Walking on a Loose Leash). For big dogs, we say this is the "your arm should not be pulled out of the socket" test. The ability to walk nicely on a leash increases the dog's chances that his owner will want to take him for walks. When a daily walk becomes a part of the routine, dog and owner get fresh air, exercise, and the significant benefit of bonding with each other.

It's true that a dog can get plenty of exercise in a large fenced backyard. However, what our canine companions get on walks that even the largest yard doesn't provide is socialization with other dogs and people. When a dog is taken for walks in the community, he not only gets exercise but also is exposed to new stimuli and experiences; this is critical for developing the dog's intelligence and emotional well-being. This chapter provides tips for teaching your dog to walk on a loose leash.

◀ **This Great Dane has the horsepower to drag someone down the street, but thanks to Canine Good Citizen training, she is under perfect control.**

▲ **An excellent example of a "loose lead." There is no tension in the leash, and you can see the "J" shape.**

What Do You Mean by "Loose Leash"?

A loose leash is one that is not pulled tight. In the CGC Test, the Evaluator will be able to see some slack in your leash. When walking, there may be a gentle "U" curve in the leash. When the dog is sitting at your side, there should be enough slack in the leash that the Evaluator can see a "J" that begins where the leash snaps to the dog's collar. The ultimate goal of Out for a Walk will be that you can take your dog for a walk and he will not pull on the leash.

Starting Position: Left or Right?

In the CGC Test, handlers may walk with their dogs on the left or right side, whichever is preferred. Unless you have a disability, we suggest that you train your dog to work on your left side. As mentioned earlier, this is the side required in AKC competitive obedience events (accommodations are made for handlers with disabilities) to ensure that the exercises are standardized. For example, when you walk in a circle with a dog at your side, if you circle to the right, the dog is on the outside. If you go to the left, it becomes a completely different exercise with the dog on the inside.

We've mentioned that the tradition of dogs working on their handlers' left sides comes from the early days of hunting, as most people are right-handed and would have their guns in their right hands and their dogs on their left sides. Further, when handlers walked with dogs and horses together, the horses were typically on the right and the dogs on the left. We're hoping that preparing for the CGC Test will result in your getting hooked on training, so working with your dog on your left side will prepare both of you for training for and competing in fun events such as Rally and obedience.

▶ **Working with your dog on the left side will prepare you for activities such as competitive obedience.**

◤ In the CGC Test, the dog does not have to be in the *heel* position required in formal obedience. This dog is behind the owner, but the leash is loose, so the dog would pass.
◀ In formal obedience competition, the dog would be penalized for walking a little wide. In the CGC Test, this is acceptable, especially since this owner does an excellent job of keeping slack in the leash.

Teaching Out for a Walk Using Food or a Toy as a Lure

■ Use a toy to play with your dog and establish the toy as a reinforcer (something the dog wants and will work for). You can also do this with a preferred treat.

■ Start with your dog at your side.

■ Hold the lure in your hand (at the center of your waist).

■ Walk forward as you give the verbal command you've chosen, such as *walk* or *heel*. It's a good idea to start working on *heel* now, although your dog does not have to be in the *heel* position during the CGC Test.

■ When the dog starts to walk along, you can praise him, ("Good dog!").

■ Periodically give the dog the treat or toy as a reward for walking nicely on the leash. In the beginning, you will use the reward more often and will eventually phase out the food or toy. Your praise, along with the enjoyment of going for a walk, will eventually be the reward.

■ A good natural progression of walking on a loose leash is to start with short distances in a straight line. During your training, begin with ten to fifteen steps and then gradually lengthen the distance.

■ Finally, when your dog walks well on leash in a straight line, add unusual patterns such as walking in a circle (both clockwise and counterclockwise), weaving in and out of objects, making quick turns to the left and right, and stopping. Eventually, you should teach your dog to sit when you stop.

THE *HEEL* POSITION: A GOOD GOAL

Teaching *heel* is a good method of control for dogs that want to lunge at other dogs, chase cars, or otherwise get themselves into trouble. The *heel* position, as defined in the *AKC Obedience Regulations* (Chapter 2, Section 18) "applies whether the dog is sitting, standing, lying down, or moving at heel. The dog should be at the handler's left side, straight in line with the direction the handler is facing. The area from the dog's head to shoulder is to be in line with the handler's left hip. The dog should be close to, but not crowding, his handler so that the handler has freedom of motion at all times."

Advanced Exercise: Teaching Heeling

One trick to teach the dog to work close to your left side is to start in a hallway or along the outside of a long building. Put the dog on your left side against the wall and say "Heel" as you begin to move forward. The wall keeps the dog in position.

To teach heeling in an open room or outdoor area, do the following:

■ Begin with the dog sitting on your left side. Have small bits of food rewards in your right hand.

■ Step off with your left foot as you say "Heel." The reason for stepping off on your left foot every time is that the dog can easily pick up on the motion of the left leg (which is beside him) moving forward. Eventually, you will be able to start walking without any verbal commands, and the dog will respond to your consistent body cues.

■ Keeping your body (shoulders and trunk) facing forward, walk along a few steps, praising the dog for being in the *heel* position ("Good dog, heel!"). If

▲ **After your dog walks well with you in a straight line, add turns and stops to your training.**

you are training with food, you can also give a food reward every few steps in the very beginning of training. Brisk walking is a good way to get the dog moving forward. When you are slow and tentative, the dog may not get the message that the point of heeling is to move along beside you.

- After several steps, stop by taking your last step on your right foot. Then, bring your left foot in next to your right foot. Your dog should stop walking.

- You can also work on having the dog sit each time you stop.

- Repeat the process until your dog will heel nicely in a long straight line, then add other patterns (left turn, right turn, circles, about turn).

- Have your dog heel in a place where there are distractions, such as children playing nearby, other people walking by, and so on.

Don't Be a Drag: Two Techniques to Stop Pulling on the Leash

If your dog pulls on the leash to get to where he wants to go, and you allow him to pull you along, you've reinforced him for pulling. He got what he wanted, which was the forward motion he needed to get to another dog or a great new smell, and once allowed to do this, he will do it again. Don't reward the dog (albeit unintentionally) for pulling!

Technique 1

1 When he starts to pull, stop.

2 Stand still. Don't move forward with the dog.

3 Wait. The dog will pull, but eventually he'll stop.

4 When he stops pulling, you can praise him and move forward. Uh-oh. He is so excited that you're moving forward, he's pulling again. Now what?

5 Repeat the procedure. It won't take long until he figures out you aren't going anywhere as long as he pulls.

Technique 2

1 When your dog begins to go in his own direction, briskly turn and go in the opposite direction. He'll have to come along, and, most often, he will hurry to keep up with you.

2 When the dog begins to follow along in the direction in which you are moving, praise him and, during the beginning stages of training, give him a treat for coming. Your dog will soon learn to watch you.

Going for a Walk:
Take Time to Smell the Roses

As you plan a walk with your dog, you may have a destination in mind. You may be walking around the block, across the park, or to buy something from the world-class bakery on the corner. A part of each walk can certainly involve serious, businesslike walking from point A to point B in which the dog is given an instruction such as "Let's walk."

Remember, though, that walks are also a way for dogs to learn about the neighborhoods in which they live. Part of the time, you may want to let the dog explore new objects or scents. Verbal cues will help the dog distinguish between when he needs to trot along with you and when it is OK to read the local pee-mail. Verbal cues such as *let's walk* and *free dog* (even though the dog is on leash) help the dog differentiate between walk time and casual sniffing time.

You also have to think about proper etiquette on walks and mind your manners. Just like there are manners for attending tea parties, eating at formal dinners, and responding to e-mail (referred to as *netiquette*), there are manners for taking your dog for a walk.

First and foremost, remember the CGC Responsible Dog Owner's Pledge. In public places, always clean up after your dog. Develop the habit of putting a cleanup bag in your pocket every time you leave for a walk. If bags are kept near the dog's leash, you'll be more likely to reach for one before leaving. You can also purchase a small bag holder that can be refilled with bags. The holder clips onto the leash so that you're always prepared.

Follow the rules. If you see a sign that says "No Dogs," that includes yours. In a large city where there aren't many bathroom areas for dogs, the landscaping in front of a hotel may be tempting, but find another place. In public parks, where areas are designated for wildlife and off-trail use is not permitted, stay on the trails.

Keep in mind that not everyone is a dog lover. On crowded sidewalks, on trails, or in hallways, make sure that you have good control of your dog when someone is approaching. Sometimes, moving the dog to your other side will be a good idea. On an elevator, good manners would be putting your dog between yourself and the wall of the elevator so that the dog is not next to people who may not care for animals. When taking a walk, if a person approaching on a sidewalk also has a dog, keep a close eye on the other dog. If he is pulling or lunging, you may want to have your dog step aside until the person with the unruly dog passes by. Likewise, you also want to

make sure that your dog behaves properly in such a situation.

▲ Teaching your dog to pay attention to you and sit on command is an excellent way to manage your dog on a busy sidewalk, in a hallway, or on a hiking trail.

Being polite and using good manners when you take your dog for a walk will help all dog owners retain the right to have dogs in public places. When owners fail to clean up after their dogs, all dog owners suffer. Before you know it, dogs have restricted access to the public places in which there are problems. Walkers, hikers, and people looking for pleasant places for picnics can become extremely vocal about dogs causing problems in public parks. Responsibility begins with you. On every walk you take with your dog, you can set a good example for others.

▲ Walking into a space that is crowded with unfamiliar people can be frightening for a small dog. CGC Test Item 5 teaches dogs of every size to handle crowds.

CGC TEST ITEM 5: WALKING THROUGH A CROWD

This test demonstrates that the dog can move about politely in pedestrian traffic and is under control in public places.

The dog and handler walk around and pass close to several (at least three) people. The Evaluator can be counted as one of the three people in the crowd. Children may act as members of the crowd; however, when children participate in the test, they must be instructed on their role and be supervised by an adult. Some of the members of the crowd may be standing still; however, some crowd members should be moving about. This test simulates settings such as busy sidewalks or walking through a crowd at a dog show or public event.

If the CGC is being given for therapy-dog certification (which is not an AKC activity), most national therapy-dog groups require that at least one person in the crowd use some health-care equipment such as walkers, canes, wheelchairs, etc.

- In this test, the dog may show some interest in the strangers but should continue to walk with the handler, without evidence of overexuberance, shyness, or resentment.
- The dog may show mild interest in members of the crowd. The dog may sniff a person in the crowd briefly but must move on promptly.
- The dog may not jump on people in the crowd or attempt to go to them.
- The dog should not be straining on the leash.
- The dog should not be trying to hide behind the handler.

▶ In the CGC Test, your dog will be tested in a "crowd" of at least three people.

ur dogs adore us and they want to spend time with us. Every single one of these devoted, loving creatures deserves a rich life, full of opportunities to accompany their human companions on daily excursions and to special activities. We've already talked about the importance of teaching your dog to walk on a leash. Now it's time to take your canine companion out into the world—you've got places to go and people to meet! Chances are, many of the places you'll go with your dog involve crowds. Busy sidewalks, crowded elevators, the patio at a dog-friendly neighborhood bistro, and public events such as community fairs and dog shows are just some of many places where Test Item 5, Walking Through a Crowd, is important.

Three's a Crowd

In the AKC Canine Good Citizen Test, the simulated crowd must consist of at least three people. However, when you are training and practicing, be sure to practice with the number of people you're likely to encounter in the real world. For example, in most cases, going to dog shows will mean that your dog will need to be able to walk through a mob of people, and the three-person crowd encountered in the CGC Test is just the beginning.

Remember Your Manners

You're going to teach your dog to mind his manners while in crowds, but while he's still learning, remember that as a responsible owner, there are some things you can do to make others feel better about dog owners.

What's Up with Elevators?

When you get onto an elevator with your dog, if there is space, step to the side, putting the dog between you and the wall. If the elevator is partially full, so that you'll be stepping into the middle space in the front, you can give your large or medium-sized dog the cue to sit. Small dogs can be picked up and held when you feel it is appropriate to do so. Walking into a small space that is tightly packed with unfamiliar people is unnatural and can be especially frightening for a tiny dog.

Savoir Faire for Sidewalks

Savoir faire means knowing just what to do in any situation. When walking down a busy sidewalk, you can decide to step aside to allow someone with an out-of-control dog to pass or, as long as the approaching dog does not appear to be aggressive, you can keep right on walking as a training exercise for your dog.

If your dog is a social butterfly and likes to say hello with his front paws, be aware of this. Until your dog is trained, keep enough distance between the unsuspecting stranger and the "world's friendliest dog" so that the dog can't jump up to give an uninvited greeting.

Problems Related to Walking Through a Crowd

In the CGC Test, four of the most common reasons that an Evaluator will score this item as "Needs More Training" are jumping on a person in the crowd, pulling away from the owner to sniff a person in the crowd, reacting in a very fearful way to a person in the crowd, and (infrequently but very unfortunately) urinating on a person in the crowd.

Jumping on People

There's an old Pointer Sisters song called "Jump (For My Love)." And that is just what dogs do. Jumping on people is a friendly dog's way of saying hello. This is not a behavior problem as much as it is a misguided attempt at canine communication. The dog is excited and eager to meet the person. As far as the dog is concerned, attention from an interesting person would be the absolute best of all possible rewards.

Your first job is to teach the dog to say hello when it is appropriate in an

▲ In some situations, we want our dogs to interact with others, but in most situations when walking through a crowd, the dog should ignore other people.

acceptable way (such as to sit nicely to meet a stranger). Your second job is to teach the dog that there are some situations in which we're just going to ignore people (such as when walking through a crowd) and mind our own business.

The best approach to addressing your dog's jumping on people in a crowd is to work hard to teach your dog to act "on cue" when you say "Heel" or "Let's walk." Behavior analysts call this technique DRI (differential reinforcement of incompatible behaviors). This means that to solve one problem, such as jumping up, you reward the dog for doing something that is incompatible, such as *sit* or *heel*. This is why all of the behaviors on the AKC Canine Good Citizen Test are so important. Behaviors such as *sit*, *down*, and *stay* can be used in many situations to manage unwanted behaviors.

Sniffing People—The Nose Knows

In addition to jumping on people in the crowd, another situation will result in a dog's not passing the Walking Through a Crowd part of the AKC Canine Good Citizen Test. Depending on the specifics of exactly how it occurs, it can be somewhat embarrassing for the owner and the crowd member involved. What we're talking about here is when the dog decides to sniff a person in the crowd. If your scent-loving hound takes a quick whiff as he walks by a human, it's usually not a problem. The problem comes when the dog begins to smell certain areas of the person's body as if to say, "I need to check your name, rank, and serial number." Again, this is simply how canines get information about one another, and the clever dog (who belongs to the owner with the beet-red face) is simply trying to learn about the people in the crowd.

The tricks to preventing this are to teach the dog the *heel* (or *let's walk*) and *leave it* commands. When you are greeting someone outside the CGC Test, the dog can be instructed to sit or lie down.

Fearful of Someone in the Crowd or the Crowd Itself

There are times when a dog might be afraid of a person in a crowd, and this can pertain to a real crowd or the "crowd" in a CGC Test. The trick to dealing with this problem is providing plenty of socialization. If there is any sign of your dog's being afraid of people, you should set up situations for him to meet new human friends. Beginning with quiet, calm people who understand dogs and making the experience very positive will set the stage for a secure dog that is ready to meet a group of teenagers or a person with a loud voice.

Urinating on a Person in the Crowd—
Understanding Your Dog

Depending on the individual dog and his personality, there can be a few reasons why a male dog would lift his leg and sprinkle the pants of someone in the crowd. This behavior can be related to dominant dogs that are marking their territory and leaving scent-laden memos for other dogs that will come along later. But what we see most often in the CGC Test are young dogs that are beginning training and may be nervous in a new situation. In the middle of the test ring, the nervous male dog feels the need to lift his leg and urinate, and, as it happens, the nearest vertical surface is someone's leg. If this happens, apologize to the person (who will most likely be a sympathetic, experienced dog person who has been there, done that) and move on. Don't yell at your dog or make a big fuss. Practice this test item with friends and family who are willing to act as the crowd.

Teaching Your Dog to Walk Through a Crowd

Some owners are dealing with upbeat dogs that have been able to do this exercise with no problems from the day they were born. Other dogs, including dogs that want to greet the crowd and dogs that are afraid in a crowd, need some instruction.

▲ If your goal is to eventually have your dog participate in therapy work, healthcare equipment, such as crutches, should be used when training for Test Item 5.

The behavioral technique related to teaching Item 5, Walking Through a Crowd, is called *shaping*. Shaping is when you reinforce successive approximations leading to a desired behavior. For example, if you wanted your dog to walk through a crowd of fifteen people, you would start by making sure that the dog could walk close to one person, then two, then five, and so on. Shaping in this exercise can be related to (1) the dog's proximity to the people in the crowd, (2) the number of people in the crowd, or (3) the unfamiliar characteristics (raincoats, wheelchairs) of the people in the crowd.

■ Start by having your dog walk, on a leash, past one person who is 10 feet away. When the dog can do this with no problems, get closer.

- Have the dog walk past a person who is 5 feet away. The dog should not be pulling to go to the person. If necessary, remind your dog with "Watch me" or "Heel." Praise the dog for walking along with you.
- Have the dog walk by a person who is very close, such as 1 foot away. Have the dog circle this person.
- Add a second person to your "crowd." You can have your dog walk by 2 people who are milling around from 5 feet away, then 3 feet away, and so on.
- Add the third person to your crowd.
- Now have your crowd help you by moving toward your dog as they would if they were walking down a sidewalk on a busy street. Go several feet, turn around, and repeat.
- After your dog has mastered walking around a small number of people in training sessions and in the real world, you can begin to add experiences that involve a greater number of people, such as walking on a busy sidewalk, taking your dog to a dog show, or attending a community event.

Exercise for a CGC Class

To prepare dogs to walk close to people in a class situation, students can help one another. Begin with the students in a line, with about 6 feet between each person. With the dog on leash, the handler at the end of the line begins and weaves in and out of the line of students.

The next task is to have the students in a circle with enough space between them for a handler and dog to pass through. The handler and dog weave in and out of the circle of students. In an advanced class, for dogs that have no trouble weaving in and out of the line and circle of people, the students who are helping can have their own (well-controlled) dogs on leash, sitting at their sides, as the handler and dog do the exercises.

An Unusual Crowd: Hats, Raincoats, Shopping Bags

By now, your dog is able to walk close to several people with no problems. It is time to add things to your practice sessions that the dog has never seen. Consider adding someone wearing a raincoat or hat to the crowd. A crowd member can walk along with a shopping bag or purse. If you are a single female who lives alone and your dog has few opportunities to interact with men, you should practice this exercise with men in the crowd. If you live in a neighborhood with children, you should also

provide opportunities for your dog to get to know children during training. Make sure that the dog is under good control before approaching a child, and be sure to obtain the permission of the child's parent.

▲ **A dog may initially act fearful of things he has never seen before, such as a hat or raincoat. Exposure to unfamiliar items is a key part of CGC training.**

Therapy Dogs: Special Skills for Special-Needs Settings

The AKC Canine Good Citizen Program is a great place to start if you aspire to have your dog certified as a therapy dog. The CGC Department has good working relationships with a number of therapy-dog groups. Many therapy-dog groups require that dogs pass the CGC Test as a prerequisite to their own therapy-dog screenings.

If you will be volunteering with your dog, you'll find out that therapy dogs need to be able to walk through a crowd. The crowd could be in the hallway of a school for special-needs children or in a dayroom of an assisted-living facility. People in the crowd in a therapeutic setting may be using special equipment such as walkers, canes, wheelchairs, IV poles, crutches, and electric carts. Incorporating healthcare equipment into practice sessions is essential for a dog that will be taking a therapy-dog test and working in a special setting.

▼ **Beyond CGC training and testing, therapy dogs are screened in the presence of equipment such as wheelchairs, scooters, and walkers.**

If you have a shy dog that loves people but is afraid of healthcare equipment such as wheelchairs, you may need a special training program to desensitize your dog to the equipment. Remember that desensitization involves taking small, slow steps toward the desired behavior. To accustom a dog to a wheelchair, you would begin with the wheelchair on the opposite side of the room. Bring the dog into the room and praise him for calm behavior. Move a few steps closer to the wheelchair. Praise the dog. Repeat this process until you are close to the wheelchair.

Next, have someone sit in the chair and talk to the dog. The volunteer who is helping you can offer the dog a treat. Finally, when the dog is calm around the chair, the volunteer can begin to slowly move the chair.

Hiding Behind the Handler

Dogs that attempt to hide behind their handlers during the Walking Through a Crowd exercise are most often dogs that are in need of more socialization to feel comfortable around people. These may be dogs whose owners work all day, exercise them in the backyard, and don't really get around to introducing them to new people. Or these may be rescue or shelter dogs that got very rough starts in life. Their owners should be applauded for giving these dogs another chance.

To work with a dog that is afraid of people in a crowd, remember how to break the task into smaller parts using shaping. Start with introducing your dog to one new person. The helper can begin by sitting on the floor and allowing the dog to approach. Eventually, the helper should stand up and begin to move around. Your helper can give the dog a treat so that the dog learns that good things can come from people. After the dog is working well with a single person, you can introduce the dog to a second new person, and, eventually, more than one person at a time can be invited to meet your dog.

In Summary

Item 5 of the AKC Canine Good Citizen Test ensures that a dog can move with his handler while in public places that may be crowded and busy with people. Teaching your dog to walk through a crowd and perfecting this skill will expand your dog's world by increasing the chances that he'll be invited to tag along when you go places. Sharing experiences with your canine best friend will strengthen the bond between you and enhance the wonderful life you have together. 🐾

▲ CGC Test Item 6 builds skills that can be used to manage your dog's behavior.

This test demonstrates that the dog has training and will respond to the handler's commands to sit and down, and will remain in the place commanded by the handler. The dogs needs to (1) sit on command (2) and down on command (3) then, stay in a *sit* or *down*.

For the Stay in Place test, the handler may choose to leave the dog in a *sit* or *down* position.

So, it looks like this: "Show me your dog can sit on command. Great! Now show me your dog will go down on command. Great! Now it's time for the *stay*—you choose the position, *sit* or *down*, leave your dog, and walk out to the end of this line."

Prior to this test, the dog's leash is removed and replaced with a 20-foot line (or a 15-foot line attached to the dog's leash). The handler may take a reasonable amount of time and use more than one command to make the dog sit and then down. The Evaluator must determine if the dog has responded to the handler's commands. The handler may not use excessive force to put the dog into either position, but may touch the dog to offer gentle guidance.

When instructed by the Evaluator, the handler tells the dog to stay and walks to the end of the 20-foot line, turns, and returns immediately to the dog at a normal pace. The dog must remain in the place he was left (he may change position such as stand up).

- The 20-foot line is used for safety. If the CGC Test is indoors in a secure area, the Evaluator may choose to have the dog drag the leash or work off lead in this exercise. Any time the test is given in an outdoor area, the Evaluator should keep in mind that the safety of the dog is critical.

- There are no breed-specific exceptions for sitting.

- Pulling the dog's front legs out from a sit position (so the dog automatically drops into a down) is beyond gentle guidance and the dog should not be passed.

- To prevent beginning handlers from tugging on the 20-foot line as they leave the dog (and pulling the dog out of the stay) Evaluators can do the following: (1) lay the 20-foot line stretched out on the floor, (2) instruct the handler to attach the line to the dog's collar, (3) after the handler attaches the line, give the handle end of the line to the handler, and (4) instruct the handler to walk to the end of the 20-foot line (holding on to the end).

- The dog is left for the stay in a sit or down. As the handler returns, if the dog simply stands but does not leave the place he was left, the dog passes the test. Dogs that walk forward to the handler should not pass.

- Dogs that do not sit or down after a reasonable period of time need more training and should not be passed.

- Do not have handlers go to the end of the line and call the dog; they should return to the dog.

The sounds of "Stars and Stripes Forever" were blaring from a CD player in the backyard, and children splashed in the pool. Matthew and Susan were hosting their annual Fourth of July cookout. As guests arrived in festive red, white, and blue attire, they would ring the doorbell and immediately hear a few quick barks from Lady, a three-year-old German Shepherd. Each time Lady barked to announce another visitor, Matthew would say to Lady, before opening the door, "Good girl; it's OK. Sit." The door was opened, and Lady politely greeted the company.

When the food was served, Lady approached the first person she saw at the table who looked like he might relinquish a few bites of hamburger to a German Shepherd with big, brown eyes. Matthew was quick to intervene. "Lady, come," he said. He quietly called the dog to an area away from the table, said, "Down," and then said, "Stay." Lady calmly watched over the meal from her vantage point. When everyone was finished eating, Matthew went to Lady and said, "Good girl! Come get a treat!" The reward for staying in a down earned her several tasty bites of hamburger.

Now, can you guess what the guests said about Lady? Nearly every person who observed this well-behaved German Shepherd throughout the party said, "That dog is so smart." Smart? Probably. But smart had nothing to do with what they were seeing. What these lucky guests witnessed was the long-term benefits of training and behaviors such as sit, down, and stay that were perfectly applied in practical situations.

This is the picture of how life with a dog should be. Our dogs should be well-mannered and a joy to have around visitors and family members. Lady wasn't born with good manners. She attended CGC classes and earned the CGC award. And then, her owner continued with training classes and practiced the skills nearly every day at home. That Matthew is so smart!

Special *Sit* Considerations

In CGC Test Item 2, Sitting Politely for Petting, we explained how to teach the dog to sit. We also described the two primary uses of the *sit*, which are (1) as a skill in daily activities, such as sitting to get a treat, and (2) as a behavior-control technique. In particular, *sit* can be used as a DRI procedure when sitting is incompatible with a problem behavior (such as jumping up on guests).

There are two additional topics related to teaching *sit* that are related to the CGC Program. The first topic deals with breed-specific exceptions to the *sit* in the CGC Test. There are no breed-specific exceptions—all dogs must pass all ten test

▶ **In the CGC Test, the dog must sit on command.**

items in order to pass the CGC Test. The second topic relates to dogs that are being shown in AKC conformation shows and whether or not teaching the *sit* in CGC training will affect a show dog's performance in the ring. Should conformation dogs be taught to sit on command?

Conformation is the event in which the physical structure of a dog is evaluated by a licensed judge. The dog begins in the standing position, and when the handler is given the instructions by the judge, the dog is moved around the ring so the judge can observe the dog's movement and gait. After moving, the dog returns to the standing position in the lineup of dogs so that any time the judge looks at the whole lineup, all of the dogs can be evaluated at once. In conformation, judges assess dogs on areas that include physical structure, general appearance, condition of coat, gait/movement, and temperament.

"Hello, AKC, I have a problem. My dog needs to pass the CGC Test to do therapy work, but I have not taught him to sit. He is being shown in conformation, and if I teach him to sit, he will sit in the ring. Can he pass the CGC Test without sitting?"

Just as there are no breed-specific exceptions to CGC test items, there are no exceptions made for dogs that owners believe the time is not quite right to teach all of the skills. If the time is not right for your dog to learn all of the CGC skills, we would suggest waiting to try to earn the CGC award until you can train him for all of the ten required skills.

However, with some behavioral know-how, there is no reason why a conformation dog can't be taught to sit for the CGC Test. The behavioral principle that comes into play here is called *stimulus control* (or *stimulus discrimination*, which is the process for teaching stimulus control). Examples of stimulus control in the real world include the following:

■ the child who has learned that yelling on the playground is fine but that it is not acceptable to scream in a library;

◀ **After the dog sits in Test Item 6, he must also demonstrate that he will respond to the handler's *down* command.**

■ the driver who knows she can fail to stop at a stop sign if no one is around but realizes that running the stop sign is never a good idea, especially if there is a car nearby that has blue lights on top; and

■ the high-school student who has learned the distinction between which teachers will allow him to get away with sleeping in study hall and which ones will report him to the principal for choosing snoring over studying.

Dogs are keenly intelligent, amazing creatures that can easily be taught to know what is expected of them in different situations. One trick for teaching dogs to discriminate between an activity that requires standing and one that allows sitting is to use different collars for different activities. For example, a fine, light show lead signals to the dog that it is time for the conformation ring, whereas a thicker buckle collar signals that you're getting ready to do obedience.

A second trick for ensuring that your dog will know what is expected is to teach the words (verbal cues) that are relevant to each activity. In preparation for the CGC Test, a dog learns words such as *sit*, *down*, and *come*. A conformation dog can be taught the word *stand*, and the conformation handler can learn to give the dog the verbal reminder to stand as soon as there is any sign that the dog is beginning to sit. With a few reminders paired with food rewards for standing, any attempts at sitting in the conformation ring will soon disappear.

DOGS WITH DISABILITIES

Dogs with disabilities are the only dogs for which exceptions are made in the CGC Test. Dogs that use carts because they don't have use of their back legs may not be able to sit or lie down. These dogs are welcome in the test, and accommodations are made so that they can participate.

Teaching *Down* on Command

Knowing how to lie down on command is another basic must-have skill for all dogs. Like the *sit* command, *down* can be used in practical settings when you need your dog to take a break, and it can also be used as a behavior-control technique.

For many dogs, *down* is harder to learn than *sit*. The good news is that the *down* is an easier position for most dogs to maintain than the *sit*. The dog can become more relaxed (even to the point of falling asleep) in the *down* position, and many dogs are more likely to stay in the *down* position during competitive events. When you need to put your dog in a control position for a longer period of time (such as while you eat a meal), it's more humane for you to request him to lie down than to sit, as he will be more comfortable.

▼ **Giving the dog a hand signal to sit or down is permitted in the CGC Test.**

Steps to Teaching *Down*

There are several methods for teaching *down* on command. The main consideration is to choose a method that is not traumatic for the dog, which means that you should absolutely avoid using force—no pushing or pulling the dog into position. Using force will do nothing to enhance your relationship with your dog, and pushing hard on the dog's hips can cause physical damage.

1 First, get ready. As you've done when teaching other skills, choose a time when you have about twenty minutes of uninterrupted time that you can devote to a training session. You can do this lesson indoors, in which case you don't need to have the dog on leash unless you need the leash for some control (e.g., when the dog says "Bye-bye, see you later."). If you are training outdoors in a public park, keep your dog on leash.

2 Get your treat bag or put a few pieces of a favorite food in your pocket.

3 Maintain a good attitude. For canines, *down* can be a position of submission. When you first begin training, a strong-willed dog may not be eager to lie down and might be resistive. You'll have to balance being consistent and firm with making the training session seem like fun. Make sure you have identified a reinforcer (treat) that the dog wants. Shy dogs and dogs that are extremely fearful (particularly shelter or rescue dogs that may have been abused) might resist lying down because they have not learned to trust people and thus will not want to assume a vulnerable position. As a part of the whole training package, these dogs will need a lot of confidence-building activities and a rich schedule of reinforcement.

▲ **If you're going to train with food, you can give the dog a taste of the treat to start so he will know what is coming and will be motivated to get it.**

4 Begin with your dog in a *sit* at your left side. You can give the dog a taste of the treat when you begin so he'll know what is coming. Then, hold the treat in front of the dog's nose. The treat should be close to his nose (about 1–2 inches away).

5 As you say "Down," move the treat in a straight line down to

◄ **As you begin to move the food toward the ground, the dog might try to stay sitting while leaning over to get the treat. If this happens, move the food so the dog needs to drop into a *down* to get the treat.**

the ground, right in front of the dog's front feet. Keep your palm down and your hand closed.

The speed with which you move the food to the floor will depend on the speed of your dog. You can experiment with this. With a fast-moving, hyper dog (think of a wound-up Labrador Retriever), you may be able to move your hand a little faster. With a slower-moving dog (think of a Basset Hound), moving more slowly may help the dog focus on the food.

With a small dog, you may want to put the dog on a table to teach him so that you don't have to bend over. If you decide to use a table, make sure it has a nonslip surface. Or, if you are in good physical shape, you can get on your knees to work with a smaller dog. With a larger dog, you'll have to bend over to move the food in your hand to the floor. Remember to use good body mechanics and bend your knees rather than bending forward with a rounded back, or you may find yourself with a back problem.

6 Remember the "L" shape. As soon as you say "Down" and lower the food, most dogs will start to drop into the *down* position to follow the food. If your dog is bunched up and not all the way down, move the food out, away from the dog, on the floor. This will get the dog into the *down* position.

7 Timing is everything. As soon as the dog is in the correct position, praise him ("Good dog, down!") and, at the same time, give him the food reward. Remember to praise and give the food immediately as soon as the dog is in the *down* position.

▲ **The dog receives the food reward when he's completely down, with his head up in a natural position. Once the dog has learned the skill, the frequent use of food will be phased out.**

8 End on a high note. Have the dog get up. Put the dog in a *sit* and repeat the previous steps a few times. Quit while you're ahead. After a few successful responses, end the training session and have fun playing with the dog.

9 Phase out the food. As your dog gets more proficient with the *down* on command, things will happen faster and you'll be able to eliminate the food lure and simply use your empty hand to signal the dog to lie down. Hand signals are permitted in the CGC Test. Eventually, your dog will respond to the *down* command from the word alone without food or a hand signal.

10 Change your position. As your dog learns the *down* on command exercise, practice moving

▶ **While hand signals are permitted in the CGC Test, ideally your goal will be to teach your dog to respond to verbal commands without accompanying hand signals.**

around and giving the command from the side of the dog, from the front of the dog, and from a distance.

Choose Your Words Wisely

A final word about the *down* on command. When you are teaching the dog to lie down, you are most likely to use the verbal command *down*. This means that the dog will pair the word *down* with dropping into the *down* position. If you have a dog that jumps up, don't also use the word *down* to indicate that the dog should stop jumping on people, your priceless antique sofa, or whatever else he is jumping on. Use a word such as *off* when your dog jumps up; restrict the use of the word *down* to when you want him to lie down. This will eliminate confusion for the dog.

Teaching Staying in Place

Combined with a reliable *sit* and *down*, having the dog stay in place is another powerful tool when it comes to sharing a peaceful life with your dog. We want you to spend plenty of time training, exercising, playing with, and loving your dog, but there are times when dogs need to lie down and stay there.

The *stay* command is important for keeping your dog safe and out of trouble. A reliable *stay* can be used when you want your dog to wait before crossing the street, when he needs to stay in position for a veterinary check, when you and your dog are around a child who is afraid of dogs, or when you want your dog to stay while you receive a delivery or talk to the postal worker. A reliable *stay* actually gives the dog far more freedom because once you have this skill perfected, you'll find that you can take your dog to many more places.

▼ Once your dog has mastered the *stay* so that it is solid and reliable, this is a behavior that can keep your dog safe.

Sit
Down
Stay in place

Steps to Teaching *Stay*

You can teach your dog to stay in the *sit*, *stand*, or *down* position. For the CGC Test, you will choose *sit* or *down* and then leave the dog, walk out 20 feet, and immediately return. If you go beyond CGC to AKC obedience training, the dog will be required at the Novice level to do a one-minute *sit-stay* and a three-minute *down-stay*. It's a good idea to teach both a *sit-stay* and *down-stay* from the beginning. You can also work on *stand-stay* because this skill has many practical uses, such as when the dog needs to be groomed or visit the veterinarian.

◀ In the Staying in Place part of Test Item 6, you will leave your dog in a *stay*, walk out 20 feet, turn around, and immediately return to the dog.

SIT-STAY

1 Be prepared. Have your food rewards ready. If you are outdoors in a park or location without secure fencing, keep the dog on a leash. Otherwise, you can teach *stay* without the leash, although you might need it if your dog decides to go AWOL in the middle of a training session.

2 Start with your dog sitting beside you on your left side. Put your left hand, with the palm facing the dog's face, about 6 to 12 inches from the dog's nose and say "Stay." Make sure that your dog can see your hand signal. This is an easy step, as the dog was already sitting and staying. Reinforce the *stay* with praise, such as "Good stay."

The hand you use for the *stay* signal is optional. Some instructors will teach you to use your left hand; others

▲ Teaching the *stay* command begins with the handler standing close to the dog.

prefer the right hand for the *stay* command. In the method described here, we suggest that you use your left hand so that you don't have to reach across your body with your right hand. Further, if you are working with the dog on a leash, it is likely you will be holding the leash in your right hand, so using your left hand to signal *stay* will be easier.

3 With the dog still sitting at your side, give the hand signal as you say "Stay." This time, you are going to pivot to stand right in front of the dog. To pivot, you'll lift your right foot and swing it around so it is in front of the dog, then bring your left foot next to your right foot. Say "Good stay."

4 Reverse the procedure to pivot back so that you're beside the dog again. Move your left foot back into position beside the dog, then swing your right foot around to be beside your left foot. Praise the dog and give him a treat for staying.

5 Next, you are going begin working on gradually and slowly increasing your distance away from the dog while he remains in a *stay*. Give the *stay* command and pivot to again position yourself in front of the dog. Then take one step back so that you're about 18 inches away from the dog. Stay in this position for about five seconds.

▶ **When teaching a dog to stay, the handler slowly increases the distance between her and the dog.**

Reinforce the dog for staying with praise and a treat.

6 Continue this process, each time moving back a little farther—two steps, four steps, and so on. Return to the dog each time. At this point in training, do not call the dog to come to you after you have instructed him to stay. This is confusing and will result in a dog that predicts that you'll always ask for a recall (when the dog comes to you) after the *stay*. You'll end up with a dog that breaks the *stay* in order to get to you.

7 If you are using a leash, you'll eventually be beyond the length of the 6-foot leash. If you are working outside, you can use a long line to ensure that your dog does not run away.

The *down-stay* is very much like the *sit-stay*. To give the *stay* hand signal, you'll have to bend over for larger and medium-sized dogs and you'll have to bend *way* over for small and toy dogs. With the dog in a *down*, repeat the steps in the *sit-stay* exercise.

▲ **Using a 20-foot line means letting it drape on the ground with slack between you and the dog.**

THE 20-FOOT LINE

In the CGC Test, if the test is outdoors, the Evaluator will ask you to attach a 20-foot line to your dog's collar. You may want to practice this before the actual test. The main things to remember when using the 20-foot line are (1) don't reel your dog in or out as though he is a prize-winning bass in a fishing contest and (2) don't do anything to tug on the line. If you are clumsy when handling the 20-foot line, you can pull a dog that is just beginning training out of the *sit* and cause him to not pass the CGC Test. In situations where there is adequate supervision, an Evaluator may decide to leave the line lying on the ground rather than have you try to manage the line.

Too Far Too Fast:
A Common Mistake in Teaching *Stay*

When a dog is not successful at learning to stay on command, chances are there is an overzealous owner at the other end of the leash. Distances of 10, 15, and 20 feet don't sound so far to the average human, so some beginning trainers will take a beginning dog, say "Stay" for the very first time, and instantly move 20 feet away from the dog. This is in the category of "too far too fast."

Remember that teaching every new skill should begin with very small steps so the dog can be successful. In teaching *stay*, you should very gradually lengthen your distance away from the dog and the length of time you expect the dog to remain in a *sit-stay* or *down-stay*.

◀ The 20-foot *stay* exercise in the CGC Test builds the foundation for *stays* that are done for longer periods of time and at greater distances from the handler.

Advanced Exercises

Once the dog knows *sit*, *down*, and *stay*, you can practice so that he's rock-solid when it comes to *stay*. Set up situations so the dog has to stay in the presence of distractors such as family members walking by, children at a park, someone playing ball (especially if the dog is ball-crazy), and people who are eating.

If the dog breaks the *stay*, meaning he gets up before you release him (by saying something such as "OK, let's go!"), don't respond with emotion. Quietly go to the dog and take him back to where he was supposed to stay. Put the dog in a *stay* and walk away. Praise the dog when he stays.

If you continue training classes beyond CGC, there are many exercises in which you'll practice the *stay*. Here are some *stay* exercises done in classes:

■ The handlers, with their dogs on leash, form a large circle. Following the instructor's directions, the handlers tell their dogs to stay and then leave their dogs and circle all the way around the ring. When the handlers return to their own dogs, the dogs are praised if they have stayed in place.

 ■ The handlers, with their dogs on leashes, get in a long line, side by side, with about 5 feet between each dog-and-handler team. One handler, with his dog on leash, begins at one end of the line and weaves in and out of the other handlers and their dogs. A very advanced version of this exercise is to have the lined-up handlers put their dogs in *down-stays* and then leave their dogs. The handler/dog team then weaves in and out of the line of dogs that are in *down-stays*. An experienced instructor can decide when a training class is ready to try this.

 ■ Your instructor may teach some of the competition obedience exercises. You'll start slowly and work up to the *stay* exercises in Novice, then Open, obedience. The Novice level will require your dog to *stand-stay* (called the Stand for Exam) for a brief examination by a judge. You will stand your dog and step away, and the judge will walk up to the dog and lightly touch the dog's head, body, and hindquarters. In Novice obedience, the dog will also be required to do a one-minute *sit-stay* (called the Long Sit) with you standing on the opposite side of the ring. After the *sit-stay*, the Long Down requires that your dog stay in the *down* position with you standing on the other side of the ring for three minutes.

When it comes to the *sit-stays* and *down-stays*, the Open obedience class really ups the ante. In Open obedience competition, the *sit-stay* is three minutes long and the *down-stay* is five minutes long. Not so much harder than the Novice class, you're thinking? In the Open *stays*, the dogs are in a line with 4 feet between them. Handlers put their dogs in the *sit* or *down* (as directed by the judge), walk to the other side of the ring, and then are led out of the building. Some handlers say that these are the longest three and five minutes of their lives.

Foundations of Obedience

Along with walking on a leash and coming when called, *sit*, *down*, and *stay* are the trained behaviors on the AKC Canine Good Citizen Test. These behaviors form the cornerstone of training, and they provide the necessary foundation for progressing to more advanced skills. While these skills may seem simple, they're the canine equivalent to learning the alphabet and counting to ten. *Sit*, *down*, and *stay* will be skills you'll call upon in other dog-related activities, such as Rally, obedience, agility, and therapy work, and in your day-to-day life with your dog. 🐾

▲ In CGC Test Item 7, the dog is on a long line and is called by his owner from a distance of 10 feet.

CGC TEST ITEM 7 — COMING WHEN CALLED

This test demonstrates that the dog will come when called by the handler. With the dog still on the 20-foot line from Item 6, the handler will walk 10 feet from the dog, turn to face the dog, and will call the dog. The handler may use body language and encouragement when calling the dog.

Handlers may tell the dog to "stay" or "wait" (or another similar command) or they may simply walk away. The dog may be left in the *sit*, *down* or standing position. If a dog attempts to follow the handler, the Evaluator may distract the dog (e.g., petting) until the handler is 10 feet away. This exercise does not test "stay;" this exercise tests whether or not the dog will come when called.

The test is complete when the dog comes to the handler and the handler attaches the dog's own leash.

- Dogs that attempt to follow the handler should not be failed. The Evaluator should distract the dog. The test begins when the handler calls the dog.
- The handler can bend down to call the dog, pat his or her legs, and make encouraging sounds.
- Handlers may call the dog more than once (two or three attempts) but if many, repeated prompts are required, the dog should not be passed.
- Dogs should not be passed if handlers have used the long line to "reel in" the dog. Dogs should come on their own when called. The Evaluator who sees that a handler is starting to reel the dog in may stop the exercise, give instructions to the handler, and start over.

With one of the most adorable personalities in the world, Dixie was a Bichon Frise who was the darling of her neighborhood. On nightly walks with her owners, this little white Miss Congeniality would prance down the street, ready to greet any other people and dogs that were out for an evening walk. Frequently invited to doggy play dates in the neighborhood, confident Dixie would swagger into a yard of bigger dogs with her canine body language clearly saying, "OK boys, let me tell you how it's going to go." She made everyone laugh when she played with Max, the Vizsla. They would run and chase, run and chase, run and chase, and then suddenly, the much faster Dixie would run under long-legged Max. He would stand and look totally befuddled, with a look on his face that said, "Where'd she go?" Dixie would be standing as still as a statue directly under the bewildered bigger dog that simply could not figure out how his playmate had vanished into thin air.

Dixie's owner, Patricia, loved spending time with her. The little dog was the princess of the household, sleeping in Patricia's bedroom, wearing a pink rhinestone collar, and having many activities during the day that were planned just for her. Dixie was loved like a member of the family. She was not spoiled and, very unfortunately, she was also not trained.

When Patricia worked in the yard, Dixie was allowed to run around the front yard off leash. She never wandered far from Patricia—until one day. Patricia was fully engrossed in her yardwork, and Dixie wandered into the street. A young man driving a large pickup truck barreled down the street. Patricia looked up, saw what was about to happen, and screamed at the top of her lungs, "DIXIE, COME HERE!" Dixie stood and looked at her, and the driver of the truck screeched on his brakes, but it was too late. Dixie was gone.

If only Patricia had kept her beloved dog on a long line while she worked in the yard. If only she let Dixie off leash in the fenced backyard but not in the front unfenced area. If only the reckless teenage driver of the truck had not been breaking the gated community's 25-mile-per-hour speed limit by driving nearly 50 miles an hour down a residential street. And, if only Dixie had responded to her owner's command—"Come!"— her life would have been saved.

Adding Coming When Called to the CGC Test

Coming When Called, Item 7 of the AKC Canine Good Citizen Test, is perhaps one of the most important skills an owner can teach a dog. This is a command that can be used to save a dog's life or remove a dog from a potentially dangerous situation. Coming when called is also a practical skill that is needed many times each day when living with a dog. The dog is called to get his collar on to go for a walk. The dog is called into the kitchen to eat. The dog is called to come into the backyard, to come to his owner at a dog park, or to come to his owner for brushing. Coming when called is a necessary prerequisite skill for participation in so many activities, and having this as a reliable response in the dog's repertoire is another behavior that can give the dog more freedom. The list of instances in which a dog should respond to coming when called is endless.

The AKC Canine Good Citizen Test was adopted in 1989 and, in an early version of the test, Coming When Called was not included. The developers of the test believed that by the time a dog was ready to take the CGC Test, he would certainly be coming to his owner when called and, therefore, the item was not really needed on the test. These were the days before the Internet, when if you wanted to express your opinions about something, you had to take the time to

▼ In the CGC Test, it is acceptable for owners to clap their hands, bend over, and otherwise encourage their dogs to come when called.

locate the right person and his contact information, write a letter, address an envelope, and find a stamp. Yet despite the time and trouble it took to do this, in the first few years that the CGC Test was in existence, hundreds of people wrote to say that coming when called was one of the most important behaviors that a dog needed to learn and that the test was incomplete without it. In 1994, the Coming When Called test item was added to the CGC Test. It replaced the Praise and Interaction exercise, as, after a few years of observing this test in action, the AKC felt that it didn't make sense to encourage owners to praise their dogs during one of the test items only. Praise should be given throughout the test, and owners are encouraged to praise their dogs throughout the test.

Coming When Called: It's Worth the Work

When an owner begins working with his puppy very early, bonding occurs (that sometimes looks like imprinting) and the result is a puppy that will follow his owner and come when called from anywhere, at any time, on or off leash. For most dogs, however, teaching a reliable *come* (or recall) takes some work. Even with an owner who practices with the dog every day, has a good instructor, and keeps a log of progress, it can take a year to get the dog to the point that he will come when called when he is in a large area such as a field or park. But the work that goes into this level of training has a significant payoff that will last for the lifetime of the dog.

How to Teach Coming When Called

As with many of the other CGC skills, coming when called should be taught using the behavioral principle of shaping. In shaping this skill, you'll begin by teaching your dog to come to you from very short distances. Over time, you'll gradually lengthen the distance. In the initial stages of training, your dog may come from only a few feet away. For the CGC Test, your dog will be required to come when called from 10 feet away. Hopefully, you'll continue your training, and your dog will ultimately respond to the *come* command from across a field.

Another part of the shaping involved in teaching your dog to come when called involves the introduction of distractions. In the beginning, your training will be done in quiet sessions with few distractions. As training progresses, you should add distractions, such as other people moving around as you call your dog, someone playing with a ball, birds flying as you practice in a field (a big distraction for sporting breeds), and other dogs moving around.

METHOD 1: Kneel Down to Call the Dog

One method for teaching a dog to come is to make yourself seem very interesting by kneeling down, opening your arms or clapping, using a very happy and enthusiastic voice, and calling your dog. When the dog gets to you, you should praise him and give him a treat. This method is particularly suitable for puppies in the early stages of training.

▲ This little Dachshund came to her owner when she was called. She could be a little closer to her owner, but she would still pass this item of the CGC Test.

METHOD 2: Teaching Coming When Called When Out for a Walk

You've been working on having your dog walk on a loose leash and, hopefully, you have been going on some nice walks with your dog. Now it's time to add the Coming When Called exercise. Get your dog and leash and start walking.

1 Walk along with the dog on your left side. When the dog is not quite expecting it, quickly begin backing up, saying, "Come!" When the dog comes to you, praise him and give him a treat.

2 To make the exercise seem more like a game and to build a quick recall, walk along with the dog on leash. When he is not expecting it, run backwards several steps, saying, "Come!" Give him a treat and praise for coming.

METHOD 3: Teaching Coming When Called from the *Sit-Stay*

1 Put your dog in a *sit-stay* at your left side. The dog's leash should be attached to his collar.

2 Tell your dog to stay (or wait, whatever command you use to tell the dog to stay in position).

3 As you did when teaching the *stay*, pivot so that you are standing in front of your dog.

4 Step back one step. Say "Come," calling your dog. If the dog does not move, give a little tug on the leash to have him come to you. When the dog comes to you, praise and give him a treat. If your dog comes to you in slow motion, as though he is not eager to do this, run backwards a few steps, enthusiastically calling him to come. Most often, when you move faster, the dog picks up on it and will begin to trot to get to you.

5 Walk in a small circle with the dog and set him up again in a *sit-stay*.

6 This time, go to the end of your 6-foot leash to call the dog. Call him, and praise him when he comes to you.

7 Mix it up—don't be predictable. If every time you leave your dog in a *stay*, you go out some distance and then call him to come, he will learn that he is always going to come to you after being told to stay. In obedience competitions, dogs are often disqualified for coming to their handlers who intended for them to stay. They are victims of this training mistake. To prevent this problem, even when you are training your dog to come when called, you should sometimes tell the dog to stay and then return to the dog without calling him to come. Reinforce the dog for staying.

8 Phase out the food. Remember, if you choose to use food, it is a good initial reinforcer for teaching a new skill, but the ultimate goal is for your dog to want to come to you when you call him. After he has learned to come when called, start phasing out the food rewards to an intermittent schedule (so the dog will get plenty of praise but will only get food every now and then; this is called a *variable schedule of reinforcement*).

9 Add a new behavior to the chain— the *sit in front*. Your dog has already learned to sit. As you work on coming when called, begin to have your dog come and then sit in front of you before you reinforce him. This is an example of the behavioral procedure called *chaining*, in which you combine behaviors in a planned sequence. If you decide to compete in formal obedience, your dog will need to come to you, sit in front of you, and then "finish" by returning to the sitting position at your left side.

▲ If you decide to compete in obedience, you should polish your recall skills so that you can stand up straight and call your dog to "sit front," as shown here.

METHOD 4: Coming When Called on a Long Leash

This method is really a variation of Method 3, with the main difference being that you will work with a long line or retractable leash to teach the dog to come when called from a longer distance, such as 20 feet. A retractable leash has a mechanism in the handle that allows the line to be extended or to roll up inside the handle. The handler can push a button to lock the leash so that no more line can be released or so that the length of line already released does not automatically retract. The idea is much like a fishing line that can be reeled in and out.

1 Choose the equipment that you will use. A long line is inexpensive and may be easier to use than a retractable leash. The disadvantage is that the line can get tangled. Retractable leashes do not easily tangle; however, if you are clumsy in handling the leash, you can pull the dog out of a *sit-stay*.

2 Put the dog at your left side. Tell the dog to stay (or wait), walk out to the end of the line, wait a few seconds, and call the dog to come. What you don't want to do is walk to the end of the long line and immediately call the dog every single time. The dog will quickly learn that as soon as you get out 20 feet, he will be called to come, so he'll start anticipating the recall and will come before he is called. Vary the length of time that you wait before calling the dog. And remember, sometimes you are going to walk to the end of the line and return to the dog without calling him. Varying the length of time that the dog needs to wait along with varying the recalls will teach your dog to pay attention to you.

3 As you did with the shorter leash, you'll use shaping with the long line. Start with having the dog come 5, then 10, then 20 feet. If the dog is moving slowly when coming to you, run backwards, excitedly calling him (you can also clap your hands) to you.

4 You can give a small tug on the leash if the dog stays in the *sit-stay* and does not come to you when called.

5 When your dog comes when called, don't forget the praise (and treats if you are training with food rewards).

6 Work to phase out food rewards, eventually offering them on an intermittent schedule. *You* should be the reward.

7 If you are using a hand signal to get the dog to come, you'll start by pairing the hand signal with the verbal cue *come*. Eventually, if you compete in obedience at the advanced levels, you will drop the verbal cue and will use a hand signal only.

What's Happening When Dogs Won't Come When Off Leash

Have you ever been to a park or hiking area and seen an off-leash dog running across a field with an out-of-breath, frustrated owner following far behind, screaming at the dog to come back? What's gone wrong here? There are numerous reasons why a dog that is moving faster than a speeding bullet across an open area has gone "selectively deaf" and chosen to ignore his owner's pleas to come.

To help you troubleshoot any problems you might be having related to your dog's not coming when called, here is a list of the most common issues.

■ The dog is not ready to be off leash in a large, open outdoor space. More systematic training on recalls is needed. Go back to the basics and move forward from there.

■ There may be competing reinforcers. Perhaps you have a trained dog that is usually happy to come to you when called, but if you have a sporting dog in a field where there are birds, or a sighthound in the woods where there are rabbits, you may have lost the competition for your dog's attention. It is important to know your dog well. This means that you know when it is safe to take the leash off and, more importantly, when it is a good idea to leave the leash on.

■ Sometimes the dog won't come to you because you have not established yourself as a reinforcer. Sorry to hurt your feelings, but the dog would say you're no fun.

■ At home, if the only times you call the dog to you are to clip his nails, clean his teeth, and do other procedures that the dog doesn't enjoy, he may be reluctant to come to you when called.

■ There might be no history of positive reinforcement for coming when called. You call the dog. He comes to you. You don't say anything to him, you put on his leash, and you put him in the car to leave the park and go home. It's no surprise that the dog is not too excited about coming to you the next time you call him.

■ You may not be understanding the dog's needs. Sometimes a dog won't come when called because you have not allowed his basic needs to be met—the dog may need to run, sniff around to gather information, or search a little longer for a good place for a bathroom break.

▲ **A 20-foot long line is used in the Coming When Called test item.**

What Should You Do if the Dog Won't Come When Called?

What is it with a dog that won't come when you call? When this is a dog that you've fed, walked, played with, cleaned up after, and done everything a good owner should do for his pet, there's a good chance you'll be embarrassed, frustrated, or angry if the dog completely ignores you. No matter how you feel, it is important that you don't get emotional. Never, ever call a dog and punish him when he comes to you. This will destroy your relationship with your dog and will ensure that your dog will never do well at coming when called.

If you are in a park or open field where off-leash exercise is permitted and the dog won't come to you, do not chase him. Chasing causes animals (dogs included) to run away from you. Instead, in the emergency situation where your dog is moving away from you, look like you're having plenty of fun where you are. Make a high-pitched, interesting noise as you move away from the dog. There is a good chance that he'll come to see what is going on, and then you can praise and reward him for coming to you. Once you've got your dog back and know that he is safe, you can put the leash on him and do some training on coming when called. If you are in a situation where there are just too many temptations for the dog (such as other off-leash dogs), you may need to keep your dog on leash for the remainder of the time. You can go back to off-leash training in safe, controlled places such as your house, a fenced yard, or a training class. 🐾

▲ Canine Good Citizen training results in dogs that react appropriately to other dogs.

This test demonstrates that the dog can behave politely around other dogs. Two handlers and their dogs approach each other from a distance of about 15 feet, stop, shake hands and exchange pleasantries, and continue on.

- The dog should show no more than a casual interest in the distraction dog. If the dog attempts to go to or jump on the distraction dog, he should not pass the test.
- The dog may move slightly toward the other dog/handler, then stop. The dog must stay back from the other dog/handler.
- The dog can stretch his neck and sniff without moving forward to the other dog/handler.
- When the handlers stop to shake hands, the dog does not have to sit. He can remain standing beside the handler. If the dog remains standing, he should not cross over in front of the handler to go to the other dog.

- The conversation between handlers can be brief, "Hi, good to see you again. Give me a call sometime."
- As the handler leaves, if the dog turns around and begins pulling as if to follow the other dog/handler, the dog should not pass the test.
- If the distraction dog causes a disruption, the dog can be tested again with a more appropriate distraction dog. The distraction dog should have been observed or evaluated before the test to ensure that he is reliable.

emember the scene we described in CGC Test Item 4, Walking on a Loose Leash? This is where you walk down the street with your dog on a leash and everything is absolutely perfect. Perfect, that is, until another dog on a leash approaches and begins to threaten, lunge at, and bark at your dog. Fearing the worst, with your heart in your throat, you hope that the other dog doesn't get loose and turn a pleasant walk into a catastrophic event. Your heart begins to pound, your palms sweat, your dog responds by going into a protective frenzy, and a peaceful stroll is completely ruined.

Yet, as bad as it sounds, there is one thing that could cause even more distress than being frightened by a menacing, lunging dog. That is when (even though you've tried to be responsible and do everything right) you find yourself in the awful position of being the "other" dog owner, and the dog that is doing the lunging belongs to you.

CGC Test Item 8, Reaction to Another Dog, in which two dogs are required to politely walk past each other, is a necessary skill for walks in the community, therapy-dog work, visits to dog parks, and being anywhere in the presence of other dogs. Dogs that are boarded while their owners go on vacation need to have acceptable reactions to other dogs, as do any dogs participating in organized dog events such as training classes, dog shows, and "meet-ups." Sometimes, dogs don't have good reactions to other dogs, and this is a problem that should be addressed by the owners.

◀ **In CGC Test Item 8, two handlers will approach from 15 feet, shake hands, and continue on. Their dogs may show casual interest in each other, but no signs of aggression.**

Lunging Lessons: What's with the Lunging?

When a dog lunges at another dog while both are walking along on leash, the lunging is often interpreted as a sign of dog-to-dog aggression, but this isn't always the case. Behavior analysts, both those for humans and those for dogs, are professionals who study behavior. They work to understand the functions of individual behaviors by conducting *functional assessments*.

For example, consider the case of a crying human infant. It would be a mistake to assume that every infant was crying for the same reason and to address each problem in the same manner, such as by offering a pacifier to every crying baby. Babies cry for any number of reasons, and when an infant cries, a parent soon learns to run through the checklist—is the baby hungry, tired, wet, cold, or thirsty? If the baby is crying because he is cold, he needs a blanket, not a pacifier. If the baby is crying because he is wet, he needs a clean diaper, not a pacifier. Depending on the cause of the baby's crying, the solutions will vary.

Dogs are no different. There are different functions for their behaviors. Understanding that there are different functions for behaviors will help dog owners know better how to address problems.

What Are the Causes of On-Leash Lunging?

- *Dog-to-dog aggression.* Many people who see an on-leash dog lunging at another assume that the cause is dog-to-dog aggression. While there are some dogs that are truly dog-aggressive, this is not usually the cause of lunging. If your dog plays well with other dogs in the dog park or during doggy playdates in your yard, chances are, if he lunges when on a leash, the cause of the behavior is not dog-aggression but is one of the other causes listed here.

- *Fearful dogs.* Dogs that are afraid of other dogs will sometimes lunge and bark when on leash. This is often the case with small dogs that put on loud, disruptive displays in the form of raucous barking. These are dogs that, through their barking and lunging on the leash, are saying, "I'm afraid. If I make a lot of noise and jump at you, you will be scared and will not try to hurt me."

- *Dogs that are protective of their owners.* Some dogs are protective and take exception to anyone or any other dog coming near their owners. Such a dog will bark and make an assertive attempt to get between his owner and the approaching dog. This is often seen when a dog lives with only one person in the household, many times a female who may have unintentionally reinforced protective behaviors.

■ *A noisy dog that wants to play.* Some dogs that bark and pull on their leashes may look scary, but they are simply barking out of excitement. These are dogs that desperately want to play. Particularly when dogs are larger and have the accompanying louder, deeper barks of larger dogs, the canine-communication version of "Let's play! Let's play! Chase me! Chase me!" is sometimes mistakenly interpreted as a precursor to aggression. Once they get excited and wound up, these dogs can be a challenge to manage if they have had no training and do not respond to instructions. Such dogs may have been properly socialized by their owners but have not been trained in basic good citizen skills. Teaching dogs to walk nicely on a leash (CGC Test Item 4) and using the instructions "Let's walk!" or "Heel!" are some of the tricks to managing this problem.

■ **Dogs that are not socialized.** For many species, including humans, other primates such as chimpanzees, and dogs, there is a critical period of socialization when young. If dogs are not exposed to new experiences, people, and other dogs during that time, they can have difficulties responding appropriately to other dogs. Unsocialized dogs don't know how to act around other dogs, so they engage in behaviors such as pulling on the leash, barking, or lunging to get to an approaching dog. These dogs lack basic manners and canine social graces because they have never been exposed to other dogs and are uncertain about how they should approach and interact with members of their own species.

Neutering to Stop Lunging

Sometimes neutering is suggested as the solution for dogs that lunge aggressively at other dogs when on leash. Spaying and neutering have benefits, but it is important to understand that neutering is not a magic cure for behavior problems. If your dog has a long-existing behavior problem with an established history of reinforcement, neutering the dog and doing nothing else will not result in an immediate fix. Some people believe that behavior problems are testosterone-related and that simply neutering a dog will immediately solve behavior problems. If only it were that easy.

Training is the solution, and depending on the severity of the dog's behavior, you may need help from an instructor who is knowledgeable about canine behavior problems. A class designed to prepare you and your dog to take the AKC Canine Good Citizen Test is a great place to teach your dog to react appropriately to another dog so that a problem won't arise in the first place.

1 **Walking on a loose leash.** First, make sure you have successfully taught your dog to walk on a leash (CGC Test Item 4, Walking on a Loose Leash) without another dog present.

2 **Walking behind another dog.** With your dog on a leash, walk about 20 feet behind another handler and dog. Can your dog do this? If so, try 10 feet. Walking behind another dog is a good exercise for a dog that is shy and afraid of other dogs. If you attempt this exercise and your dog tries to drag you to the other dog, this may not be the exercise for you. Don't let the dog drag you; if he does, remember the exercise in which you turn and go in the opposite direction when your dog starts to pull.

3 **Parallel walking.** With your dog on a leash, walk parallel to another dog on a leash. The other dog should be 20 feet away, then 10 feet, then 5 feet. In parallel walking, you are walking side by side with another person and dog on a leash at the distances specified, and you are both going in the same direction. Can your dog do

▼ **From the dog's perspective, walking behind another dog is a much safer thing to do. This is less likely to trigger undesirable reactions such as barking, lunging, or fearful behavior.**

▲ Parallel walking is less threatening to a dog than approaching another dog head-on.

▶ Shape your dog's appropriate reactions to another dog by starting at a distance and gradually getting closer.

this? Walking parallel to another dog is less confrontational than walking toward another dog, as he will do in the CGC Test. If your dog begins to bark or lunge, widen the distance between the two dogs until your dog is comfortable. Gradually have the dogs walk closer to each other.

4 Walking toward another dog. Now it's time to have your dog walk toward another dog that is approaching; both dogs are on leash. Start about 20 feet apart, and you and the other handler will simply walk by each other, not stopping or saying anything. Can your dog do this? If so, gradually (in 3- to 5-foot increments, getting closer as your dog is successful at each new distance) close the gap so that you and the other handler get close enough to shake hands. When you can do this, your dog has learned the Reaction to Another Dog exercise of the CGC Test.

A SAFE DISTANCE

For safety, dogs remain on the outside of their handlers (on their handlers' left side) during the CGC Test. They do not go nose to nose. When the dogs are close enough that the handlers can shake hands, the handlers should shake hands and exchange pleasantries (as specified in the CGC Test). Each handler should keep his dog's leash shortened enough so that the dog cannot pull across the handler and go to the other dog.

What if My Dog Lunges at the Other Dog?

If your dog barks, lunges, or has any other trouble with any of the aforementioned exercises, remember *shaping*. Baby steps. Go back to the previous step or make the exercise easier. If your dog cannot tolerate walking beside a dog that is 5 feet away, go back to 10 feet, then 9, then 8, and so on. Remember to use plenty of praise and reinforcement (including food rewards) for successful responses. For most dogs, with a systematic approach and lots of reinforcement, it won't be long before passing other dogs on busy sidewalks and in class will not present a problem.

For a highly reactive dog that has had no socialization, you might need to do your training outside with a helper and another dog on leash to get enough space between the dogs. You might need to follow behind the other dog at a distance of 50 feet or more until your dog settles down.

For dogs that are having a hard time not lunging or barking excessively when another dog approaches on a leash, there are two other techniques that can be helpful.

1 *Only move toward the other dog when your dog is behaving.* When it comes time to approach another dog, if your dog jumps and lunges, turn around and go back in the opposite direction, away from the other dog. When your dog settles down, turn and approach the other dog again. You may need to repeat this multiple times, so choose one of your more patient friends to help you. This could take a while, so in the beginning you'll need to set aside time to make this a designated training session.

2 *Use a "sit and watch" technique.* By now, you've taught your dog a *sit-stay*. As soon as you see another dog approaching, move your dog some distance away and instruct him to sit. You can reinforce the dog for sitting. As soon as the other dog

passes, you can go on your way, but do not allow your dog to drag you as if to chase after the other dog. When your dog can sit and watch another dog go by, you can graduate to having the dog stand and watch. Eventually, you'll be able to have your dog walking as the other dog approaches. Start a good distance away when your dog first does the "sit and watch" procedure and gradually get closer.

WHY THE HAND-SHAKE?

▲ **The handlers and dogs will eventually get close enough so that the two people can shake hands.**

We'll occasionally get the call from the person who says, "I don't shake hands with people I meet on the street—why do you do this in the CGC Test?" When the CGC Test was developed, there was a long period of field testing. When observers would give handlers the instruction to pass by the other handler at a distance of about 3 feet, some would be at a distance of 3 feet, others would be closer, and still others would be as far as 6 feet from the other handler who was passing by with a dog on a leash. The handshake was implemented to help standardize the test. If handlers have to shake hands, they will be roughly the same distance apart when they stop in the Reaction to Another Dog exercise.

▲ Using a "sit and watch" procedure will help a reactive dog learn to tolerate other dogs as they pass by.

Making New Friends (For Your Dog)

If your dog is having trouble with Reaction to Another Dog, don't get discouraged. If you have a dog that missed out on socializing with other dogs as a pup, you can develop an organized plan to help him win some canine friends. Try some of the aforementioned suggestions along with the following tips to develop a dog with world-class social skills.

■ **Start slowly.** If your dog is nervous around other dogs, going to a dog park may be too much for your dog's first step at getting acquainted, especially when there are twenty other canines, including the canine schoolyard bully, racing around at top speed.

■ **Be systematic.** Start by planning to meet one friend with only one dog at a designated time. Choose a dog that is well mannered and polite. If your dog is rowdy and dominant, and you are afraid that he might hurt another dog, have an experienced dog trainer with you during the initial interactions. Your dog can detect when you are nervous, and the presence of a confident, skilled observer will help you relax.

■ **Expose your dog to all types of dogs.** If your purebred Papillon has only ever met others of his breed, your dog will get a real surprise the first time he encounters an Irish Wolfhound. Training classes provide you with an excellent place to expose your pup to small dogs, large dogs, quiet dogs, active dogs, dogs with long hair, and dogs with short hair.

I Just Want to Say Hello

Lunging is not the only problem seen in the Reaction to Another Dog exercise. Sometimes dogs just want to cross in front of their owners to get to another dog. They want to say hello, sniff, find out who the dog is, or initiate play. To pass the CGC Test, your dog will need to be trained well enough that this won't happen.

Basically, whether you are a dog or a person, getting along well with others and understanding the boundaries has a lot to do with experience and exposure. If you haven't done it already, attend an AKC dog show. You'll see many dogs of every breed that are standing within inches of each other, waiting to go into the ring. You'll see unflappable dogs of all shapes and sizes on leashes, being rushed past you through noisy, crowded areas. The handlers and owners of dogs shown in conformation have usually done an excellent job of socializing these dogs to other dogs, people, and loud noises. The dog show itself provides training opportunities that are endless.

Generalization: Fixing Problems in Group Classes

Generalization is the behavioral term that refers to behaviors being seen in contexts other than those in which they were originally taught. For example, if you teach your dog to sit when a visitor comes to the front door, and the dog later sits when he meets someone in a park, we would say that the "sit for greeting" behavior has *generalized* across settings (however, with most dogs, this is not likely to happen). If you taught your dog to run and get his favorite stuffed animal when you come home, and he begins bringing the stuffed animal to visitors, we would say that the behavior of bringing the toy has *generalized* across people.

When a dog has a behavior problem, such as reacting inappropriately to another dog (by barking, lunging, or shying away), many people will tell you to take your dog to training classes. The idea is that your dog will have a chance to socialize with other dogs and will soon be ready to sail through CGC Test Item 8, Reaction to Another Dog, with flying colors.

In general, the suggestion to start attending classes when your dog has a behavior problem is excellent advice. In a class with a competent instructor, you'll learn to better communicate with your dog; your dog will be exposed to many new stimuli, including other dogs; and you'll learn new skills, such as *sit*, *down*, and *stay*, that can be used to manage behavior.

Here's what you need to watch out for, though. If you go to a group class where most of the dogs get along well with other dogs and the emphasis in the class is on other skills, such as teaching heeling, there's a good chance that your dog will not learn to interact appropriately with other dogs (or to perform Test Item 8). If you spend an hour each week in a circle, with the instructor saying, "Forward, halt. Forward, about turn, halt," your dog may be no better off at the end of the eight-week session when it comes to meeting another dog. You'll join the ranks of disappointed people who tell others, "I tried obedience training and it didn't work."

Behaviorally, it is highly unlikely that generalization will occur across markedly different behaviors such as the dog's learning to sit on command and suddenly knowing how to react acceptably to an unfamiliar dog. A reliable *sit-stay* can keep your dog out of trouble when another dog approaches, but you also need actual practice with the specific Reaction to Another Dog test item.

If the class is not addressing your dog's problems, you might need to approach the instructor, talk about your specific issue, and ask to have some relevant exercises incorporated into the class. If this is not possible, ask if you can practice with other students and their dogs before the class begins.

At the Dog Park

Dog parks can be great places to provide opportunities for your dog to socialize with other canines. There are a few things you should watch out for if you decide to take your dog to a dog park. One of the main concerns is that, unfortunately, some dog owners use the dog park as a break for themselves. Oblivious to what is going on, they sit and laugh and chat with other owners or bury their noses in books. Getting to know other dog owners who frequent a dog park is fine, as long as you supervise your own dog.

To make sure your dog is safe, keep an eye on the activity in the dog park. If you see a dog being overly rowdy with other dogs, ask the dog's owner if he can get his dog under control. Your Shih Tzu has not learned a good lesson about socializing with other dogs if he spent his time at the dog park quivering under a bench while being intimidated by a larger dog.

Canine Couture: Nice Dress, But I Can't See What You're Saying

The $43 billion pet industry is just one sign that people really love their dogs. Another sign is the rapidly increasing number of products for canines, including fancy dresses, boots, shoes, hats, coats, jewelry, and designer outfits.

In places where there is cold and rainy weather, canine coats and boots can serve the very functional purpose of keeping dogs warm and dry. Other times, owners simply enjoy outfitting their dogs in canine clothes that range from everyday wear to expensive formalwear that comes complete with pearls and diamonds.

For photo opportunities, special events such as Dog-o-ween, and the occasional indulgence of the owner, putting clothes a on dog for short periods of time probably doesn't hurt anything. But here are some things to remember about clothes on your pup:

■ Dogs are already wearing fur coats, and they can get easily overheated if you expect them to wear sailor suits or ruffled dresses when they are running around outside.

■ Dogs need to move around to sniff, explore, and make sense of their world. Some clothing for dogs can restrict movement or present safety risks by getting caught on objects.

■ Dogs are dogs; they are not babies or fashion accessories. We hope that if you put clothing on your dog, it's not a signal that you aren't letting the dog run through the grass, chase a bird off the fence, or do all of the other things dogs were bred to do.

■ Dogs communicate with each other using body language. This issue is very relevant with regard to CGC Test Item 8, Reaction to Another Dog. Clothes and costumes can mask the subtle signals that one dog sends to another to communicate. Other than coats needed for harsh weather, you should leave the canine couture at home when your dog is at the dog park or interacting with other dogs. As much as you may like dressing up your dog, remember to keep his canine traits and needs in mind.

Peace of Mind

CGC Test Item 8, Reaction to Another Dog, is the test item that ensures that dogs will behave politely around other dogs. This is the skill that gives you the peace of mind that comes from knowing that your dog will be calm, composed, and collected in the presence of other people and other dogs. 🐾

▲ Walking your dog around the neighborhood will expose him to a variety of distractions.

This test demonstrates that the dog is confident at all times when faced with common distracting situations.

The Evaluator will select two distractors from among the following (since some dogs are sensitive to sound and others to visual distractions, it is preferable to choose one sound and one visual distraction):

- A person using crutches, a wheelchair, or a walker (5 feet away).
- A sudden opening or closing of a door.
- Dropping a pan, folded chair, or other object no closer than 5 feet from the dog.
- A jogger running in front of the dog.
- A person pushing a cart or crate dolly no closer than 5 feet away.
- A person on a bike no closer than 10 feet away.

A note about distractions: distractions such as gunshot, the rapid opening of an umbrella close to the dog, walking on a metal grid, etc., are temperament test items that are typically seen on formal temperament tests. The CGC Test should not be confused with temperament testing. While instructors may use a variety of distractions (e.g., a person in scuba gear) in training classes, in the CGC Test, distractions should be items that are common occurrences in the community.

- The dog may show casual interest and may appear slightly startled. The dog may jump slightly but should not panic and pull at the leash to get away.
- The dog may attempt to walk forward slightly to investigate the distractor.
- Dogs that become so frightened that they urinate (or defecate) should not pass.
- Dogs that growl or lunge at the distractor should not pass.
- An isolated (one) bark is acceptable. Dogs that continue to bark at the distractor should not pass.
- Handlers may talk to dogs and give encouragement and praise throughout the test. Dogs may be given instructions by the handler ("Sit…good boy…watch me…")
- Several national therapy-dog groups use the CGC as a part of their therapy-dog evaluations. These groups specify which distractors should be used. Evaluators who conduct the test for therapy-dog groups will have this information.
- The distraction cannot simply be noise in the background (dogs barking, cars). Distraction stimuli should be consistent for each dog.

ne of the American Kennel Club's most popular and well-known weekend dog shows was underway on a crisp fall day. Both dogs and people were enjoying the beautiful autumn weather, and across the show grounds, there were activities of every type. Conformation, obedience, Rally, agility, the AKC Canine Good Citizen Test, and a puppy match at the end of the day were just some of the many reasons that eager spectators streamed in droves through the gates of the show.

In the Novice obedience class held in a building on the grounds, spectators watched as a Border Terrier who had done a great job heeling was called by his owner in the recall exercise. At a brisk trot, the frisky, small, rough-coated dog started coming to his handler. Halfway there, he slammed on his brakes. He was visibly upset, he wasn't moving another inch, and he was eventually disqualified.

In another building, entering a conformation ring with her handler, an aristocratic young Weimaraner who had been showing beautifully at previous shows was reluctant to move around the ring with her handler, who had been telling the proud owners for weeks that "she shows like a dream."

And outside, in the grassy field where the agility competition was being held, an attractive, fun-loving Golden Retriever was doing a superb job completing an advanced agility course until she went into the tunnel, came out the other side, stood perfectly still, and began to stare at something outside the ring. Because she completely stopped working, she did not qualify in the fast-paced competition.

For each of the three dogs, most spectators just chuckled and attributed the mistakes to "dogs will be dogs." But in each situation, the trained observer could see what was happening.

The Border Terrier was doing just fine on the recall (coming to the handler) exercise when he slammed on the brakes. Halfway to his owner, on the wall right beside where the recall took place, was a large red fire extinguisher. The dog had never seen anything like this and was not about to go past it. After all, who knew what such a strange contraption might do?

There was not a fire extinguisher on the wall where the Weimaraner was competing. There was nothing on the wall. Looking around, nothing seemed out of the ordinary. What most people missed was what happened as the young gray dog waited to go into the ring. A worker came by with a large flat cart that was heavily loaded with folding chairs. The chairs were stacked so high that when the worker pushed the cart over a bump in the floor where a thick electrical wire was taped down, three metal chairs fell from the cart, making a horrific noise and nearly hitting the Weimaraner. After the mishap, this sensitive dog wanted no part of being anywhere near this particular show ring.

And finally, in agility, there was nothing hanging on the wall (there were no walls) and no loud noises or objects falling from carts. What happened here? The Golden Retriever was a dog whose greatest reward in life was playing with a tennis ball. Dog trainers have a term for dogs like this—they would say that the Golden is "ball crazy." Just as the Golden came out of the tunnel, she looked up, and what did she see? A ten-year old boy was standing at a vendor booth near ringside, tossing a small yellow ball into the air.

What happened with these dogs perfectly illustrates that the world is full of unpredictable sights, sounds, and moving objects. CGC Test Item 9, Reaction to Distractions, is the test item that assesses your dog's ability to respond appropriately in the presence of distractions.

What Are Distractions?

Distractions are basically just the stimuli (including, sights, sounds, people, and things) encountered in the world. Most people think of distractions as those events that divert your attention from what you were doing, such as "I'm sorry my report is late, but I looked out the window, there was an elephant in the yard, and I could not concentrate." In the Golden Retriever's case, the yellow ball presented a distraction for the dog at the agility trial.

Distractions can be stimuli or activities that are pleasing and entertaining. For humans, this can be something like a person's going to a movie to get his mind off being overloaded with work. When a dog that is being trained in the backyard to perform an off-leash obedience routine runs to the opposite corner of the yard and chases a squirrel, the dog has found a distraction that he considers far more entertaining than what his trainer is asking him to do.

Distractions can also be upsetting stimuli (e.g., things or conditions in the environment) that can cause emotional turmoil or uncertainty or serve as obstacles to paying attention or completing a behavior. The accountant who is trying to balance a budget might have a difficult time completing the task if there is a worker using a jackhammer outside his office window. The small dog that has nicely walked on leash down the sidewalk of a particular street every day might suddenly notice that balloons have been attached to the railing of an outdoor café, and they are blowing in the breeze. Not so sure about this new distraction, the little dog plants her feet and decides there is no way, no how, she is walking

▲ **The Evaluator will present the dog with distractions such as dropping a chair and making noise.**

any farther. How to react appropriately to distractions is one of the most beneficial skills you can teach your dog.

Exposing Your Dog to Distractions

When puppies are nine to twelve weeks old, although an exploratory phase begins weeks before this, they get very serious about exploring new spaces and objects around them. Taken outside at this age, a group of puppies will scatter, each one busier than the next with very important exploring. Pick up a young puppy who is exploring, and he is likely to kick his feet and squirm as if to say, "Put me down! I am very busy right now." Jumping into the tall grass, working to get his round, roly-poly puppy body up a low step on the porch, and running with unabated joy to any new human who appears are typical puppy behaviors. If the puppy goes straight from this idyllic existence into a home with an owner who understands the critical importance of continuing to expose the puppy to new experiences (which is basically CGC Test Item 9, Reaction to Distractions), the pup will grow into a dog that is confident and self-assured. Very unfortunately, dogs sometimes don't get that perfect start in life or they somehow develop fearfulness and other inappropriate reactions to distractions. When this happens, the good news is that, with systematic procedures, dogs at any age can learn to have appropriate reactions to distractions.

The following list of distractions shows some of the many stimuli that your dog will encounter at home and in the community. The list can be used both as (1) an assessment (would your dog have an acceptable reaction to these items?) and (2) a list of exercises that can be used in classes and in training sessions that you do with your dog. There is some overlap in the categories; for example, a stimulus may be listed as both a noise and a motion distraction. The "places" category is listed so you can think about a variety of places that you can take your dog, but the distractions presented (such as noise and visual distractions) in this category are also listed separately. It's important to note that before taking a puppy into the community on a regular basis, make sure that the puppy has had all necessary vaccines and that you've been given the green light from your veterinarian to begin daily excursions to new places.

Types of Distractions

People as Distractions

■ *Immediate family.* When you first bring your dog home, he will meet you and the immediate family. Your dog may need a special, slow introduction to certain family members, such as your newborn baby who screams at the top of her lungs, Grandpa with his gruff voice, and ten-year old Billy who is clinically hyperactive.

■ *All shapes and sizes.* People come in all shapes and sizes. Expose your dog to babies, children, men, women, teenagers, older people, people with shrill voices, and people with gruff voices. Clothing can present a problem—here at the AKC, we

can tell you about a lot of dogs that were disqualified at rainy outdoor shows when they did not want a judge, who happened to be wearing a raincoat and hat, to touch them. In cities, teenagers on skateboards, people walking along with shopping bags, or joggers present your dog with people-related distractions.

▲ **Your dog will be faced with many distractions in the real world. In the CGC Test, your dog demonstrates that he is confident around distractions that are presented by the Evaluator.**

Places as Distractions

When it comes to places, the first place your dog will see distractions is with his breeder or initial owner.

■ *Distractions at home.* Once your new dog comes home with you, your home will be the place that distractions (i.e., new stimuli) will be introduced. Balls that roll, toys that squeak, a new bed, a crate, doors that slam, and kitchen noises are all distractions in the home. If your dog was born on a farm and lived outside, you may have a dog that is nervous when he is first exposed to carpeting, tiled floors, or steps. If you have added a dog that has been living in a kennel to your family, the dog may be familiar with concrete and gravel surfaces but not grass or dirt. While we don't usually think of dirt as a distraction, the key concept here is that early exposure to a wide variety of stimuli will result in a steady dog that is better able to deal with other kinds of distractions.

In addition to becoming accustomed to the inside of the house, your dog will find plenty of distractions outside in the yard. Wind blowing, squirrels running along the fence, water in the swimming pool, chimes on the back porch, the yelling of the neighbor's children as they play football, and the noisy lawnmower are some of the many distractions in the dog's own backyard.

■ *Distractions in the community.* The community provides an endless source of distractions for dogs. Cars driving by, cabs, people and other dogs on busy sidewalks, people playing tennis with a ball like the one the dog has at home, and trips to the vet, groomer, training class, and corner pet-friendly bistro are all common distractions in the community. Ideally, your dog will be an integral part of your life and will go many places with you. Staying in a pet-friendly hotel provides new experiences, such as concrete stairs and elevators. As your dog reacts acceptably to the common distractions in your neighborhood, you can practice with distractions that are a little more challenging, such as opening and closing an umbrella or having the dog walk on an unusual surface such as wire grating. Helpers in your training class can wear unusual costumes and make strange noises.

Noises

At home, there are plenty of noise distractions. Pots and pans, televisions, radios, washing machines, vacuum cleaners, doorbells, telephones, lawn mowers, doors that slam, and the seventh-grader who is practicing his trumpet are all examples of noise-related distractions. In public places such as a park, there will be children laughing and yelling, birds chirping, balls bouncing, and water sounds from swimming pools, fountains, and lakes. Sporting dogs are trained to work in the presence of gunshots, a noise not commonly heard.

When it comes to noise, thunder and fireworks are in a category of their own. Animal-control agencies across the country submit articles to local newspapers before the Fourth of July to remind people to keep their dogs inside. Dogs that are left in backyards can become so traumatized and panicked over fireworks that they dig out of their yards and run away. The best thing you can do to keep your dog safe on the Fourth of July is to keep him inside. Desensitizing a dog to actual fireworks is a little bit difficult since the training opportunity occurs only once a year. For the other 364 days of the year, you can work with your dog on tolerating a variety of noises so that fireworks are more tolerable.

Some dogs are afraid of thunder. Thunder is more than a noise problem. Thunder is paired with driving rain, the sky lighting up, an increase of static charges in the air, and the ground and windows shaking.

To handle both thunderstorms and fireworks, make sure that your dog knows he is safe. Bring him into the house with you. Close the curtains if there are flashes of lightning paired with the thunder. This is a good time to provide some planned distractions. Noise from a movie on television or music can help. You can play games with your dog or provide another distracting activity.

In a relatively small number of cases, dogs cross the line from simply being afraid of thunder to having full-blown phobias. (A phobia is a fear that is so extreme that it changes the way the animal functions.) Such a dog, if crated, can go into a frenzy to get out of the crate, biting and breaking his teeth on the crate. Or, he may engage in excessive panting, pacing, and drooling. When the reaction to a stimulus is this severe, the owner needs to work with the dog's veterinarian or an animal behaviorist to address the problem.

For puppies that have not been exposed to storms, and mildy fearful dogs that do not have potentially dangerous reactions to storms, you can purchase a CD of thunderstorm noises. The behavioral principle behind these sound-effects CDs is desensitization. The CD of storm sounds should be played at a low volume, with the volume gradually increased as the dog becomes comfortable with the noises.

Stationary Visual Distractors

Stationary visual distractors are things the dog sees that aren't moving. Furniture, strollers, and wheelchairs (that don't even have to move to be frightening) are examples of visual distractors. The Border Terrier who was afraid of the fire extinguisher on the wall was reacting (not in a good way) to a visual distraction.

Dogs that are extremely sensitive when it comes to their environments can have negative reactions to anything new. The delivery service has just dropped off a large box, and you've placed it in the middle of the living room. Your Whippet puppy, who is highly reactive to visual distractions, starts to enter the room. She stops, stands in the doorway, and nervously looks at the package as if to say, "What is *that*? That does not belong here—I'm not going near it!"

Laddie was a Border Collie who was raised on a farm. When he was sixteen weeks old, he got a new home in a residential neighborhood. Until then, he had never been exposed to anything outside of the barn and barnyard. The first time his new owner took him for a walk, his body shook, he looked miserable, and he went into a military crouch with his belly on the ground as he crawled down the street. The culprit? Mailboxes. Lots of them. There they were, on their poles, lining the street and waiting to jump out and attack when he least expected it. The mailboxes were visual distractions, and a key part of Laddie's therapy was for his owner to take him somewhere different every day so he could learn that the world is a good place and mailboxes would not kill him.

▲ Smells that only a dog can appreciate are distractions that you'll find everywhere you go. Decide when it is okay for the dog to sniff and when he needs to walk along with you.

Scents

Scents are another category of distractions, and for a dog with a good nose, scents can be a problem. Dogs that are competing in tracking events follow scent on the ground. Sometimes, the dogs are working a track and, without warning, off they go! They have picked up the scent of a small animal and, when given the choice between earning a tracking title and "goin' crittering," they're going to find the critter.

In the community, you may choose to take your dog (who has earned the CGC award) to a lunch with a friend at a dog-friendly bistro. Sitting on the outside patio, you realize how great it is that your dog has learned a reliable *down-stay*. A waiter passes by and the dog stands up, no longer wanting to stay at your feet. Aaahhh! The smell coming from a tray of hamburgers presented a scent distraction that competed with the *down-stay*. Practicing the *down-stay* and providing your own tasty reward is the trick to dealing with this problem.

One of the most common instances of scent being a distraction for your dog is when you take the dog for a walk. There are you are, trying to do the right thing by walking briskly and burning all of the morning's doughnut calories. But it seems as if your dog feels the need to stop and sniff every two steps. You'll have to find a happy balance when it comes to letting your dog sniff on walks. If you provide training and allow sniffing "on cue," you'll be able to let the dog sniff sometimes and at other times say "Let's walk!"

Most of the time, scent distractions involve scents that are pleasing to the dog. Every now and then, a dog has an unusual reaction to a person. This can happen when the dog lives in a smoke-free environment and the person who is trying to pet the dog is a heavy smoker, or when the person is wearing strong-smelling aftershave or perfume.

Motion Distractors

Motion distractors are things that are moving; the movement is what causes the dog's reaction. Joggers, children on bicycles and skateboards, carts, moving strollers, moving wheelchairs, crate dollies, balls, cars, and other animals, such as dogs, cats, and squirrels, are examples of distractions that can take a dog's attention away from doing what he is supposed to be doing or cause an inappropriate reaction. Motion distractions are particular problems for high prey-drive dogs, those who like to chase.

To address problems with moving distractions, consider the following tips:

■ *Start with the distraction being still.* Walk the dog around the distraction. Chances are, there won't be a problem. The problem is motion. It's when the car moves or the cat runs that the dog's prey drive kicks in and the chase begins.

■ *Use systematic desensitization.* Start with the dog far away from the object, and gradually get closer. Or, start with the object moving very slowly, and gradually increase the speed. Obviously, you can't practice this with squirrels and cats. Both species are unlikely to cooperate during desensitization exercises with your dog.

For example, if a tennis ball is a problem, take your dog, a tennis ball, and a helper outside. Begin practicing with the dog on the CGC skills—heeling on leash, walking in a circle, and so on. At a distance across the yard, have your helper throw the ball up and catch it. Instruct the helper to slowly and gradually move closer. You should continue working with the dog and give plenty of praise and rewards for paying attention.

If a fast-moving object is what causes the problem (usually in a high-prey-drive dog), you can start by slowing rolling a ball or moving a toy as you tell the dog to stay. Gradually increase the speed, and reward the dog for staying in position.

In these types of training exercises, be fair to beginning dogs. A dog with an advanced level of training will sit-stay while you throw his favorite tennis ball in the air. For dogs that are just starting their training, use a neutral toy to start. Give your dog every chance to be successful.

■ *Use DRI techniques.* DRI is a particularly effective technique for dogs that chase cars. On leash, the dog is taught to heel, sit, and stay as cars drive by and is rewarded for the appropriate behaviors (that are incompatible with chasing).

■ *Use a "sit and watch" procedure to control the dog.* Ideally, your dog will learn to follow your instructions ("Let's walk," "Sit," "Come," and so on) even when there are moving distractors present. But until the dog is well-trained, a good *sit-stay* is your friend. You can have your dog sit and watch when distractors are a problem. There is something about having the dog in a *sit* or *down* that stops the momentum and decreases the chances that the dog is going to chase the moving distractor.

■ *As an advanced exercise, in a safe, enclosed area, take your dog off leash.* When the dog begins to run toward the distraction, do a recall (call your dog to come to you). When the dog comes, give plenty of praise and a treat.

■ *Practice around cats, squir-rels, and other small animals.* Some breeds have been bred for centuries for hunting. It's in their genes. A very well-trained dog can be called off a

▲ Distractions that move can be tempting for some dogs. Having a reliable *sit-stay* is a good way to manage a dog that barks at moving objects or is afraid of them.

squirrel, cat, or other small animal. However, until your dog is very well trained, use leashes, fences, and plenty of good sense to keep other animals safe.

Pay Attention

Reaction to Distractions, CGC Test Item 9, plays an important role in making sure that dogs are well-adjusted, confident canines. As soon as a dog joins your family, he needs training aimed at paying attention and following commands in the presence of the many types of distractions that he will see and hear in the world around him. 🐾

▲ In a training class, you'll be able to practice for CGC Test Item 10 with your classmates.

SUPERVISED SEPARATION

This test demonstrates that a dog can be left in the presence of a trusted person and will maintain his training and good manners. Evaluators are encouraged to say something like, "Would you like for me to watch your dog?"

An Evaluator will hold the leash of the dog while the owner goes out of sight for three minutes. In the early days of the CGC Program, Evaluators were asked to not talk to the dog so that the testing of this skill could be standardized across Evaluators. We realize that most owners would not leave their dogs with someone who did not talk to the dog. Evaluators may talk to and pet the dog but should refrain from giving the dog excessive attention, playing with the dog, etc.

- The dog does not have to stay in position.
- If the dog continually barks, whines, or howls, he should not be passed.
- The dog should not pace unnecessarily and should not show signs of agitation.

- A dog that simply walks back and forth and looks for the handler is passed. There should be no signs of extreme stress, including panting, breathing hard, etc.
- If a dog begins to look very upset or distressed (barking, whining, panting, pacing, pulling), the test should be terminated. The CGC Test is an activity that should be fun. We do not want dogs or handlers to have a bad experience with the CGC. If a dog is extremely distressed, training is needed. (This training should not be done during testing.) This one incident of giving in to the dog's insecure behavior is not enough to cause any lasting effect. The owner should be told nicely that separation is an issue for the dog and that some training would help the dog feel more secure.
- If a dog pulls on his leash (trying to get away), he should not be passed.
- Any dog that urinates or defecates during testing should not be passed. The exception to this is in Test 10 when the test is held outdoors, or between exercises outdoors (e.g., the dog urinates on a bush while being walked to the next test station). Dogs should not stop to relieve themselves while they are working with the handler in the exercises.

As much as we might like to spend every minute of every day with our dogs, there are times when our beloved canine family members need to spend time alone. CGC Test Item 10, Supervised Separation, involves your dog's staying with a trusted person for a short period of time. This is the first step toward your dog's tolerating a separation from you.

In the real world, examples of times when you might need another person to watch your dog while you are not in the dog's sight include leaving the dog with a groomer, leaving the dog with the veterinarian while you step out of the room, and stepping away to make a call on your cell phone, go to the restroom, or go into a store.

Eventually, your dog will need to stay without you for longer periods of time, such as if he requires an overnight stay at the veterinarian's office or at a boarding kennel.

▼ In the CGC Test, the owner will leave the dog with the Evaluator and go out of sight for three minutes.

Teaching CGC Test Item 10: Supervised Separation

As a prerequisite to the Supervised Separation exercise, a great game for group puppy-training classes is "Pass the Puppy." Everyone sits in a circle and holds his or her puppy. When the instructor gives the cue, everyone passes his or her puppy to the next person. The instructor continues to give the signal to "pass the puppy" until everyone has held every puppy and each person has his or her own puppy back. This exercise exposes puppies to a lot of new people, and they learn at an early age that humans other than their owners will not hurt them.

Some dogs will have no trouble staying with another person, but other dogs, particularly if they have no experience staying with another person, may not want to leave "Mom" or "Dad." If your dog does not want to stay with another person, try the following:

1 Stand beside the other person. Hold your dog's leash.

2 Stand close to the other person. Don't leave, but let the other person hold the leash.

3 Stand beside the other person, and with the person holding the leash, step back one step and then return to the dog. The other person is praising the dog and giving a food reward if the dog will take it. The dog should receive attention only if he is calm.

4 Repeat Step 3, but step back two steps. Anytime the dog fails by whining, pacing, panting, appearing stressed, etc., go back to the previous step.

5 Teach this skill systematically, adding one step at a time. The biggest mistake people make is trying to make progress too fast, which can cause the dog to panic. For example, the owner gives the leash to a helper and immediately walks across the room to the doorway.

6 Once you've worked up to getting across the room, it is time to step outside the door (for one second) and then return. Add a few seconds at a time until you can be gone for three minutes. If a few seconds at a time is too many, add one second at a time.

Dogs benefit from consistency and routines. If you say the same thing (such as "I'll be right back" or "Wait here") every time you leave the dog, he will learn that when you say this, it means you are coming back.

7 When you return, if the dog acts like you have been gone for twenty years and goes into a hysterical fit of joy (jumping, spinning), be very calm and don't reinforce his excited behavior. Wait and then praise and reward the dog when he is calm.

Home Alone: Please Don't Leave Me!

Ultimately, in the real world, "supervised separation" will progress to the separation that occurs when you leave your dog unsupervised. You might have heard stories about what can happen when dogs with separation problems are left home alone.

Urinating/Defecating When the Owner Leaves

Some dogs urinate or defecate on the floor every time their owners leave home. For example, Spot was a Dalmatian that would urinate in his owner's bed when the owner left to go to work. We don't mean scent marking, in which a dog sprinkles the

▲ **In training for this test item, leaving your dog with a friendly, dog-savvy person will help the dog adjust to your absence.**

corner of the bedspread. Spot got in the bed when Dad went off to work and left a large puddle in the middle of the bed.

Destruction Zone: Destroying Things When the Owner Leaves

Sometimes, destruction is the primary problem related to separation. Sasha was a beautiful Siberian Husky whose owner did not believe in crate-training or using a kennel. Sasha was free to roam about the house, and in addition to frequently chewing things, on occasion she would pull the curtains down when her owner left. Once the drapes were on the floor, Sasha seemed to systematically chew at least one hole in each curtain panel so that all of them needed to be replaced. More than once, Sasha pulled so hard on the curtains that she also pulled the curtain rods out of the wall, requiring drywall repair in addition to replacement curtains.

"Be Quiet!"—Noise Related to the Owner's Leaving

Noise is another problem that is often seen (or heard) when dogs have separation issues. One toy-breed owner who liked to travel had four Maltese. When she would stay in a hotel, the dogs were easy to care for, and they were all house-trained. The dogs would be fed, walked, and given personal attention, and then the owner would leave and go out to dinner. As she left the room, the four sweet, angelic darlings had halos over their heads as they watched from their crates. Just about the time that the owner got to the end of the hall and on the elevator, all four dogs started barking. And barking, and barking for hours, disturbing every exhausted traveler who was unfortunate enough to have a room nearby.

Problems for Owners and Property Owners

Urinating and defecating indoors, destroying property, and making enough noise to disturb others are issues that owners face when their dogs have problems related to separation. These are also problems that concern property owners, and they are primary reasons that pets are not permitted in many apartments, condos, and rental houses. Remember the Responsible Dog Owner's Pledge—to protect the rights of pet owners, never let your dog infringe on the rights of others by making excessive noise, inappropriately urinating or defecating indoors, or causing damage to property.

Separation Anxiety, Separation Distress, Separation Behaviors

Separation Anxiety

You may have heard the term "separation anxiety." For quite a while, this has been the term used to refer to dogs that have problems when left alone. Technically, *anxiety* is a term meaning that there are physiological changes in the animal, such as shortness of breath, heart palpitations, and increases in blood pressure and heart rate. There is also usually a certain amount of worrying and apprehension that goes along with the clinical definition of anxiety. A well-recognized type of anxiety with humans is test anxiety, where the person can panic to the point of trembling, feeling sick, and developing a migraine related to an upcoming final exam.

Because not all dogs that are left alone experience anxiety, animal behaviorists are beginning to use other terms, including *separation distress* and *separation behaviors*.

Separation Distress

Distress is simply an animal's inability to adapt to stress (or the conditions that are causing stress). In humans or animals, the result of stress is often maladaptive behaviors that include inappropriate urinating or defecating (toilet-trained children who are experiencing distress might wet the bed or wet their pants), making noise (dogs bark and whine while distressed children might cry), and destruction or aggression. In many situations, *separation distress* is a more accurate term than *separation anxiety*.

WHAT REALLY HAPPENED?

Clearly, more research is needed in the area of separation issues. These problems are often seen in rescue dogs and dogs that have been adopted from shelters. If your dog has separation problems and you can get video footage of the dog in action, it can help an animal behaviorist know how to best develop a plan of action if he can see exactly what happened.

Separation Behaviors

Some owners return home to discover toilet paper has been dragged from the bathroom all through the house and underwear is now strewn about the living room. A tornado went through the house? No, the dog was at it again. While you were gone, you're certain your dog did a canine imitation of the Tom Cruise scene in the movie *Risky Business* in which he jumped on the coffee table and played a broom as if it were a guitar.

▲ A dog that is accustomed to being separated from his owner for brief periods of time will remain calm and relaxed during the Supervised Separation exercise.

There are some differences of opinion about this, but when it comes to the topic of separation issues, some canine experts believe that there are times when the dog is neither anxious nor distressed when the owner leaves, and he is just having a good time with his mischievous behaviors. As in, if a video camera were rolling, you would see the dog sliding down the hall to Bob Seger's "Old Time Rock and Roll," shouting, "Wait 'til they see this!"

The idea that some dogs get bored and start a party when their owners are gone is controversial. What we do know is what happened—there was toilet paper all around the house, shoes were chewed, and perhaps the dog urinated on the bed. These occurrences can all be accurately referred to as *separation behaviors*.

Even if you do believe that your dog's separation behaviors are related to the dog's being bored and finding something fun to do, it is *never* appropriate to punish a dog for what he has done while you were away.

1 *Shaping is the key.* Remember shaping, in which you start with leaving the dog for a short time and then gradually add time. The mistake that owners often make is to get a puppy or new adult dog, see that he is doing fine with the new family, and then leave him alone while they go to work all day. You should leave the dog for a very short time (e.g., minutes) the first time and see how he responds.

If your dog has a problem related to separation and engages in separation behaviors as soon as you walk out the door, you may need to implement a systematic training procedure. This is a training session for which you need to have a block of time—don't start this when you are in a hurry and can only do part of the process. The systematic training looks like this:

■ Without making a big deal over leaving, tell the dog, using whatever message you choose to use every time you leave the dog alone, that you are going. You can say something like "I'll be back" or "Watch the house." What you say doesn't matter as long as you use a matter-of-fact tone and say the same thing each time. This will help the dog learn that you are coming back when you say the chosen phrase.

■ Walk out the door, close the door, and immediately open the door and return. If the dog gets excited and jumps on you, do not reward his behavior by talking to him or petting him. When the dog is calm, you can talk to him and praise him.

TEN TIPS
FOR LEAVING YOUR DOG ALONE

■ Repeat the verbal cue you established. Walk out the door, close the door, wait one second, and return. Add a few seconds each time. You may have to do this thirty times before you can start adding minutes.

This process can be time-consuming, and you might find yourself getting bored going in and out of the door. Know, however, that when done properly, this is an effective procedure for addressing separation problems.

2 *Crate training.* If you get a puppy or dog that has separation problems, and you have to leave the dog alone, the first thing to remember is that you need to keep him safe. Puppies who wander about the house chewing electrical cords or dogs that chew through back-porch screens can get in a lot of trouble, not to mention danger. There are many books that will teach you how to humanely and safely crate-train your dog. A crate should be large enough that the dog can move around comfortably. When used properly and not overused, a crate can be an effective tool for keeping your dog safe and preventing a disaster.

3 ***Toys to prevent boredom.*** For real separation distress, you will most likely need to do systematic training as previously described. For both dogs that are able to be loose in the house and dogs that are crated during the day, providing the dog with acceptable toys is a smart move

▲ **Providing your dog with a selection of safe toys can help prevent the boredom and stress that can cause separation issues.**

that can help prevent boredom. If you give your dog toys, make sure that the items you choose are not things that can be chewed up (e.g., stuffed animals) and cause problems such as choking or intestinal blockages if swallowed. There are a number of dog toys in which you can place a treat or peanut butter so the dog has some work to do in order to get the reward. If you choose not to use a crate, be sure to puppy-proof your home before leaving the dog alone so that your dog doesn't make a bad choice (such as chewing your expensive Italian leather shoes).

4 *Meeting your dog's physical needs.* Before leaving your dog alone for an extended period of time, make sure that all of the dog's physical needs have been met. This includes providing fresh water and taking him out to relieve his bladder and bowels. When a house-trained dog has not been given an adequate bathroom trip outdoors before you leave, it can be extremely stressful both physically and mentally for the dog that is trying to do the right thing by "holding it" until you come home.

5 *Exercising your dog.* Exercise is also in the category of meeting your dog's physical needs. A short walk or a chance to play before you go to work can go a long way toward having a dog that is relaxed and ready to take a rest when you are gone.

6 *Keeping a regular schedule.* A predictable schedule can help your dog with separation issues. After you've completed your own morning routines, if you let the dog outside for adequate exercise, give him a dog biscuit and fresh water, and say "Watch the house" (or whatever your goodbye cue is) every time you leave, the dog will learn that this is the morning drill. Before long, you'll be home from work and it will be time for another walk, training, and playtime.

7 *Familiar sounds.* Some owners report that their dogs are more relaxed when they hear a familiar sound such as a television or radio. When the owners leave, they make sure that their dogs have music, the Weather Channel, or a favorite soap opera. Animal shelters also report that dogs seem calmer when music is played in kennel areas.

8 *Multiple-pet households.* If you add a puppy or new dog to a household that already has other pets, make sure that you understand the dynamics between the animals before leaving the new dog alone with them. For example, you don't want to leave a large dog with a smaller dog if there is any chance that the small dog will be terrorized or injured, and you don't want to leave a dog with cats unless you are certain that the dog will not attempt to hurt the cats.

9 *Dividing and conquering.* When you have multiple dogs that bark incessantly while you are away (such as the Maltese sisters), it will be difficult to impossible to change the behavior of a group of dogs. You would probably have to divide and conquer to solve this problem, working with and getting one dog at a time under control. The best solution might be to change your own behavior. Instead of leaving the dogs in a hotel room so they can bark and disturb other guests, you would take them with you and leave them in your van while you had dinner. If the weather was not suitable for leaving dogs in the car, your solutions would be room service, having friends bring your dinner to you, or taking the dogs and getting your dinner at a drive-through. Dogs that bark and disturb others while in hotels and other public places can put the rights of all dog owners at risk.

10 *A calm return.* When you do the systematic plan (described previously) for leaving your dog, you'll go out the door and then come in, repeating this multiple times. Beginning with very short times outside the door, you'll eventually add more time until the dog barely responds when you come back into the house. If you come back inside and the dog jumps on you and goes crazy, there is a good chance that you have increased the amount of time that you are gone too quickly. You'll need to go back to being outside the door for a shorter time.

If you come back into the house and the dog is spinning, trying to jump on you, or initiating an excited greeting, ignore the dog, even if you have to turn and walk away. When the dog is calm, you can pet him and say hello. The idea here is that you already have a dog that thinks it is terrible if you leave. If you reinforce an excited, crazed frenzy when you come back, you are simply confirming for the dog that being separated is a horrible thing.

Feeling Comfortable

Dogs that receive regular training have fewer behavior problems. Training gives a dog something to wrap his mind around. When owners and dogs attend training classes together, they practice new skills each day. This provides the routine that is so helpful to dogs. Attending a six-week class is the perfect beginning, but if your dog has any signs of separation behaviors, you should continue training beyond the initial introductory class. Consider participating in an AKC sport with your dog such as Rally, obedience, or agility.

CGC Test Item 10, Supervised Separation, begins with teaching your dog to stay with a trusted person for a short period of time. In the context of your daily life with your canine family member, the supervised separation exercise serves as a foundation for a dog that eventually feels comfortable staying home alone and peacefully waiting for your return.

▲ **CGC Test Item 10 was created to prevent the separation issues to which dogs can be prone.**

▲ A dog owned by responsible owners is a true
member of the family, a friend to those of all ages.

THE AKC CGC RESPONSIBLE DOG OWNER'S PLEDGE

The AKC Canine Good Citizen concept applies to both ends of the leash. Every dog that earns the CGC award should have a responsible owner. The Responsible Dog Owner's Pledge is one of the most important parts of the CGC Program. If every dog owner followed this pledge, there would be no need for restrictive legislation pertaining to dogs, there would be far fewer dogs in shelters, and there would be a significant decrease in dog-related problems, such as bites.

Responsible dog owners agree to:

- take care of their dogs' health needs;
- ensure that their dogs are safe;
- never allow their dogs to infringe on the rights of others; and
- understand that owning a dog is a commitment in time and caring.

The CGC Responsible Dog Owner's Pledge is signed by each owner before owner and dog are taken through the CGC Test. This chapter explains the Responsible Dog Owner's Pledge.

It is nighttime in America. Robert J., a shift-worker who routinely logs in sixty-hour work weeks, can't sleep. He tosses and turns all night long, looking at the alarm clock on his nightstand every thirty minutes. Morning is only a few hours away, and he is facing a long day at work. This isn't new; Robert's sleep has been disrupted many nights recently by the neighbor's barking dog. The dog was a new pet for the children, who soon got bored with this sweet Boxer puppy, so he was sentenced to a life in the backyard. Robert has not confronted his neighbors about the barking because he doesn't like conflict. As a result of the excessive nocturnal barking outside his bedroom window, Robert has developed bad feelings toward his neighbors and, worse yet, extremely bad feelings toward a dog that is an innocent player in this depressing scenario.

In the mountain country of Colorado, on a hiking trail with a strict no-dogs policy, Bill and Nancy R. settle down for the night in their tent. As they go to sleep, they talk about how they miss having their Golden Retriever, Bella, along on hiking trips. She's back home in a boarding kennel. Her loving owners miss her terribly and wish she was not banned from the trails because others did not clean up after their dogs.

As midnight approaches, Jill A., a weary driver who has been accompanied on her long car trip by her Cocker Spaniel, stops at a Holiday Inn in Georgia and asks for a room. She's turned away after being told the hotel no longer accepts dogs because so many rooms had been damaged and dog owners had made a habit of leaving dog waste in the hotel's manicured lawns and flower beds.

Annoying nuisance barking, the loss of privileges for dogs on hiking trails and in hotels, and unnecessary incidents involving dog bites. These are some of the consequences of irresponsible dog ownership.

Dogs want to please us, they really do. With short daily training sessions, all dogs can learn the skills on the AKC Canine Good Citizen Test in a matter of weeks. But passing the CGC Test isn't enough to make a dog a good citizen. The Canine Good Citizen concept applies to both ends of the leash, and for a dog to be well mannered, he needs a responsible owner as a partner. The Responsible Dog Ownership training portion of the CGC Program is perhaps more important than the ten-step test for the dog. Being responsible owners will ensure that dogs continue to be welcome members of our communities.

Should You Get a Dog?

The first step to being a responsible dog owner is determining if the time is right for you to have a puppy or dog in your life. When you make the decision to add a puppy to your family, be prepared to look into that puppy's eyes and say, "I'm here for you for the next fifteen years. I will do whatever it takes to care for you, keep you safe, and give you a high-quality life." Are you prepared to house-train a puppy and be patient if there are accidents on your new carpet? Are you prepared to lose sleep during the first weeks that you have your puppy at home because he cries for his littermates and needs to go outside every two hours, even when it's raining? Do you have the time to give your puppy adequate exercise several times a day? Are you prepared to invest the time that it will take to train your dog to be well behaved? If you have children who are begging for a puppy, is there a responsible adult in the family who is committed to taking care of the puppy and providing him with love and attention if the children become bored with him and move on to the next novelty in their lives? If the puppy is intended to be an integral part of a child's life, is there an adult present who can teach the child how to properly care for an animal and treat the puppy with kindness?

You may decide that you would prefer a dog that has outgrown puppyhood. Bringing an adult dog into your family also has special considerations. Are you willing to work through any behavioral issues that this dog has developed? If you select a dog from a shelter or rescue group, you may not know the dog's exact medical history. Are you prepared to pay for any unforeseen and perhaps costly veterinary expenses? If you can't make these long-term commitments, it may not be the right time for you to add a dog to your family.

Choosing the Right Dog for You

You've thought about all of the pros and cons of dog ownership. You've searched your soul. You are at a time and place in your life where a dog would be a very positive addition to your family. The next step is determining the right dog for you. Do you want to benefit from the predictable traits of a purebred dog from a responsible breeder, do you want to adopt a dog from a rescue group, or do you want to visit a shelter to find your new dog? If you decide that a purebred dog is for you, educating yourself about individual breeds is your next step. The AKC recognizes more than 160 breeds, and they are all different. Do you want a big dog or a small dog? Do you want a flat-coated dog or a dog with longer hair? Are you looking for a breed that is typically good with children? It is important to match your dog's temperament with the general "temperament" of your family. If you are an active, athletic family, you may not want a breed that is largely inactive. A Basset Hound can be a great dog, but he won't be the world's best jogging companion. If you are a quiet, stay-at-home-and-watch-television person, you don't need a Border Collie that is on a constant mission to find a job and has been bred for centuries to run all day.

Where Should You Go to Get a Dog?

Now you have some ideas about the type or breed of dog that you're looking for. Where will you get this dog? First, you can get a purebred dog from a responsible breeder. Responsible breeders are well versed in canine genetics. They breed dogs in order to improve the quality of an individual breed, and they have organized breeding plans. Responsible breeders are involved with their national breed clubs (parent clubs) and are educated about any physical or genetic problems related to their breeds. Responsible breeders will be able to tell you about the past generations in your dog's bloodline, leading up to his breeding. Responsible breeders participate in conformation shows, which are designed to reward those dogs with superior physical structure and screen out those with structural and physical problems. Dogs that do not meet their breed's written standards are not bred.

In most cases, responsible breeders will have homes (and waiting lists) for every puppy months before each litter is born. Litters are planned well in advance, and finding the sire or dam who will be the best match in a mating may involve a dog that lives all the way across the country. A responsible breeder will have done a number of health screenings on any dogs to be bred. Some of these screenings include the OFA's (Orthopedic Foundation for Animals) hip dysplasia evaluation, the Canine Eye Registration Foundation's tests for eye problems, and thyroid checks. Most responsible breeders will have contracts, stating that if anything happens in the lifetime of a dog so that the owner cannot keep him (or if the dog has any problems), they will take the dog back and either care for him or find him a loving home for the remainder of his life. Responsible breeders will want to stay in touch with owners of their dogs so they can hear from time to time how the dogs are doing. Your breeder is available to you as a resource if you have any trouble raising or caring for your dog. Many people find that the breeders of their dogs become their friends and mentors.

This is far different treatment than what you will get if you purchase a dog from a "backyard" breeder. Backyard breeders are the local breeders you may see advertising in the newspapers. A backyard breeder usually breeds his dogs either to make money, to get a puppy from a dog he likes, or to allow his children to witness the miracle of birth. When such a breeder decides to breed his dog, he finds a local dog of the opposite sex and same breed. Just about any local dog of that breed will do. After purchasing a puppy from a backyard breeder and leaving the premises, the dog is *your* dog, and any of the dog's problems are yours, too.

Reinforcing backyard breeding by buying a dog from such a breeder perpetuates the problem of uneducated breeders. Backyard breeders often know nothing about the history or characteristics of the breed of dog they're selling.

▲ **Your first step on the road to responsible ownership is the selection of a puppy from a reputable source.**

Another place to get a dog is from a rescue group. There are breed-specific rescue groups and all-dog rescue groups. Rescue dogs are usually adult dogs; however, rescue groups sometimes have puppies. Dogs from rescue groups are loving, wonderful dogs that deserve homes, but be aware that some have behavioral issues, so you should be prepared to handle these issues and address your new dog's training needs.

Finally, you can go to your local shelter to get a dog. Shelter dogs, like rescue dogs, may have some behavioral issues. Depending on the part of the country in which you adopt a shelter dog, the shelter may not have much, if any, information on the dog's previous owners or living environment. However, very carefully selected shelter dogs can make wonderful pets. You can find both purebred and mixed-breed dogs in shelters, and both will benefit from Canine Good Citizen training and a loving owner.

You can find a responsible breeder and a list of purebred rescue groups and read about individual breeds at www.akc.org.

▲ If you obtain your puppy from a breeder, she should provide the pedigree, registration, contract, health documentation, and all other relevant paperwork.

What Is Responsible Ownership?

The first thing you'll be asked to do when you enter a Canine Good Citizen Test is to complete the registration form and sign the Responsible Dog Owner's Pledge. In signing the pledge, you'll agree to the two primary components of responsible dog ownership: (1) to be responsible for your dog's health needs, safety, and quality of life throughout his life and (2) to never allow your dog to infringe on the rights of others.

Being Responsible for Your Dog's Health Needs

Say "Aahh"—Obtaining a Veterinarian for Routine Care

By signing the CGC Responsible Dog Owner's Pledge, you'll agree to be responsible for the healthcare of your dog. Healthcare includes, first and foremost, selecting a veterinarian and taking the dog in for an initial evaluation and to establish a medical record at the clinic. The veterinarian will work with you, as the dog's owner, to determine the most appropriate vaccine schedule for the dog. It was once an expectation that all dogs would be vaccinated annually; however, there is currently some debate in the veterinary community regarding vaccines. For this reason, owners and their veterinarians should work together to develop appropriate vaccine plans for individual dogs. In addition to providing vaccines and medical treatment when needed, your veterinarian can help you develop preventative-care plans that will improve your dog's quality of life. Preventative plans include protecting your dog from worms and external parasites such as ticks and fleas.

With the increased costs of veterinary care, it is wise to consider health insurance for your dog. You can find helpful information from PetPartners, Inc., at www.akcphp.com.

Let's Eat—Providing Adequate Nutrition

Responsible dog owners provide adequate nutrition for their dogs. Adequate nutrition comes from quality dog food with the proper amounts of protein, fat, fiber, vitamins, and minerals. Your dog's breeder or veterinarian can recommend a food, you can learn about dog foods at your local pet-supply store, or you can ask your dog-savvy friends for recommendations. There are specialty foods for puppies, older dogs, and dogs with weight or health problems. Adequate nutrition will help your dog maintain a healthy weight and good coat.

In addition to a good dog food, dogs should have access to clean water at all times. A word about water—indoor dogs should always have water in the house. If your dog spends part of the day outdoors, clean water should also be provided outside. Dogs are like humans in that they can get dehydrated when they do not get enough water.

Looking Good—Daily Exercise and Grooming

Daily exercise is needed to keep your dog healthy. Exercise is good for the dog's heart, lungs, circulatory system, and muscles. Regular exercise will play an important part in maintaining your dog's weight and avoiding the many health problems that arise from obesity.

Grooming also plays a role in your dog's good health. Routine grooming tasks, including brushing, bathing, and caring for the feet, nails, eyes, and ears, will keep your dog free from external parasites and skin infections. While bathing should be done on an "as-needed" basis, daily brushing helps your dog's coat maintain good condition. Brushing cleans the coat and stimulates the skin oils that create a healthy shine. Brushing not only improves the coat but is also a way for you and your dog to bond; tactile stimulation is very reinforcing to animals. When brushing doesn't remove the dirt and excess oiliness, it's time for a bath to keep your dog clean.

Being Responsible for Your Dog's Safety

Fence Me In—Controlling Dogs with Fences and Leashes

As simple as it seems, leashes and fences are the answers to many of the problems related to dogs in our communities. Even for an avid dog lover, it can be frightening to be walking in the park and have an unknown dog approach at a fast run. Your heart begins to race and you begin to worry that the dog will bite you or attack you or your dog (who is on a leash). Even though we may be dog lovers, when a dog is barreling toward us at light speed, it is irritating for many of us to hear the owner yelling from halfway across the park, "It's OK, he's friendly" (or "He just wants to say hello," or "He just wants to play."). It doesn't matter if he's friendly. The irresponsible owner and his out-of-control dog didn't have the right to make others feel uncomfortable or to interrupt other owners' walks with their own dogs.

A responsible dog owner will properly confine or control his dog at all times. This involves using leashes in public, fences at home when the dog is outside, and reliable voice commands when the dog is in an approved off-leash dog area. If you think there's a chance that a person who is out walking his dog would like his dog to have an opportunity to play with yours, approach the person and ask permission.

Having a yard that is fenced (or, if you live in the city, taking your dog to a fenced dog park) gives your dog the chance to run and get the gross motor exercise that all dogs need. This kind of exercise cannot be provided with just a walk around the block on a leash. With the exception of geriatric dogs, dogs that have physical problems, or toy breeds that can get much of their exercise indoors, dogs need exercise in order to expend energy.

High-energy breeds are often mistakenly reported by their owners as having behavior problems because they're so "hyper." These dogs don't have behavior problems; their owners simply do not understand the level of exercise required for dogs that have been designed to work all day. An owner of a Border Collie complained about her dog's inability to settle down in the house. She said, "Yes, he gets exercise. I walk him around the block every day when I get home from work." This owner's response underlines why responsible dog owners must take it upon themselves to become well educated about their breeds. If this owner truly understood Border Collies, she would know that she could walk her dog around the block five times and he wouldn't even be warmed up.

Sometimes, even when owners try to be responsible, dogs just don't cooperate. So you follow the AKC's advice and get a brand-new chain-link fence. The dog digs out of the fence, the dog jumps over the fence, or the dog does something that you never saw a dog do—he climbs the fence. Now what? If you have a canine Houdini on your hands, you'll have to do your best to dog-proof your fence with extra height at the top and/or concrete reinforcement at the bottom. However, the best solution is to train the dog so that he responds to your instructions, such as *come*; engage him in activities; and provide supervision when he is in the yard. If you have to leave, bring the dog into the house. This also prevents someone from stealing your dog, the dog's barking and disturbing the peace while you are gone, or the dog's getting bored and digging a tunnel to freedom.

If your dog is destructive, he should be crate-trained to stay in the house when you are gone. You'll rest easy knowing that your dog is in a climate-controlled environment and that he can't be getting into trouble. A crate provides safety for both your dog and your belongings.

Some owners who don't have fences decide they want a large dog but they don't want the dog in the house. Their answer to keeping the dog outside is to chain their pet to a stake. This is *not* a good idea. Dogs are companion animals. They want to be with you. It is inhumane to have a dog living alone in the yard with no human contact most of the time. If your goal is to have a dog for protection, and you are thinking of chaining your dog, invest in a good electronic alarm system instead of a dog. Dogs that are chained for long periods of time can become seriously aggressive. Chaining a dog does not protect the child who may wander up to pet the dog.

Dogs and Children

The use of reliable fences and leashes will protect your dog and keep him safe. Leashes and fences also prevent incidents. The data clearly shows that most tragic incidents could have been prevented if people simply did two things: (1) fenced their dogs and (2) supervised their children.

As a responsible owner, a key part of keeping your dog safe is maintaining an environment that sets your dog up for success. Even though parents should supervise their children, when there is a dog bite, it is often the dog that pays the price with a dangerous-dog classification and the accompanying restrictions or, in the worst case, mandatory euthanasia.

"Where, Oh Where, Has My Little Dog Gone?"—Identification

As a responsible dog owner, you will do your best to supervise your dog and keep him on your own property. Unfortunately, no matter how hard you try, sometimes accidents happen. For example, the front door is open and your black Lab looks out and sees a squirrel across the street—in a flash, he's gone. Or a friend comes to visit, and her child is playing in the backyard. Too late, you realize that your Whippet was in the yard and the child left the gate open. For times like these, when accidents happen, you should use some form of identification for your dog to maximize his chances of being returned home.

Collar tags are readily available and inexpensive forms of dog identification. The downsides of collar tags are that they can be broken off, the dog may not be wearing his collar when he makes the great escape, and a collar that is worn all the time can be a safety hazard if it gets caught on something. Further, if a dog is stolen, his collar tags will be simply removed and thrown into the nearest trash bin, giving you no proof of ownership if you locate your dog.

Microchips and tattoos are good permanent forms of identification. Many veterinarians will microchip or tattoo dogs. Using microchips to permanently identify

dogs, the American Kennel Club's Companion Animal Recovery (AKC-CAR) program has reunited over 360,000 lost pets with their owners. Founded in 1995, AKC-CAR has enrolled over four million animals.

▲ **A dog must be well behaved to be off leash in public, and a responsible owner allows her dog off leash only when regulations permit.**

Microchips are rice-sized, and each microchip is encoded with a unique and unalterable identification number. The chip is typically implanted just under the skin in the scruff of the dog's neck and lasts for the life of the pet.

If your dog has a microchip and is lost, the dog can be scanned at a shelter or participating veterinary clinic to determine if a microchip is present. If the animal is enrolled in the AKC-CAR program, the owners will be notified immediately.

The 100,000th dog to be reunited with her family after being lost was Belle, a puppy whose nose and sense of adventure led her out of her yard and away from home. Belle belonged to the Akowski family in Tucson, Arizona. The Akowskis had Belle microchipped shortly after bringing her home from the animal shelter. As closely as the Akowskis watched Belle, the day came where someone accidentally left a gate open. Belle followed her canine sibling—a known escape artist—out of the yard. Belle got lost, and a kind person eventually found her covered in cactus spines. She was taken to the veterinarian, where she was scanned and identified. AKC-CAR was called, and the Akowskis were contacted shortly thereafter. Belle was safely returned to her family after an adventure that lasted thirteen days. Without the microchip, Belle might not have been reunited with her family.

Never Allowing Your Dog to Infringe on the Rights of Others

Who Let the Dogs Out?—No Running Loose

On May 13, 2004, the Caraway City (Arkansas) Council met to discuss a new ordinance about loose dogs. The meeting was in response to a number of dog bites from at-large dogs. Caraway's mayor said, "If people would keep the dogs in a pen or on a leash, there would have been no need for a new ordinance." Because of the dogs running loose, one alderman added, "I am concerned about the elderly and children who are so defenseless." The mayor continued, "If we don't do something, we could be liable for not protecting our people." The police chief was present and gave his opinions on the proposed new ordinance, "… the dogs that are here now are giving us problems. Too many problems with these three breeds of dogs. Kids can't ride down the street without the dogs chasing them. People are scared to death to even go out to their mailboxes. We have had problems getting out of the Jeep for fear of attack."

The council then voted and passed Ordinance 2004-03, thereby banning all Pit Bulls, Rottweilers, and Doberman Pinschers from Caraway. Owners of these breeds were given only ten days to find new homes for their dogs.

A key part of being a responsible dog owner is never letting your dog infringe on the rights of others. Dogs should never be permitted to run loose in a neighborhood. When some dog owners are irresponsible, other dog owners lose their privileges, and in a growing number of locations, the privileges lost may include the right to own a dog.

Silent Night: No Nuisance Barking

We all want our neighborhoods to be peaceful places where we can enjoy the restful havens that our homes provide. It is hard to relax or sleep when there is a constantly yapping dog nearby. Responsible dog owners do not permit their dogs to disturb others by engaging in excessive barking. If your dog is a barking fanatic, consider a behavior program to put barking "on cue," meaning that the dog learns both *bark* and *no bark* commands.

If you stay in pet-friendly hotels with your dog when you travel, and your dog is a barker, assuming the neighborhood is safe, there are people to keep an eye on the car, and the temperature is moderate, take him with you when you go to dinner. Park your car in the shade and turn on a battery-operated fan or do whatever you need to do to keep the dog comfortable in the car. Chances are your dog will be perfectly quiet in the back of the SUV that is familiar territory. If it's hot weather, leave your barker at home with a trusted dogsitter. Whatever you do, don't leave your noisy dog in a hotel room to bark the entire time you are gone. Responsible dog owners work hard to maintain good relationships with pet-friendly hotels, and hotel managers do not want to lose business because of barking dogs.

"Excuse Me, You Forgot Something"—Picking Up Waste

When dogs defecate in public places such as parks, hiking trails, and wilderness areas, and their owners do not clean up after them, the first response of city, county, or park officials is to say, "That's it! No more dogs."

Cleaning up after your dog is the right thing to do. Other people enjoy clean recreation spaces, and they should not have to look at or step in your dog's waste. Responsible dog owners carry plastic bags with them on walks and hikes. If your dog soils in a public area, use a bag to clean up after him. You can dispose of the bag in the nearest garbage can.

Being Responsible for Your Dog's Quality of Life

Good Dog! Good Owner!—Basic Training

Responsible dog owners understand that basic training is beneficial to all dogs. Training maximizes dogs' abilities, and, through training, owners enhance their relationships with their dogs. The data on dogs that are returned to shelters shows that over 90 percent of dogs surrendered to shelters by their owners have had no training. This is an indication that training results in the bonding that makes an owner committed to the dog.

When your dog is under control and responds to commands such as *sit, come, down,* and *stay,* you've given your dog the skills he needs to have additional freedom. Canine Good Citizen training is the foundation for all other training that follows in your dog's life. Every dog deserves at least the training required to earn the Canine Good Citizen award. In a one-hour class that meets weekly for six to eight weeks, with about fifteen minutes of practice at home each day, you and your dog can earn the CGC certificate, which shows your ability to teach your dog new skills and your commitment to being a responsible dog owner.

Let the Games Begin: Attention and Playtime

Like young children, puppies learn about the world around them through play. The love of play will continue into your dog's senior years if you make games and playtime fun, reinforcing events. Having your dog run to fetch a ball or soft Frisbee or find things that you've hidden are examples of games that will provide exercise, fun, and mental stimulation for your dog. Every day should include some playtime during which you and your dog can enjoy each other.

▼ Dog ownership means a commitment to spending time with your dog, and well-trained dogs are a joy to be around.

Have I Told You Lately that I Love You?— A Commitment in Time and Caring

Owning a dog is a commitment. If you provide your dog with quality care, basic training that begins with the CGC skills, daily playtime, and plenty of attention, your dog will become the kind of companion and friend who can make you happy every day.

You are in charge of your dog's quality of life. The saying among dog trainers, "people get the dog they deserve," seems to be true. Dogs are wonderful, remarkable creatures; they give us their love and devotion, and they deserve no less than a responsible, committed owner in return. 🐾

CANINE GOOD CITIZEN OWNER'S COMMITMENT TO RESPONSIBLE DOG OWNERSHIP

When you and your dog take the AKC Canine Good Citizen Test, one of the first things you'll do is sign the Responsible Dog Owner's Pledge. The AKC CGC Responsible Dog Owner's Pledge follows.

I understand that to truly be a Canine Good Citizen, my dog needs a responsible owner. I agree to maintain my dog's health, safety, and quality of life. By participating in the Canine Good Citizen Test, I agree:

I will be responsible for my dog's health needs. These include:
- routine veterinary care including check-ups and vaccines
- adequate nutrition through proper diet; clean water at all times
- daily exercise and regular bathing and grooming

I will be responsible for my dog's safety.
- I will properly control my dog by providing fencing where appropriate, not letting my dog run loose, and using a leash in public.
- I will ensure that my dog has some form of identification (which may include collar tags, tattoos, or a microchip ID).
- I will provide adequate supervision when my dog and children are together.

I will not allow my dog to infringe on the rights of others.
- I will not allow my dog to run loose in the neighborhood.
- I will not allow my dog to be a nuisance to others by barking while in the yard, in a hotel room, etc.
- I will pick up and properly dispose of my dog's waste in all public areas such as on the grounds of hotels, on sidewalks, parks, etc.
- I will pick up and properly dispose of my dog's waste in wilderness areas, on hiking trails, campgrounds, and in off-leash parks.

I will be responsible for my dog's quality of life.
- I understand that basic training is beneficial to all dogs.
- I will give my dog attention and playtime.
- I understand that owning a dog is a commitment in time and caring.

Owner's Signature_____ Date_____

▲ When you arrive to take the Canine Good Citizen Test, the first thing you'll do is sign in.

FINDING CGC TRAINING AND TESTING NEAR YOU

Benefits of CGC Training

The benefits of owning a dog that has passed the AKC Canine Good Citizen Test are many. By teaching your dog the CGC skills and earning the CGC award:

- you will be the proud owner of a dog that responds to your instructions and is easier to manage;
- you will have identified yourself as a responsible owner;
- in CGC classes, you will be introduced to the wonderful world of dog training and all of the exciting activities that come after CGC, such as Rally, obedience, and agility;
- depending on where you live, you may have additional privileges, such as admission to dog parks, discounts at veterinary offices, homeowner's insurance benefits, and the ability to participate in therapy-dog groups because of your dog's CGC status; and
- perhaps most important of all, through CGC training you will develop a bond with your dog that will last forever.

The first step is to teach your dog the skills on the AKC Canine Good Citizen Test. If you know how to train dogs, you can teach the skills yourself and then find an AKC-approved CGC Evaluator to test your dog. Or, you can attend a training class. Some classes will be called "Canine Good Citizen" classes, but a basic obedience training class can also prepare you for the CGC Test. All you have to do is tell your instructor at the beginning of the course that passing the AKC CGC Test is a goal.

We strongly suggest attending a class to teach your dog the CGC skills. In a class, dogs will have opportunities for socialization that they won't have if you train on your own. You'll be able to practice the distraction dog and meeting strangers exercises with other people and their dogs. This experience is invaluable when it comes to teaching your dog to be steady around other people, other dogs, and distractions.

The list of skills on the CGC Test is provided in earlier chapters. The ten-item CGC Test is also on the AKC's Web site at www.akc.org/events/cgc. When you get onto this page, look on the left side and click on "Training/Testing."

Meet Your AKC-Approved Canine Good Citizen Evaluator

To earn the AKC Canine Good Citizen award, dogs must pass the AKC CGC Test. The test must be administered by an AKC-approved CGC Evaluator. Evaluators are experienced dog trainers.

To be approved as an Evaluator, the applicant must have at least two years' experience teaching other people and their dogs, be at least eighteen years old, be in good standing with AKC, and have experience working with a variety of breeds and types of dogs.

Choosing the Right Instructor
for You and Your Dog

Dog training has changed tremendously in the last several decades. Whereas dogs and horses were once trained with heavy-handed punishment-based procedures, current training philosophies are aimed at using positive reinforcement and scientifically-based procedures. What seems to vary from trainer to trainer is the extent and level of positive reinforcement and whether or not corrections are used in training (and, if so, what type).

Many people who decide to take their dogs to classes have seen ads in the paper or have heard about classes in their area. They call to register, and they show up on the first night of class with their dogs. This is not the best way to start a dog-training class. When you are ready to enroll your dog in a training class, we strongly suggest that you call several instructors and ask if you can come and observe before you sign up. Go to the class without your dog, sit and watch the other students, and take note of how the instructor teaches. Many people would have made different choices about their training classes if they had observed the instruction firsthand before enrolling.

The goal is for you to find a class, a training school, and an instructor with a philosophy that is suited to who you are and how you want your dog to be trained. Obviously, you'll want to find a competent instructor, but you also should be on the lookout for a person who will treat you and your dog with the care and respect you deserve.

WHERE TO FIND CGC TRAINING AND TESTING

1 Look up Evaluators by state on the AKC's Web site: www.akc.org/events/cgc/cgc_bystate.cfm. You can contact the ones near you and ask about training and testing.

2 When your dog is ready to be tested or if you want to watch a test while you're training for CGC, visit www.akc.org/events/cgc/cgc_schedule.cfm to find upcoming CGC Tests.

3 Go to www.akc.org and click on "Clubs" to find the AKC obedience club near you.

4 Inquire at your local pet-supply superstore; it may offer CGC classes and testing.

5 Find a private trainer in your area. Any good basic obedience class will prepare you and your dog for CGC.

Ask the instructor some questions. Examples of questions include:

- How long have you been training dogs?
- What kinds of classes do you teach?
- Have you put any titles on your own dogs?
- What dog sports do you participate in or have you participated in?
- What is your basic philosophy of training?
- What kind of equipment will we be using in class (e.g., collars, etc.).

- Do you use food rewards? Corrections? If so, can you tell me about these?
- Are all sizes of dogs together in class?
- Do you know your dropout rate? How many students graduate from your classes?
- After the beginning class, do many students go on for additional training?

When you observe the instructor, think about the following:

- The instructor's skill level in teaching humans.
- The instructor's knowledge of dogs.
- The instructor's communication style with students—pleasant and reinforcing or bossy and sarcastic?
- The organization of the class, i.e., how long is spent on each topic, how many dogs/owners, etc.?
- The curriculum—does it teach all you want to learn?
- The attitude of the dogs—do they look happy and eager to work or do they seem bored or nervous?

- The attitude of the human students—are they enthusiastic or are they frustrated?
- The way that the instruction is presented and sequenced—is the class set up in such a way to encourage success?
- The teaching methods—do you spend the entire class listening to the instructor talk?
- The instructor's ability to handle any behavior problems or student questions.

If at First You Don't Succeed—Retesting

Some dogs do not pass the AKC CGC Test on the first attempt. If your dog does not pass the CGC Test the first time, don't be embarrassed or disappointed. This could mean that you have a dog that is somewhat challenging to train, or it could mean that you just need to work on a specific behavior a little longer. The important thing is that you've committed yourself to being a responsible owner, you love your dog, and you are working to earn the CGC award. In the grand scheme of things, it won't matter how much training the dog needed.

The story on the next page was printed in the June 2007 issue of our *AKC CGC Evaluator News*. The story is heartwarming because a very hyper, hard-to-manage dog with some behavioral issues had the potential to be great. He found himself in the hands of a loving owner who would not give up. This is what the AKC Canine Good Citizen Program is about.

Raising Radar:
A CGC Accomplishment

by Llona Geiger

At the meetings of my local obedience club, there is a part of each meeting for "brags." Owners are given the chance to stand up and tell everyone about the accomplishments of their dogs since the last meeting. People brag about getting the Obedience Trial Championship (OTCH) award, they brag about getting 198 out of a possible 200 points in a recent trial, and they brag about having the only dog in their breed to have a certain combination of advanced titles. These members are good at what they do, and they deserve to brag. Most would never brag about their dogs passing the AKC Canine Good Citizen award. For them, this would be super easy.

But not for me. My dog, Radar, is a highly athletic male German Shorthaired Pointer. GSPs are known to be athletes. I have owned and loved this breed for more than thirty years. Radar came to me after my dog,

◀ **Llona Geiger and Radar. Radar earned the CGC award thanks to Llona, who was willing to be persistent and not give up on a dog with some behavioral issues.**

Chip, died. Very unlike Chip, Radar was mostly white with a stubby tail that moved in circles over the tiny liver spots on his rear end. It looked like a radar-screen image of the Atlanta airport.

We started by taking Radar to puppy training. Then we went to a manners class, not once, but twice. After that, we went on to advanced manners ("Manners and More"), not once, but twice. It seemed that Radar was a dog that was repeating every class that other dogs sailed through. We enrolled in a Novice obedience class at my local dog club, and, you guessed it, we needed to take it twice. We then took basic agility (twice) as well as Rally obedience (twice—I'm thinking there is a pattern here). When my son calls from Arizona, he always asks if Radar has his PhD yet. I just laugh and ask him if his experimental airplane is flying yet. We agree that we both spend considerable sums of time and money on the smallest glimmers of hope and the slightest signs of progress.

Training Radar has sometimes resulted in hurt feelings and more. I recall being told not to return to one class until my dog was more mature (translation—until he behaved and I could control him better). The irony of this was that if anyone needed to be in the class, it was me and Radar.

Radar has never given up on me, so having to do everything twice won't cause me to give up on him. I'm getting older now, but I am still stuck on this sporting breed that I love so much. I like our long walks in the woods. I like the GSP's inquisitiveness and affection. I like the breed's antics, desire to work, grace, agility, and good-natured tolerance of other dogs. And, this may sound strange, but I like the trainability of the breed. Radar, trainable? You bet. I finally have the CGC award to prove it. And it may be *twice* as meaningful to me.

Update on Radar: In the spring of 2009, the AKC Canine Good Citizen Department checked in to see how Radar was doing. Llona was hooked on dog training and was assisting in an obedience class where Radar was the demo dog. Radar had earned a title in AKC Rally in three straight shows. He also completed the Companion Dog (CD) title in Novice obedience, earning a second place and a very impressive first place. Radar is currently preparing for advanced obedience competition. ❧

THE AMERICAN KENNEL CLUB

This certifies that

"Wyn"

Owned by

Jon S. Bailey

successfully passed the Canine Good Citizen Test on

May 1, 2003

and has been listed in the Canine Good Citizen (CGC) Archives

by the American Kennel Club

VP of Companion Events

▲ Earning the Canine Good Citizen award is an accomplishment for both the owner and the dog.

BEFORE AND AFTER CGC

The AKC Canine Good Citizen Program is the place to go to teach your dog basic canine manners and to learn how to be a responsible dog owner. But hopefully, Canine Good Citizen training will be only one important part of the education that you and your dog experience together. Both before and after CGC, the American Kennel Club is ready to help you have a lifetime of learning and fun with your canine companion.

If you've purchased this book and you have a puppy that is too young for CGC training, that's OK. You can get started in the AKC S.T.A.R. Puppy Program. After CGC, there are many fun activities you can do to continue training your dog, including Rally, obedience, agility, tracking, and a number of performance events for specific breeds. Eligible dogs can also participate in conformation or Junior Showmanship.

▲ The puppy level of Canine Good Citizen training is an exciting new program called AKC S.T.A.R. Puppy.

Before CGC: AKC S.T.A.R. Puppy

The AKC S.T.A.R. Puppy Program is an exciting program designed to get dog owners and their puppies off to a good start. The S.T.A.R. Puppy Program is an incentive program for caring dog owners who have taken the time to take their puppies through a basic training class that is at least six weeks long. S.T.A.R. is an acronym for all of the things puppies need to have a good life—socialization, training, activity, and a responsible owner.

We know that classes are a very effective way to teach owners to communicate with their puppies. They provide the knowledge that owners need to raise a puppy, including information on housetraining, chewing, and the most practical way to teach basic skills, such as coming when called. The AKC S.T.A.R. Puppy Program is a natural lead-in to the AKC Canine Good Citizen Program.

When you and your puppy complete a basic training class that is taught by an AKC-approved CGC Evaluator, your puppy is eligible to be enrolled in the AKC S.T.A.R. Puppy Program. Your instructor will administer the twenty-item AKC S.T.A.R. Puppy Test at the end of the course. Upon passing the test, you'll send in your application for enrollment in the program. Your puppy will receive the AKC S.T.A.R. Puppy medal and be listed in the AKC S.T.A.R. Puppy records. And, to ensure that owners continue learning beyond puppy class, the S.T.A.R. Puppy Program provides them with the *AKC Puppy Handbook* and an ongoing free monthly newsletter with training tips and up-to-date information.

More information on the AKC S.T.A.R. Puppy Program can be found at www.akc.org/starpuppy.

After CGC

If you decide to continue training after your dog earns the Canine Good Citizen award, the American Kennel Club can provide you with a wide variety of training opportunities. To learn more about any of the AKC activities discussed here, all you have to do is go to www.akc.org and type the name of the activity (e.g., "obedience") in the search box.

Conformation

There are more than 160 AKC breeds and varieties of breeds that can compete in AKC conformation dog shows. In these shows, the emphasis lies on the *conformation*, or physical structure, of the dog. Dogs are judged on qualities including body structure, general appearance, gait, and temperament. After examining each entry, the dog-show judge decides how closely, in his or her opinion, the dog measures up to that judge's mental image of the perfect dog as described in the breed's written standard.

In conformation, dogs compete for points toward their championships. It takes fifteen points to become a champion of record, and the points must be won under at least three different judges.

At an all-breed show (where all AKC breeds can enter), each Best of Breed winner competes for four placements within his Group. In the final competition, seven dogs (the first-place winners from each Group) compete for Best in Show.

Dogs in conformation shows may not be spayed or neutered. The purpose of conformation competition is to improve purebred dogs by identifying those that are quality representatives of their breeds and thus desirable for breeding.

Junior Showmanship

Junior Showmanship is the AKC activity that teaches young people between the ages of 9 and 18 how to exhibit dogs at shows and develop good sportsmanship. In Junior Showmanship, the competition is judged solely on the skills of the young handlers, not on the dogs' actual conformation. Juniors may also complete with their dogs in Companion Events (such as obedience and agility) and Performance Events (those events designed for certain breeds, such as lure coursing and earthdog events). There is no minimum age for young people who wish to compete in Companion Events.

Agility

If you didn't blink, you might have seen agility on television. Agility is the fast-paced activity where dogs run at top speed around a course with equipment that includes tunnels, tire jumps, weave poles, bar jumps, broad jumps, the dog walk, the A-frame, the seesaw, and the pause table.

Dogs in agility are judged on both speed and accuracy, and all breeds can participate. Because agility is an extremely physical and athletic activity, it is important for both handlers and dogs to receive proper training. Agility is a good source of exercise for active dogs and a great confidence builder for shy, timid dogs.

Obedience

Obedience training provides dogs with a basic education that will help them be better companions. With their abilities to follow instructions and their

understanding of many commands, obedience-trained dogs excel at other canine sports. AKC obedience clubs across the country can help you train your dog to be a better family pet or to compete in obedience competitions.

▲ **Programs for handlers and judges foster professionalism and ethics in those who participate in conformation showing.**

AKC Obedience is divided into several levels for competition. Novice, Open, and Utility are three of the levels at which dogs can earn obedience titles.

■ *Novice.* In Novice obedience competition, the exercises are Heel on Lead and Figure 8, Stand for Exam, Heel Free (off-leash), Recall, Long Sit (one minute), and Long Down (three minutes). The title that is earned is the Companion Dog (CD) title.

You can see that the skills in Novice obedience are more advanced versions of many of the skills on the AKC Canine Good Citizen Test.

■ *Open*. After the dog earns the Companion Dog title, he can compete in Open obedience to earn the Companion Dog Excellent (CDX) title. Open obedience exercises include Heel Free and Figure 8, Drop on Recall, Retrieve on the Flat (the dog retrieves but does not have to go over a jump), Retrieve over High Jump, Broad Jump, Long Sit (three minutes) and Long Down (five minutes).

UNLEASHED

In the Canine Good Citizen Test, every exercise was on leash. In Novice, the dog progresses to the point that some of the exercises (such as Recall and Heel Free) are done off leash. In Open, as soon as the handler walks into the ring, the steward takes the leash away and everything is done off leash.

■ *Utility*. The most advanced level of obedience is Utility. Dogs in Utility compete to earn the Utility Dog (UD) title. The exercises in this class, which are also done off lead, include the Signal Exercise, Scent Discrimination, Directed Retrieve, Moving Stand and Examination, and Directed Jumping. Beyond the UD, the Utility Dog Excellent (UDX) and Obedience Trial Champion (OTCH) are additional titles that can be earned.

At each level, the dog needs three qualifying scores (at least 170 out of 200 points) under three different judges to earn the available title at that level.

Rally

AKC Rally is a relatively new sport, and both dogs and their owners are giving it rave reviews! Rally is a good next step after AKC Canine Good Citizen.

In Rally, the handler/dog team enters the ring. After the instruction from the judge to begin, they move at their own pace through a series of signs that designate exercises to be performed. The handler can communicate with the dog throughout the course by talking, clapping, and providing praise. In cases where there is a tie on accuracy, the tie is broken by the speed with which the handler/dog team completed the course.

Examples of directions on Rally signs include "Stop and Down," "Moving Down and Walk Around Dog," "90-degree Pivot Right," and "Leave Dog, Two Steps, Call to Heel and Forward."

Tracking

AKC tracking is the activity that teaches dogs to track and follow human scent. You might have seen K9 police officers (in real life or in a movie) using their dogs to track a lost child or a suspect who has run into the woods.

There are three main tracking titles that can be earned. The first is Tracking Dog (TD), in which the dog must follow a track from 440 to 500 yards long with three to five changes of direction. Each track is aged for thirty minutes to two hours before the test starts. The Tracking Dog Excellent (TDX) title requires the dog to complete a track that is three to five hours old, 800 to 1000 yards long, and has seven changes of direction. In TDX, there are cross-tracks, meaning that a person makes the dog's job of following the track more difficult by walking across the original track. The Variable Surface Tracking (VST) title is the urban tracking title in which dogs track over different surfaces (such as a parking lot, around a building, and down an alley) in the community. Finally, dogs that earn all three tracking titles earn the title of Champion Tracker (CT).

Performance Events

The AKC's Performance Events showcase purebred dogs in the jobs that they were originally bred to do. Earthdog tests, herding, lure coursing, coonhound tests, field trials, and hunting tests are the events that make up the AKC's Performance Events. Basset Hounds and Dachshunds can enter field trials. Beagles, retrievers, pointing breeds, and spaniels can participate in field trials and hunting tests.

Earthdog Tests

Earthdog trials are for dogs that "go to ground." Originally, the terriers involved in today's earthdog events were bred to go into the dens, holes, or dirt tunnels of underground quarry, such as rats or badgers. The long, low shape of many of the breeds who participate in earthdog events is well suited for crawling into and getting out of tunnels.

Breeds that participate in earthdog events are Dachshunds, Australian Terriers, Bedlington Terriers, Border Terriers, Cairn Terriers, Dandie Dinmont Terriers, Fox

Terriers, Parson Russell Terriers, Lakeland Terriers, Manchester Terriers, Miniature Bull Terriers, Miniature Schnauzers, Norfolk Terriers, Norwich Terriers, Scottish Terriers, Sealyham Terriers, Skye Terriers, Welsh Terriers, West Highland White Terriers, and Silky Terriers.

The titles that can be earned are Junior Earthdog (JE), Senior Earthdog (SE), and Master Earthdog (ME). Introduction to Quarry is the level for beginning handlers and dogs.

Herding

The herding instinct developed in the herding breeds as a result of centuries of breeding. Herding tests are noncompetitive events in which dogs are judged against a performance standard to evaluate their abilities. In herding trials, dogs compete for prizes and placements. The stock used for herding includes sheep, goats, ducks, and sometimes cattle.

The most basic herding title is Herding Tested (HT). There is also a herding instinct test, which is an entry-level test to demonstrate that a dog has the ability for herding; a certificate can be earned in this test.

Lure Coursing

Lure coursing is the fun-to-watch event in which dogs follow an artificial lure around a course on an open field. The lure (that often looks like a white handkerchief) is attached to a wire and is moved mechanically at varying speeds. The dogs see the lure move, their centuries-old hardwiring kicks in, and the chase begins.

Lure coursing is for the sighthounds, the breeds that use their sense of sight to locate game and then run after it. These dogs work differently than dogs that trail game using their sense of smell. Sighthounds that compete in lure coursing are Afghan Hounds, Basenjis, Borzois, Greyhounds, Ibizan Hounds, Irish Wolfhounds, Italian Greyhounds, Pharaoh Hounds, Rhodesian Ridgebacks, Salukis, Scottish Deerhounds, and Whippets.

Coonhound Tests

The six purebred coonhounds (Treeing Walker, Black and Tan, Plott, English, Bluetick, and Redbone) all participate in field trials, bench shows, water races, and nite hunts. These events evaluate the dogs' conformation and test their ability to follow the scent of raccoons in different scenarios.

Field Trials and Hunting Tests

Separate events are held for Beagles, Basset Hounds and Dachshunds, pointing breeds, retrievers, and spaniels. This is because each of these dogs originally had a slightly different purpose and style when working. All of the sport-

▲ Although classified in the AKC's Working Group, the Rottweiler is permitted to compete in AKC herding events as a nod to the breed's heritage.

ing breeds were bred to hunt, but they work in different ways, and the differences are quite interesting. For example, spaniels "flush" game (drive it out of cover), whereas pointing breeds will "point" to mark the game. If you have a sporting breed, watching your breed work in the field is a joy. 🐾

▶ **Izzy, of the United States Department of Agriculture's Beagle Brigade, proudly wears her CGC tag when she goes to work.**

SPECIAL APPLICATIONS OF THE CGC PROGRAM

In a relatively short period of time, the AKC Canine Good Citizen Program has become far more than a ten-item test. This chapter describes some of the many special applications of the Canine Good Citizen concept.

In 1989, the American Kennel Club introduced the Canine Good Citizen Program to reward responsible dog owners and to recognize well-mannered dogs. No one dreamed that in only twenty years, the CGC Program would dramatically influence the expectations that our culture has regarding the manners of our canine family members. In a growing number of widely diverse settings, the Canine Good Citizen Program is being adopted as a universal standard of behavior for dogs in our communities.

Animal Control

One of the many jobs of animal-control agencies is to enforce ordinances that pertain to animals. Many ordinances are created to handle problems such as dogs that injure other people or animals, act in a threatening manner, bark incessantly, or otherwise infringe on the rights of others, as well as owners who do not clean up after their dogs in public places.

Depending on the nature of the violation, ordinances range from requiring dogs to wear muzzles to mandating that owners attend classes with their dogs. An increasing number of animal-control agencies are requiring Canine Good Citizen training (followed by passing the CGC Test) as a rehabilitative measure for dogs and their owners.

Certainly, CGC training alone will not fix a dog with an aggression problem. But, in these cases, it shows that the owner is willing to make a good-faith effort to get the dog under control. Further, the owner signs the Responsible Dog Owner's Pledge, agreeing to properly confine and control the dog.

Beagle Brigade: Detector Dogs

The United States Department of Agriculture's National Detector Dog Training Center (NDDTC) has used the CGC Program as part of its training for detector dogs. Located in Orlando, Florida, the NDDTC trains airport Beagles as well as cargo and border dogs. The CGC Program of the "Beagle Brigade" first started in 2001 at the NDDTC when instructor Susan Ellis trained four handler-and-dog teams to pass the CGC Test. For a while, the CGC Program was optional training for detector dogs in

addition to the basic classroom and scent-detection work. After a while, Ellis reported that she noticed an increase in the bonding between teams that had CGC training. Ellis, who is no longer at the NDDTC, said, "I felt the CGC created far more focused and confident teams."

◀ **The Beagle Brigade also includes Labs who have passed the CGC Test.**

Director Michael L. Smith recently described the continued development of the CGC Program at the National Detector Dog Training Center. "Many of our detector dogs have achieved their CGC certification. Some of our well-known airport Beagles have passed the CGC Test as well as our Labrador Retrievers who work in cargo and border inspections. These dogs inspect palletized cargo and conveyances of all types, and they work in international mail facilities. Because they have to be well behaved around people, the AKC's Canine Good Citizen Program has been incorporated into our basic canine handler's curriculum. We have a Beagle working as a detector dog in Taiwan who trained for and passed the CGC Test. Our dogs are using their CGC skills here in the United States and around the world."

Boy Scouts

If there ever was an organization that stresses good human citizenship, it is the Boy Scouts of America. Founded in 1910, the Boy Scouts of America provides recognition to scouts who have earned awards and merit badges related to many practical skills. The AKC's Canine Good Citizen has been added to the "Dog Care" merit badge curriculum, showing that the Boy Scouts truly recognize the merit of the CGC Program.

Community Colleges

In a number of cities, the Canine Good Citizen Program has graduated and gone to college. To meet the needs of citizens, an increasing trend is for community colleges to add adult basic-education classes to their curriculum. Mary Leatherberry is an AKC-approved CGC Evaluator who has a model CGC Program at Santa Fe Community College (SFCC). Serving 14,500 students each year, SFCC's non-credit Continuing Education Program offers classes in everything from Japanese poetry to web design. When Leatherberry proposed a CGC class in 2002, Gordon Fluke, SFCC's Director of Community Education, was willing to give it a try.

Since then, dog-training classes at the college have become among the most popular continuing-education offerings. Once students complete the basic class, they can enroll in the intermediate class, which features the ten CGC test items as the framework of the class. Each class has eight dog/handler teams. The tuition is inexpensive ($75 in 2009) and the course meets for six weeks, one hour each week. CGC testing is offered at the end of the class and monthly thereafter, so if the dog does not pass, he can try again a month later.

Leatherberry understands that the lecture method is not the best choice when it comes to teaching motor skills such as dog training to adult learners. Therefore, her classes are active and fun for both dogs and their owners. Coming when called may involve having the dogs jump through hoops or over hurdles, and heelwork might be performed to disco or rock music.

Many owners continue with further training after CGC and go to AKC clubs or private trainers for additional instruction in Rally, agility, or obedience. "When people ask me 'Where can I go to learn advanced agility?'" says Leatherberry, "I know I've succeeded in helping owners see that training their dog is fun and rewarding."

Santa Fe has long been known as a dog-friendly city, but that's not without some controversy. When citizens wrote letters to the editor to the local newspaper, complaining about inconsiderate dog owners who ignore leash laws or fail to pick up after their dogs, a ban was enacted that prohibited dogs from accompanying their owners on patios of outdoor restaurants, something that previously had been allowed.

Ben Swan, a newspaper reporter for the *Santa Fe New Mexican*, took up the cause and promoted Leatherberry's CGC class and test offerings as a way to "bring dog-friendly back to Santa Fe." Leatherberry said, "That really resonated with dog owners here. People want to be part of the solution, not part of the problem."

4-H

The first 4-H clubs began in the early 1900s to benefit rural youth. When many people hear "4-H," they think of a young person showing a cow or goat at the county fair. While agriculture continues to be an important part of 4-H, this a modern organization that has kept up with the times and is no longer focused primarily on farm-related training. Currently, more than 6.5 million children aged 5 to 19 are members of 4-H. These young people are working on projects related to the four Hs—head, heart, hands, and health. With the U.S. Department of Agriculture as the parent organization, 4-H has maintained as its slogan: "Learn by Doing."

4-H training addresses practical skills in the areas of citizenship, leadership, healthy living, science, and technology. And don't forget the dog training! More than 150,000 young people in 4-H clubs across the country are busy learning about dog care, dog training, 4-H dog shows, Rally, obedience, and agility. The AKC's Canine Good Citizen Program also has a presence in 4-H. The Canine Good Citizen Test has been added to the *4-H Leader Guide* as a starting point for beginning dog trainers.

Housing

It can be difficult to find an apartment to rent or a condo to purchase in a multi-unit building if you own a dog. Fortunately, more and more property managers are realizing that the bond that people have with their pets is important. The AKC's Canine Good Citizen Program has been used as a part of the pet policy in an increasing number of housing situations.

In some cases, the management meets with owners, and all owners simply sign the CGC Responsible Dog Owner's Pledge. In other cases, dogs are required to undergo training and actually pass the CGC Test. That's the case at the Tanner Place Condominiums in Portland, Oregon. Developed by Hoyt Street Properties, Tanner Place is part of the revitalization of Portland's Pearl District neighborhood. The upscale condo complex includes studios, one- and two-bedroom units, and penthouses. Owners can have dogs at Tanner Place, but they need to show proof of passing the Canine Good Citizen Test.

▲ In 4-H programs across the country, children work to earn the AKC Canine Good Citizen award with their dogs.

In housing situations, the Canine Good Citizen program (particularly the Responsible Dog Owner's Pledge) helps property managers and owners say, "We know you love your dogs. You can have them here, but these are the conditions."

Kennels (Boarding)

Kennels used to be places where you dropped off your dog when you went on vacation. The dog was given a run to stay in along with food and water, and that was the extent of the services. Not any more. The times they are a-changin', as the song says, and nowadays an increasing number of kennels are super-facilities that can meet all of your dog's needs.

Rio Gran Kennels in Hastings, Minnesota, is one such state-of-the-art facility. Rio Gran is a 15,000 square-foot pet resort that includes 50 luxury themed suites. If you have a rough-and-tumble Bulldog, he will appreciate a weekend in the Harley

▲ **Rio Gran Kennels in Hastings, Minnesota, is an exemplar of modern-day kennels that offer a full range of services—including Canine Good Citizen training and testing.**

Davidson suite. The building has a city theme, making the hallway of suites appear like something straight out of a Disney hotel for humans.

The owners of Rio Gran are on to something. They understand two things about today's dog owners: (1) they love their dogs and (2) they want to have fun with their dogs. Rio Gran also has a training academy where dog owners can bring their dogs for lessons, or the dogs can attend classes while being boarded. Some of the classes offered include obedience, trick training, flyball, Rally, disc dog, and, of course, preparation and training for the AKC Canine Good Citizen Test.

Rio Gran owner Karen Beskau said about CGC's role at Rio Gran, "We're here to help owners enjoy their dogs and feel good about when the dogs stay with us. Our ongoing CGC classes and CGC testing provide an excellent first step in training. The CGC award is something owners and dogs can achieve together. When dogs have basic training and good manners, we find that our job is much easier when it comes time to board the dog."

Legislation

In 1990, Florida dog fanciers were working hard to get a statewide dangerous-dog law passed that would protect citizens and meet animal-control needs while at the same time not penalizing responsible dog owners. During many of the legislative committee meetings, legislators would say things to the effect of, "We can pass restrictive legislation, but what kind of programs can we implement that are positive, proactive, and designed to educate the public about dogs?" The answer every time: the AKC Canine Good Citizen Program.

The next year, in 1991, the Florida legislature passed the country's first Canine Good Citizen resolution. If you think back to your high-school civics days, you might remember that a resolution is not a law; it is simply an endorsement or acknowledgment. A law has enforcement power, so if you break a law, you can be punished with a fine or jail time. While legislative resolutions (some states have passed CGC proclamations rather than resolutions) have no enforcement power, they are an excellent vehicle for educating legislators about what the CGC Program is, what responsible dog ownership means, and the benefits of training.

As of 2009, 40 states and the United States Senate had passed Canine Good Citizen resolutions, acknowledging that problems related to dogs are really problems with owners who need to be more responsible, and that training for dogs and people is the solution.

State of Florida
HOUSE OF REPRESENTATIVES

House Resolution 2521

By *Representative Bob Sindler*

A resolution endorsing the "AKC Canine Good Citizen" program.

Whereas, dogs play an important role in the lives of many Florida citizens by serving as companions and assistance animals, and

Whereas, it is recognized that the "bad dog" problem is most often an irresponsible owner problem, and

Whereas, responsible pet ownership is encouraged in this state and responsible owners should properly confine and provide adequate training for their dogs, and

Whereas, "Canine Good Citizen" programs identify and officially recognize those dogs that behave as members in good standing with the community, and

Whereas, the Canine Good Citizen concept was developed to teach pet owners that dogs should exhibit functional, "good citizen" behaviors in the presence of other people and animals, in both the home and the community, and

Whereas, because 35,000 Floridians are the victims of animal bites each year, there is a need for dogs to be well-behaved community members, NOW, THEREFORE,

Be It Resolved by the House of Representatives of the State of Florida:

That the Legislature of the State of Florida endorses "Canine Good Citizen" programs as a means of teaching owners responsible pet ownership, and as a means of teaching dogs canine good citizen behaviors in the community.

BE IT FURTHER RESOLVED that the Legislature of the State of Florida encourages dog training programs and kennel clubs to provide training and education for community pet owners that emphasizes the importance of properly confining and controlling dogs and providing training which results in "Canine Good Citizens."

This is to certify the foregoing was adopted on April 10, 1991.

Speaker of the House: T.K. Wetherall

Primary Sponsor: Rep. Bob Sindler, DVM

Initiated by: Dr. Mary Burch, CGC Evaluator (volunteer)

Licensing

In many cities, licensing programs are used to partially fund animal-control services. Years ago, as a result of the work of local AKC clubs and AKC Field Representative Bill Holbrook, the city of Sequim (in Clallam County, Washington) was the first city to offer licensing discounts when dogs passed the AKC Canine Good Citizen test. Currently, Clallam County offers a 10 percent discount on licenses to owners of dogs that have earned the CGC award.

In July 2009, the Board of County Commissioners in Clackamas County, Oregon, authorized Dog Services to implement a new dog-licensing incentive program. Owners of dogs that have passed the CGC Test are eligible for a 25 percent dog-licensing discount annually for the lifetimes of those dogs. Diana Hallmark, Manager of Clackamas County Dog Services, reported, "The initial response to the CGC incentive program has been very positive. Dog Services has been receiving requests about CGC and dog training from both community dog owners and our community veterinarians. Our hope is that more owners will spend quality time with their canine companions and provide the training necessary to ensure their dogs are excellent neighbors, which in turn will reduce the number of complaints and service requests to which Clackamas County Dog Officers must respond."

Military

Families who live on military bases often have pets. Canine Good Citizen testing has been encouraged and supported by military veterinarians (with assistance from local CGC Evaluators and dog trainers) at a number of military bases, including Fort Bragg (North Carolina), Fort Rucker (Alabama), and Fort Polk (Louisiana).

Movies

"Quiet on the set! And…action!" Everyone on the set of movies and Broadway productions needs to follow the director's instructions, and that includes the canine actors. Housed on the campus of the Los Angeles Center Studios, Hollywood Paws prepares animals for professional studio work in movies, television, and commercials. Hollywood Paws trainers work with owners and their dogs from basic obedience to advanced on-film performances. Hollywood Paws recognizes the importance of good manners for canine movie stars and beloved pets alike, and administers the AKC Canine Good Citizen Test on a regular basis.

Hollywood Paws currently has seventy dogs ready to do production work (including movies and television) and fifty more in training. If a pet owner has a dream of making his dog a star, Hollywood Paws is the place to go. Training focuses on overcoming the challenges unique to movie sets and working in front of a camera. The dog's ability to work at a distance from the handler and perform complex chains of behavior (sit, then move back 20 feet and quickly lie down) are critical.

The CGC Test has an exercise related to distractions. On a movie set, dogs must go from CGC-level distractions to more difficult distractions, such as lying down and playing dead while food service walks by with lunch and an actress is shrieking and crying.

▲ **Trainer and CGC Evaluator Joel Norton directs a dog and owner at Hollywood Paws, a California program that prepares animals for film work. At Hollywood Paws, the CGC Test is administered regularly.**

In CGC training, dogs learn to follow their owners' verbal commands. In Hollywood, this skill advances to a behavior called a *work away*, meaning that the dog must work with his owner out of sight and listen for the owner's verbal cues. There are three levels of classes at Hollywood Paws, and dogs take the CGC Test at the end of the first level. Graduation from Level Two means that dogs are eligible to be submitted for production jobs.

Joel Norton, the head trainer at Hollywood Paws, explains why the AKC Canine Good Citizen Test has been adopted. "The CGC is important to us because it allows a third party to check the progress of our dogs in terms of basic obedience," says Norton. "Since the CGC test revolves around control of one's dog, it is a perfect fit for a graduation test for our Level One program. CGC testing is not a requirement for movie dogs from the standard animal-rental companies, but because we use dogs belonging to private citizens, CGC testing provides peace of mind that everyone appreciates."

So, who are some of the canine movies stars who have earned the AKC Canine Good Citizen award? Perhaps Norton's most recognizable actor is the Golden Retriever named Scout from the movie *Air Buddies*. Step aside Brad Pitt, Scout has also appeared in an Orkin commercial, in blood-pressure medication ads, and in the CBS show *NUMB3RS*. Other canine celebs who have earned the CGC award at Hollywood Paws include dogs that have performed in a pilot show with William H. Macy, a movie called *Stiletto* with Tom Berenger, *Next* on MTV, *Big Movie Premiere* on E!, and ads for Verizon, Microsoft, Burger King, and Nick at Night.

Parks

Dog Parks

Dog parks are fenced areas where owners can take their dogs to run off leash. Some dog parks are fenced areas within larger town parks, some are attached to residential areas such as condos or apartments in large metropolitan areas, and some are privately owned parks for which dog owners can purchase memberships. Dog parks range from simple fenced-in grassy areas with no amenities to areas that resemble canine country clubs.

Dog Wood Park (Florida)

Dog Wood Park, located in Gainesville, Florida, is everything a dog could dream of. This 15-acre privately owned dog park is clearly in the "top of the line" category. Owners pay a membership fee so their dogs can have access to a place to run and socialize with other dogs in a safe, controlled environment. There are two large swimming pools (much appreciated in the Florida summer!), numerous large shade trees, a dog shower for muddy paws, shaded walking and jogging trails, dry areas for those days when you don't want your dog to get wet, benches, swings and hammocks, picnic tables, a "dog mountain" sand pile for digging and climbing, tunnels and other obstacles, and, of course, plenty of tennis balls.

In addition to all of these fabulous activities for owners and their dogs, one of the greatest things about Dog Wood is the emphasis on and commitment to educating owners. AKC Canine Good Citizen training and testing is done on-site, and after CGC, owners can advance to obedience, Rally, and agility training. Owner Janet Hobson encourages visitors to come by and have a look at the park during office hours or to visit online at www.dogwoodpark.com

Misty Pines Dog Park (Pennsylvania)

Misty Pines Dog Park in Sewickley, Pennsylvania, is another outstanding dog park. Dogs can enjoy the fenced playgrounds, hiking trails, agility courses, and water activities that include swimming and dock diving. Misty Pines has separate areas for small dogs and puppies.

As with most dog parks, to keep everyone safe, aggressive dogs are not allowed. However, there are occasionally "dog bullies" who sometimes come to dog parks. Dog bullies don't bite and they don't physically harm people and other animals, but they are pushy and overbearing. This might be the bigger dog that keeps a little Shih Tzu cornered under a bench unless someone intervenes. Misty Pines staff will work with the owners of the bully to teach them how to handle their dog (beginning with using a leash) so that everyone, including the problem dog, benefits.

The AKC's Canine Good Citizen Test is a goal for many owners who are members at Misty Pines. Judith Fox, an AKC CGC Evaluator who conducts CGC Tests at the dog park said, "For everyone to fully enjoy a dog park, both dogs and their people need to have good manners. The CGC Program provides a really great format for talking about what it means to be responsible and for teaching dogs the basic skills they need to be around other people and dogs." For more information on Misty Pines, see www.mistypinesdogpark.com.

City and County Parks

In most places, with the exception of fenced-in dog parks or designated off-leash areas, leash laws require all dogs in public parks to be on leashes. Owners who are not responsible sometimes choose to violate leash laws. Their untrained dogs run like maniacs up to other people (and their leashed dogs) while the owners follow behind, yelling, "It's OK, he's friendly!" We described the "It's OK, he's friendly!" phenomenon in an earlier chapter.

The American Kennel Club believes that dog owners should adhere to leash laws. However, there are some cases in which it would be helpful to have a dog lawfully off leash in a public park, and that is when the dog is involved in an organized sport (e.g., agility demonstration) or training activity. With the help of dog fanciers, dog trainers, and a supportive city staff, Willard Bailey made a difference in Phoenix, Arizona. In doing so, the city of Phoenix established a model that can be used for parks and recreation departments in other cities.

It was once the case in the Phoenix parks that if a person practicing for an obedience trial was working with the dog off leash, he was violating the law. After many months; an uncountable number of strategy sessions, presentations, and commission meetings; and a lot of hard work, Bailey and other Phoenix dog trainers were successful in having the Phoenix Leash Law revised so that trainers could work with their dogs off leash. The AKC Canine Good Citizen Program plays a part in the updated Leash Law, known as Phoenix City Code 8-14. The ordinance now says (summarized):

Dog owners must keep their dogs on a leash when the dog is not on the owner's property. Exceptions are made for:

■ Working animals used by or at the direction of law enforcement agencies.

■ The dog is being exhibited or trained at a kennel club event or official city event.

■ The dog is in an approved off-leash area (a dog park).

■ The owner/custodian is educating and instructing a dog for any nationally recognized dog sport while meeting *all* of the following conditions:

a. The owner/custodian has a leash in their his/her possession,

b. has no other dogs off leash,

c. has the dog within sight and voice range and actively uses sufficient auditory or visual commands to ensure the dog is not harassing or disturbing people or other animals and is not displaying aggression,

d. must be able to demonstrate upon request of an enforcement officer that the dog will promptly return by direct route upon voice command. The dog must also stay by the owner/custodian after returning.

e. The owner/custodian must have in his/her possession a "dog sport performance title certificate" (e.g., obedience, agility, etc., title) from a nationally recognized dog sport organization or a "Canine Good Citizen" Program certificate from the American Kennel Club.

Rather than break the law, dog owners can work effectively with city and county officials to change ordinances so that they will permit organized dog-training activities in public parks. It's not easy to change a law or have an ordinance revised. It's a long, hard road that will involve a systematic approach and the help of many people. But it can be done—just ask the dog trainers in Phoenix, Arizona, who worked effectively to change the system.

State Parks

Summer and fall are perfect times of the year for campers to get away from the hustle and bustle of urban areas and enjoy nature in state parks and historic sites. The canine family members who accompany campers in Missouri state parks now need to have earned the AKC Canine Good Citizen award. Dogs must be on leash at all times, and owners must agree to clean up after their dogs (a part of the CGC

Responsible Dog Owner's Pledge) in order to minimize the impact of dogs on the park environment.

Campers who wish to camp with their dogs in Missouri parks can also register for campsites if they meet one of the following criteria other than CGC: current-year participation in dog shows, current membership in an AKC club, or certification as a therapy dog, service dog, law enforcement K9, or search and rescue dog. Having CGC included as a requirement for dogs in Missouri parks provides another great example of how the AKC Canine Good Citizen Program is continuing to be recognized as a standard of behavior for dogs in our communities. We know that when owners don't clean up after their dogs and infringe on the rights of others by allowing their dogs to bark incessantly, the first thing that happens is that dogs are banned from parks and hiking trails. When the AKC heard that Missouri was using CGC as a means of protecting the rights of park visitors and the natural environment, you might say that we were happy campers!

Police K9

Police K9 dogs assist police officers with many tasks, ranging from protection and bite work to bomb and narcotics detection. Because dogs working as police K9s so frequently come in contact with the public, police officers know that in addition to their advanced, highly specialized training, these dogs need to be well mannered and safe in the presence of citizens and other animals. For this reason, a number of police K9 dogs have been trained and tested for the CGC award.

Jim Faggiano is an AKC-approved CGC Evaluator. He is also a dog trainer who specializes in police dogs. Faggiano is a POST (Police Officer Standards for Training) Evaluator for the state of California. In addition to testing dogs on K9 police-dog skills, Faggiano administers the AKC Canine Good Citizen Test during POST evaluations because he believes that a standard recognized by the community is important.

Officer Mary MacQueen of the Salamanca, New York, Police Department and the Cattaraugus County, New York, Sheriff's Office is a true believer in having a K9 partner who is well mannered. Her working K9 partner, Am./Can. Ch. Nitro's Boy Wonder (known as K9 Officer "Robin"), is an unusual police dog in that he is a Golden Retriever who works for two different police agencies and is also a conformation champion.

Robin has demonstrated the ability to win in the show ring one day and find illegal narcotics that have been sealed in concrete the next day. Officer MacQueen

▶ Am./Can. Ch. Nitro's Boy Wonder, also known as K9 Officer "Robin." Robin is a CGC award recipient and the K9 partner of Officer Mary MacQueen of the Salamanca, New York, Police Department and the Catteraugus County, New York, Sheriff's Office.

is frequently asked to give public demonstrations and media appearances with her wonder dog. As the public watches Robin's crowd-pleasing demonstration in awe, Officer MacQueen tells them, "The first step to all training is having a dog that is well mannered. One of Robin's most important credentials is that he has passed the AKC's Canine Good Citizen Test."

Prisons

There are more than 100 prison programs (for men and women) in which inmates train dogs. Some inmates are puppy-raisers for service-dog programs and others train shelter dogs that will be returned to the shelter after training so they can be adopted. The Canine Good Citizen Program is used as the training standard for a number of prison-based dog-training programs.

There is perhaps no better example of a win-win situation than when inmates train shelter dogs for adoption. Inmates get a chance to give back to society and dogs get a chance to have new lives. The abbreviated article on the next page was first published in full in the April 2008 issue of *CGC Evaluator News*. Written by one of the inmate dog trainers, the article describes how the Canine Good Citizen Program is used in prison settings to change the lives of both people and dogs.

CGC in Prisons:
The Pets Educated to Survive
(PETS) Program

I t may sound like an oxymoron to some people, but educating dogs so that they'll survive is a goal of the Pets Educated to Survive (PETS) program. The PETS program began in July 2001 with two Boxers, and in 2008 it maintained about twenty dogs and ten cats with sixty handlers/trainers. To date, PETS has trained more than 575 dogs and cared for 160 cats from local animal rescue agencies. More than 270 inmate handlers have participated in the program, and they have given nearly 1 million hours of community service.

Since 2002, PETS has been fortunate to have two experienced volunteers who conduct weekly training sessions at the prison. AKC-approved CGC Evaluators Dorothy Miner and Diane Laratta provide expert instruction. PETS handlers and their dogs receive ongoing training in obedience commands, healthcare, first aid/CPR, grooming, behavior analysis, agility training, "Meet the Breeds," temperament testing, and CGC instruction. Our PETS Mission Statement declares that we are dedicated to giving rescued dogs "the best second chance possible" to find good adoptive homes. CGC is our standard for graduation.

Here's how our program works. A dog from a local rescue agency is brought into the prison and assigned to a primary inmate handler to train. (A secondary handler also works with each dog.) A typical dog stays [at the prison] for approximately six to eight weeks. During an initial bonding period with the handler(s), the dog is given a physical examination and is observed for behavioral and socialization issues. The dog receives care and grooming and is given time to adapt to his new environment. Then, if no major problems are detected, he is gradually introduced to more than twenty obedience commands over the next few weeks. Because we receive a variety of rescued dogs, we tend to divide the dogs into two general categories: those that are well adjusted and those with "special needs." We face some unique challenges when preparing dogs in both categories for the CGC Tests.

Our biggest challenges come from dogs that are rescued by shelters that are strays or neglected animals. These dogs represent a plethora of "special needs," ranging from extreme fear and/or sensitivity issues to socialization problems and/or heightened levels of separation anxiety. Many of these dogs present underlying issues through obvious signs of stress, recognizable fear, and sometimes through aggressive behaviors.

Other challenges include dogs that have taken more than twenty minutes just to walk through the front doors to the housing unit, dogs that are extremely noise-sensitive, or dogs that have had too much or too little human contact. One extreme case was a Border Collie that was here for nine months. It took her two months before she was comfortable just walking the perimeter of the dayroom when most of the inmates were in their cells. Four months later, she passed her CGC and was adopted shortly after that. The CGC Program has been an instrumental part of our PETS regimen that allows us to produce well-trained, adoptable pets.

Many "rescued dogs" end up at shelters because of troubled pasts. Some may have been mistreated as puppies and have only known an unforgiving "puppyhood." Some may have brought on their placement in a shelter by exhibiting unwanted behavior like excessive barking, digging, chewing, or, worse yet, not being housebroken. Some may have simply been left in the "streets" to fend for themselves at too young of an age, got in with the wrong crowd and made some hard choices in life that turned into trouble. Further still, some may have shown severe separation anxiety, antisocial behavior, or unacceptable forms of aggression that warranted their being banished from their communities for the safety of those around them. It is my experience that most of these animals, given the proper care, guidance, and training, respond in such a way that affords them the opportunity for another chance to succeed in life. Unfortunately, not all of these animals can be saved. That is a sad fact. Fortunately, the PETS program is dedicated to helping as many as possible. But we are only talking about the dogs, right?

It is my belief that the reason prison animal programs like PETS are so successful is that, as offenders, we understand where these dogs come from. In many ways, we've lived their troubled pasts. We may have had unforgiving childhoods, exhibited unwanted behaviors, taken to the "streets" at too young of an age, or shown severe anxiety, antisocial behavior, or unacceptable forms of aggression. Our life experiences help us understand these dogs and many of us, after being "educated to survive," become trained with the knowledge to pass a "good citizen test," showing that we can reenter society and lead productive lives. We bond with these animals and want them to succeed because, in the end, we want the same thing they do—the best second chance possible at a new life.

—*Greg W.*

Rescue Groups

Rescue groups are groups that remove dogs from shelters or problem situations (e.g., the owner died and the dog is left homeless). One of the primary functions of rescue groups is to place dogs in loving homes. In addition to providing medical care for dogs that need it, many rescue groups are beginning to place dogs that were given up because of behavior problems in foster homes where training is provided. An increasing number of rescue groups are using the Canine Good Citizen Test as a goal to demonstrate that the rescue dogs have achieved a recognized set of skills. Dogs are listed as having earned the CGC award, and adoptive owners are encouraged to continue training.

The Welsh Springer Spaniel Club of America (WSSCA) is just one of many exemplars when it comes to the incredible rescue work done across the country by devoted members of AKC national parent clubs. An example of the WSSCA's rescue results follows.

A responsible Welsh Springer Spaniel owner stipulated that her dogs would go to her family when she died. The owner died, the family took the dogs, and, within a short period of time, decided that they could not keep them. WSSCA rescue was contacted. A WSSCA rescue committee member in Kansas worked with the family to get the dogs, and she cared for them until another member could assist with their placements. A second WSSCA rescue committee member took time off from work, drove from West Virginia to Kansas, and took five dogs with her back to West Virginia. After providing each dog with grooming and a complete veterinary checkup, the WSSCA carefully screened potential adopters and eventually placed all five dogs in loving homes. This dedicated AKC national parent club and many others like it across the country work tirelessly to ensure that the breeds they love do not end up in shelters.

The American Kennel Club currently registers more than 160 breeds. Each of those breeds has a national parent club, and we are extremely proud that most have organized, active rescue groups. Volunteers are always needed to foster dogs, help with transportation to new homes, and be listed as breed resources for local shelters. To get involved in rescue with a breed you love, go to www.akc.org, click on "Breeds," and then click on "Breed Rescue."

Search and Rescue

Because of their amazing hearing, ability to see well at night, extraordinary sense of smell, and physical endurance, dogs are the tools of choice when it comes to locating missing persons. Search and rescue (SAR) dogs not only need the ability to find a missing person but they also need the good manners and training that is required to behave appropriately when the person is found. A SAR dog that is aggressive toward people or other animals would not be of much use in a search situation in which many people and other dogs are involved.

▲ **The AKC Canine Good Citizen Test is one of the accepted behavioral assessments for search and rescue dogs.**

In 1997, the National Association for Search and Rescue (NASAR) outlined a standardized curriculum for the NASAR SAR Dog Certification Program. The AKC Canine Good Citizen Test is one of the accepted behavioral assessments for dogs in the NASAR requirements.

If you are interested in search and rescue, know that this work is serious business, and the dog's work is only part of the equation. The life of a person who is injured can depend on what you, the human, do when your dog finds the person.

SAR certification requires a great deal of training for the handler. Handlers must pass first-aid courses or have medical training, complete incident-management training, receive training and certification on specific rescue techniques, and be certified in cardiac pulmonary resuscitation (CPR).

Service Dogs

Service dogs are dogs that assist people with disabilities. Earning the Canine Good Citizen award does not give your dog the same special-access rights to public places (restaurants, planes, stores, etc.) that service dogs have. People with disabilities have struggled for decades for the right to have their canine helpers with them in public places, and it would be absolutely unethical to use the CGC award for the purpose of alleging that a dog is a service animal.

Having said this, there are a number of people with disabilities who want their service dogs to pass the Canine Good Citizen Test. Even though these dogs have very advanced skills, such as opening refrigerator doors, holding and giving a check to a bank teller, and picking up a dropped cell phone, many service-dog owners want their dogs to pass the test of good manners best known to the general public—the AKC Canine Good Citizen Test.

Shelters/Humane Organizations

Sadly, one of the most common reasons that dogs are relinquished to shelters is that they have behavior problems. Many of these problems could be easily corrected with basic training (of both the dog and the owner). To help dogs get a good start toward a successful placement in an adoptive home, many shelters now have Canine Good Citizen training programs for their dogs. In cases where shelters don't have paid trainers or behaviorists, volunteers from local dog clubs or the community provide training. Some shelters allow the shelter staff to attend dog-training sessions and get involved in training. This is an uplifting and wonderful experience for the staff, who spend a lot of their time dealing with problems and difficult issues. A shelter-based CGC program generally looks like this:

■ Volunteers or staff who are identified as trainers are trained on dog-training skills and CGC.

■ Dogs are identified for the training program.

■ Training sessions begin.

■ When the dog has learned all of the CGC skills, a sign is posted on the dog's kennel door that says, "I have passed the Canine Good Citizen Test. If you adopt me, we can get my certificate from the American Kennel Club."

■ When the dog is adopted, the shelter staff or volunteer (dog trainer) gives the adoptive owner and dog a lesson. The owner is taught how to get the dog to perform the CGC behaviors. The owner runs through the CGC Test with the dog and is given the paperwork to request the CGC certificate.

■ During the training, some shelters post "report cards" on the kennel doors of those dogs being trained. "I am learning these ten skills on the Canine Good Citizen Test. If you adopt me, we can finish my training together." The skills are listed and checked off as the dog can do each one.

■ The first priority is finding the dog a loving, adoptive home, so if the dog has a chance to be adopted before training is completed, training stops and the dog goes home with his new family. The family is given information about training opportunities in the area, and the trainer selects another dog to begin training.

Therapy Dogs

Each year, tens of thousands of therapy dogs and their owners visit hospitals, nursing homes, schools, developmental-disabilities programs, and numerous other settings to make people happy and, in some cases, teach new skills. Many therapy-dog programs require CGC testing as a prerequisite for participation in their programs. Therapy Dogs International (TDI), the largest therapy-dog group in the country, has used the AKC Canine Good Citizen Test as a component of their therapy-dog screening for a number of years .

Veterinarians

The veterinarian is often the first-animal care professional that dog owners will come to know and trust. In recent years, CGC Programs have been implemented in a variety of veterinary settings.

Clinics/Offices

In 1997, Michael A. Lappin DVM implemented a Canine Good Citizen Program in his Massachusetts veterinary clinic. Featured in an article in the *AKC Gazette*, this program served as a model for many other veterinary clinics around the country. The key features of Dr. Lappin's CGC program were:

- CGC training to clients and non-clients during non-clinic hours.
- CGC testing following training sessions.
- A flyer that was given to all clients regarding the benefits of CGC.
- A 10% discount on services to dogs that had earned the CGC award or more advanced obedience titles.
- A CGC mention on the recall cards sent to clients (e.g., "Just a reminder that it is time for Tess and Buddy's annual exam and vaccines. Remember, if your dog earns the CGC award, you can receive a discount on veterinary services. Contact us for information on Canine Good Citizen training and testing.").

Dr. Lappin understood that training a dog enhances the bond between the dog and the owner. For veterinarians, there are other bonuses to well-trained dogs. An article in *Veterinary Economics* magazine pointed out the financial benefits to well-behaved pets in veterinary clinics. When a veterinarian can handle a dog without an assistant or multiple assistants, those staff members can be working on other tasks. More gets done during the day, resulting in additional revenue. When a veterinarian has to spend thirty minutes getting a dog under control so he can examine the dog, the dog is agitated, the owner is humiliated, the vet may be frustrated or at risk of getting bitten, and the whole ordeal can be costly in terms of time spent trying to manage a dog that has not been trained.

University Training for Veterinarians

University of Pennsylvania

The Canine Good Citizen Program has also had a role in university training programs for veterinarians. Dr. M. Josephine Deubler is known as one of the great women of the dog world. The first female graduate of the University of Pennsylvania School of Veterinary Medicine, Dr. Deubler received her VMD in 1938 and was a member of the faculty of the veterinary school for over fifty years. The genetic-disease testing laboratory at the University of Pennsylvania bears her name.

With decades of experience as an exhibitor, dog-show judge, and leader in the field of animal welfare, Dr. Deubler recognized the potential benefits of the Canine Good Citizen Program for dogs and their owners. She understood that many dog owners would talk to their veterinarians about behavioral issues and that proactive early training is crucial.

When she heard about the Canine Good Citizen Program during a dinner conversation at a dog show, Dr. Deubler went into action. Within several weeks, CGC materials had been requested and were sent to the University of Pennsylvania School of Veterinary Medicine. Veterinary students are now actively involved in conducting Canine Good Citizen Tests. The University of Pennsylvania veterinary students and dog owners are using the Canine Good Citizen Program to learn from each other.

University of Florida

At the University of Florida, Cynda Crawford DVM, PhD is best known as the nationally recognized researcher who is famous for her discovery related to the canine influenza virus. While most days in the lab focus on science, Dr. Crawford has also been the faculty advisor to veterinary students who administer the Canine Good Citizen Test and evaluate dogs for therapy work. These young vets will go into the world as well-respected professionals who are equipped to help dog owners understand that a healthy dog is both physically and behaviorally healthy.

Work Settings

The therapeutic benefits of dogs have been well documented. For those of us who love them, science tells us that dogs can lower our blood pressure and reduce stress. And perhaps nowhere do we need stress relief more than when we are at work.

The American Kennel Club's Raleigh, North Carolina, office has a Dogs-in-the-Building Program that has been used as a model for other programs around the country. Dogs that come to work with AKC employees must:

■ Pass the Canine Good Citizen test. The owner has to sign the Responsible Dog Owner's Pledge as a part of CGC testing.

■ Have a veterinarian certify that the dog is in good health.

■ Have proof of rabies vaccines.

■ Have a flea/tick-prevention program in place.

■ Demonstrate skills that are beyond CGC, such as the ability to stay in an office, be quiet, and not cause trouble during the day. Owners put baby gates across their doorways and use crates when appropriate.

Dogs aren't the only ones who need to follow the rules at work. Owners agree to:

■ Walk dogs only in designated areas.

■ Clean up after their dogs.

■ Identify a "backup" human buddy for the dog that can take the dog out if necessary, help if there is a problem and the owner is in a meeting, etc. A sign (with a picture of the dog, the owner's and dog's names, and the designated buddy) is posted by the office door.

■ Use only the designated "dog elevators." This accommodates people with allergies and building occupants who may be dog-phobic.

■ Respect the rights of nearby staff who may have allergies to animals. In such a case, the health of the worker with the allergy comes first.

■ Respect the rights of visitors and building "neighbors" (the Raleigh building is shared by other companies) by recognizing that some people are dog-phobic and/or do not wish to interact with a dog.

■ Not allow the dog to interfere with productivity and work progress.

■ Provide documentation of homeowner's insurance or renter's insurance (for liability).

■ Follow any recommendations of the Dogs-in-the-Building committee when there is a problem.

▲ The AKC encourages owners to take their dogs' training to the next level and enjoy the competitive opportunities that local AKC clubs provide.

HOW THE AKC HELPS EVERY DOG OWNER

Here at the American Kennel Club, we're far more than dog shows. We say that we're not just champion dogs—we're the dogs' champion. This chapter outlines some of our many services and programs that haven't been covered in earlier chapters.

Founded in 1884, the AKC has over 5,000 dog clubs and more than 22,000 events of varying types each year. The AKC is a "club made up of clubs." This means that, as an individual, you can't become a member of the AKC. The members are dog clubs from all over the country, and it is these clubs that serve as the guardians for individual breeds.

Canine Health Foundation

The mission statement of the AKC Canine Health Foundation (CHF) is to "develop resources for basic and applied health programs with an emphasis on canine genetics to improve the overall quality of life for dogs and their owners." CHF works diligently to eliminate genetic disorders in dogs. The research done by CHF benefits all dogs, purebreds and mixed breeds alike.

Clubs/Club Relations

The AKC has clubs across the country that include specialty clubs (clubs for one specific breed), all-breed clubs for conformation, performance clubs, obedience clubs (that teach obedience, Rally, and sometimes agility), agility clubs, and more. If you are interested in training your dog, check out an AKC club near you. You'll find experienced trainers who can help you achieve your training and competition objectives. You'll have the chance to meet and train with a wonderful group of people who share your love of dogs. To find the AKC club near you, go to www.akc.org and click on "Clubs."

Companion Animal Recovery

We all love our dogs, and we take every caution to protect them, but sometimes accidents happen and a dog gets lost. AKC Companion Animal Recovery (CAR) provides lifetime recovery services for pets who have a microchip, tattoo, or collar tag bearing their contact information. CAR is on the job, ready to help lost pets get home 24 hours a day, 365 days a year. Since CAR began in 1995, more than 360,000 lost pets have been successfully reunited with their families.

Customer Relations

When you have a question and need help, the helpful, friendly staff in the AKC's Customer Service call center will assist you. The Customer Service Department handles nearly 70,000 questions per month and hundreds of emails per day that range from registration issues to the ordering of Canine Good Citizen Test kits. Customer service hours are weekdays between 8:30 a.m. and 5:00 p.m. (ET).

American Kennel Club

8051 Arco Corporate Drive, Suite 100
Raleigh, NC 27617-3390
919-233-9767
info@akc.org
orderdesk@akc.org

DNA

The AKC's DNA Operations Department, part of the Compliance Division, uses the most modern DNA technology to help dogs. This department uses DNA technology to establish the genetic identity of dogs. Collecting a DNA sample is a painless process that involves using a small brush to swab the inside of the dog's cheek. Loose cells stick to the swab and are a source of DNA that can be analyzed.

Handlers Program

Dogs can be shown in conformation dog shows by their owners, friends, or professional handlers. The AKC Registered Handlers Program was started in order to ensure that the health and welfare of all dogs in the care of handlers is maintained. To participate in this program, handlers must complete an application process, meet certain criteria, and adhere to a Code of Ethics.

▲ Dogs and owners can enjoy AKC events as participants or as spectators.

Judges Education

The education of judges is obviously important for conformation dog shows, but the role of judges goes beyond the show ring. AKC judges receive intensive hands-on training at seminars and institutes around the country. They become experts on individual breeds—the breed's movement, physical structure, any health problems the breed might have, temperament, and so on. Having a cadre of well-trained experts can be beneficial to anyone who is considering getting a particular breed.

Legislation

The AKC Canine Legislation Department had a name change in recent years and is now called Government Relations. This is the department that monitors dog-related legislation and serves as a resource to dog fanciers who are addressing legislative issues.

Library

If you love dogs, a visit to the American Kennel Club's library is something you should do at least once. Housed at the AKC's New York office, the library has more than 19,000 volumes, including 2,500 rare books, magazines, stamps, bookplates, and videos. Because the library has one of the most impressive dog-book collections in the world, when you visit, there's a good chance you'll see writers and scholars who are working on their latest manuscripts.

Museum

Holding one of the largest collections of dog-related fine art in the world, the AKC Museum of the Dog is housed in St. Louis, Missouri. Supported by an annual operating grant from the American Kennel Club, the AKC Museum of the Dog is open year-round to the public. For more information, call (314) 821-3647.

PAL Program

The Purebred Alternative Listing (PAL) Program, formerly called Indefinite Listing Privilege (ILP), with its new, improved, more user-friendly name, is a program that allows unregistered purebred dogs (e.g., dogs from shelters and rescue groups who don't have "papers") to compete in AKC Performance and Companion Events.

There are various reasons why a purebred dog might not be eligible for registration. The dog may be the product of an unregistered litter or have unregistered parents. The dog's papers may have been withheld by his breeder or lost by his owner. Many dogs enrolled in the PAL/ILP Program were surrendered or abandoned, then adopted by new owners from animal shelters or purebred rescue groups.

The AKC events that a PAL/ILP dog can participate in are agility trials, Junior Showmanship, obedience trials, Rally trials, and tracking tests. Small terriers and Dachshunds can compete in earthdog trials. Herding tests and trials are open to herding breeds, Rottweilers, and Samoyeds. The sporting breeds and Standard Poodles can use a PAL number to participate in hunt tests, and sighthounds with PAL privileges can compete in lure coursing.

Once enrolled in the PAL/ILP Program, entering AKC events is easy. Instead of an AKC registration number, you simply list the dog's PAL/ILP number on the entry form. To receive an application for enrollment into the Purebred Alternative Listing/Indefinite Listing Privilege, email PAL@akc.org.

Publications

If you want to learn more about dogs, the AKC has several publications that may interest you. The *AKC Gazette* is a monthly all-breed magazine that includes articles related to all aspects of dogs. Along with the *Gazette* is the *Events Calendar,* a listing of all dog events across the country, the dates of the events, and information for entering. *AKC Family Dog* magazine is a bi-monthly publication that includes practical articles written in an entertaining style for today's busy dog owner.

▲ Some owners like their dogs to accompany them wherever dogs are welcome.

Public Education

The AKC's Public Education Division works to educate the humans in a dog's life. The goal of AKC Public Education is to teach responsible dog ownership and the joys of participating in dog activities to dog owners, the general public, educators, and legislators.

More than 1,200 volunteers from AKC clubs serve as Canine Ambassadors who visit schools and other youth programs to teach about topics such as safety around dogs and responsible ownership. In addition to the Canine Ambassadors, there are more than 3,000 Public Education Coordinators in AKC clubs who promote the sport of dogs in their communities.

Club Educational Services is another part of AKC Public Education. If you've been to an AKC dog show and seen the AKC Informational Booth, you've seen Club Educational Services at work. This department reaches more than 160,000 people each year with printed materials, videos, and Web site demonstrations.

Web Site

If you haven't yet visited the AKC's Web site, take a moment and go to www.akc.org If you are interested in dogs, you're in for a treat when you visit the Web site that has been described as the most popular dog-related address on the Internet. You can read the latest news pertaining to dog-related issues, shop at the online store, learn about breeds, find breed rescue groups, locate upcoming shows and events to participate in or attend as a spectator, or find an Evaluator or trainer for CGC or S.T.A.R. Puppy...and much more! 🐾

APPENDIX: CGC EVALUATORS (PAST AND PRESENT) ACKNOWLEDGED FOR THE 20TH ANNIVERSARY OF CGC

The AKC Canine Good Citizen Program was launched in September, 1989, and in the first twenty years has enjoyed the support of thousands of dedicated dog trainers and dog owners. The American Kennel Club is indebted to each of the CGC Evaluators in the list that follows for their involvement and dedication to Canine Good Citizen training and testing during the first twenty years of the program.

Because the CGC Evaluator list changes over time, readers who are interested in finding an Evaluator to administer a CGC test should go to the current Evaluator list at: http://www.akc.org/events/cgc/cgc_bystate.cfm.

ALABAMA

Chris L. Amick
Deneen E. Balistere
Shelby L. Becker
Paula Bowsher
Tara L. Brackin
Cynthia R. Buckman
Janet Carberry
Gregg M. Carter
Sharon Casto
Debra Clark
Cynthia J. Clark-Pesce
Rebecca Collier
Diana D. Cook
Kelly A. Cotney
Lisa C. Cox
Lesa Crowe
Frances H. Dauster
Beth W. Fitzgerald
Leah Gangelhoff
Debra Goebels
Linda C. Hall
Allison Hamilton
Darcy J. Harbaugh
Michael L. Hardy
Sarah Hatfield
Marie K. Hill
Victory Hulett
Renee S. Jones
Richard Karrasch
Norma A. Lattimore
Winona S. Leard
Rose Lehn
Susan S. Lowder
Irene Lynn
Lisa A. Mason
Shannon Medhus
Julie Moon
WIlliam C. Moore Jr.
Shelia Nicholas
Janice L. Plessner
Amanda Prince
Leslie Gene Reed
Susan Jarrett
  Robertson
Jesseca L. Sanders
Tracy Schumann
Annette G. Shepard
Laura D. Smith
Kaye C. Stevenson
Carolyn E. Tichenor

Les Tippen
Carol A. Turberville
Karlene Turkington
Jeannette V. Vega
Jamie D. Ward
Larry E. Welker
Margie P. Wiesman
Sheila Wilbanks
Susan F. Windham
Shelby Young

ALASKA

Dori Lynn Anderson
Jennifer L. Anderson
Elaine Bartlett
Candy Bartos
Maija Doggett
Sara Fann
Diane M. Fish
Catherine Hadley
Cheri L. Hagen
Lisa Haggblom
Deanna Hardin
Faith S. Hays
Deborah D. Hill
Cheryl R. Mallonee
Marty Messick
Lisa M. Moore
Anita J. Moran
Pam Nelson
Sheri Nelson
Melinda M. Patterson
Andra Rozentals-
  Burns
Susan A. Sampson
Claudia M. Sihler
Jennifer L. Taylor
Josh Waters
Elizabeth A. Williams
Donna Wojciechowski

ARIZONA

Moria A. Aicher
Donna Mae Anderson
Reshenna Andrews
Suzanne A. Applegate
Ann E. Austin
Troy Ballard
Terry I. Bankert
Dia L. Barney
Lisa Basham

J. J. Belcher
Rhonda Bell
Sandra Lynn Bello
Paula L. Bensel
Karen A. Blohm-
  Mangone
Rocky W. Boatman
Lynne Brant
Anzi Brosh
Karen Cassidy
Sandra Chipman
April Cobb
Keith Coddington
Mary Anne Coleman
Crystal A. Coll
J. R. Cook
Kathleen S. Corum
Robin Cristner
Suzanna Cullinan
Michel Dawson
Jamie J. DeBenedetto
Gary J. DeGeronimo
  Sr.
Delores DeLoera
Patricia A. Dooley
D'Arcy Downs-
  Vollbracht
Toni L. Drugmand
Carole F. Dunn
Maryse Dunn
Kelley Durham
SuAnn Dwight
Anita Rae Easley
Karen L. Edgar
Lisa Ethridge, DVM
Patti Foss-Sutherland
Carol Lynn Fox
Jayme Friedman
Janet C. Galante
Nita M. Gandara
Julie A. Garrahan
Gordon Blake Gillespy
Elizabeth S. Girard
Alice Gough
Cornelia Grabichler
Doreen Gray
Nancy Grimm
Bert A. Haagenstad
Sheila Hanna
Devin L. Harshbarger
Elizabeth Hart
Lorie Hartwick
Roy Hayes

Cheryl Henderson
Rene Hofstetter
Jean A. Hogg
Mark A. Holly
Jeri G. Holton
Lynn D. Holzner
Krystal Huston
Brenda K. Hutton
Kim A. Jacobs
Brad Jaffe
Tamara A. Jaffe
Cynthia K. James
Loralee Johnson
Myra Judd
Donna Kaplan
Lydia Kelley
Shana J. Kerr
Joanie S. King
Justin Kitts
Cecilia A. Klein
Kimberly Kowalski
Linda L. Lambert
Stacey B. Larsen
Marcia L. Malsack
Marjorie F. Mansell
Cindy McArthur
Tawni McBee
Ruthann McCaulley
Jack McCoy
Mindy A. Merkle
Gail Meserve
Cheryl L. Miller
Stephen W. Miller
Carol Mitchell
Katherine A. Morris
Linda Mueller
Erica Nelson
Helaine Prince Nelson
Roger Nelson
Ric Newman
Kristi Nolde-Morrissey
Susan M. O'Driscoll
Lars Peter Oja
Nancy A. Parker
Clacie Payne
Dawn R. Peetz
Varsha Prasad
Toni Prothero
Deborah L. Raymond
Jenifer Raypole
Lucy A. Reynolds
Nancy J. Reynolds
Louis W. Robinson

Darcy A. Rohats
Alleyn Rossomando
Marsha Rute
Ayda A. Sandoval
Joyce Sanford
Ronald D. Schoenwald
Summer Severin
Jamie Smith
Kristi Smith
Leah Snavely
William D. Somerville
Jewell Stapley
Connie R. Stoddard-
  Baddgor
Shawna Swanson
Jan Tomlinson
Linda J. Triplett
Laurie J. Tully
Diane Turner
Lauren Van Buren
Marilyn R. Vinson
Michael A.
  Wiederhold
Steve Wood
Angelina S.
  Woodberry
Laura E. Woolsey
Alice Wright
Marilyn S. Wright
Teri Yool
Kathy Zavodjancik
Mary H. Zepeda
Kathy A. Zmudzinski

ARKANSAS

Sharon Avery
Kimberly Burnett
Cameron Chapman
Margie O. Cox
Suzanne Crites
Wendy J. Ethier
Debra Gefell
Sherry L. Gibbany
Ben H. Goff
Nancy Grimm
Dick Hefner
Kat Hinsen
Carol Hobbs
Janice L. Holden
Terry Huffstetler
Julie S. Jarrett
Rose Klein

Kathryn Kopreski
Barbara L. Laule
Joy E. Lucchesi
Justin McGrew
Suzanne K. Olsen
John Pope
Irene Porsch
Melisa Powell
Stephanie Rogers
Joan M. Rosemier
Anita Sedberry
John Segars Jr.
Rosemary L. Semon
Karen M. Valle
Cherri R. White
Hermine S. Wilkins
Kathleen Zasimovich

CALIFORNIA

Kate Abbott
Nancy Abeyta
Andrea Acosta
Ellen J. Adams
Barbara A. Adcock
Luciano A. Aguilar
Elizabeth Akers
Andrea Lynne Albright
Maryl Aldrich
Krista Alexander
Alison Alimbini
Harvey S. Allen, II
Jo Ann B. Allen
Elizabeth Allen-
  Garland
Pat A. Alley
Dorothy J. Ambrose
Teah Anders
Shannon R. Anderson
Julie E. Apostolu
Valerie M. Appell
Barbara S. Arine
Arline Armendariz
Kim Armitage
Lynne Armstrong
Nan K. Arthur
Gina L. Arthurs
Mary Ash
Andrea M. Ashbaugh
Megan Ashbaugh
Dan R. Atkinson
Darlene L. Atkinson
Erika Ault

Audrey E. Austin
Russell S. Avison
Stacey Ayub
Ann Azevedo
Jourdan B. Bacon
Jennifer Bailey
Jeana M. Barlow
Candice S. Barner
Mary Virginia Barnes
Valda L. Barr
Mary Barrett
Karen Barta
Connie Bartlett
Janet Bates
Linda Bates
Roxanne Baudry
Mary E. Bayley
Pamela H. Bechtold
Pam Becker
Jean R. Beeler
Bree Beery
Trina M. Began
Pamela Behrens
Janice C. Bell
Jeanette Beltran
Ellen Benner
Bruce Bertholf
Steve Bettcher
Ronald John Bevacqua
Cynthia Binder
Laurie E. Bischoff
Verrenia Bishop
Tracy Bivins
Clarissa Black
Joni J. Black
Denise C. Blackman
Margaret A. Blair
Donna Blake
Tiffany Blakeman
Kellae Blessing
Suzi Bluford
Elana Rose Blum
Daniel R. Boggs
Julie C. Bond
Maria Bond
Cathy Bones
Sandra C. Bonifield
Paul A. Bosley
Judith Bowman
Rochelle M. Bowman
Anita L. Boyce
Vikki Boyd
Randi K. Boysen-Carl

Jamie Bozzi
Amanda L. Bradley
Cynthia M. Brevik
Tania Brodowski
Sarah Brookes
Linda R. Brooks
Barbara Ann Brown
Judith A. Brown
Kienan Brown
Lindia L. Brown
Bonnie L. Brown-Cali
Rita Browne
Barbara A. Browning
Betty Burden
Claudia L. Burk
Kathy Kline Burk
Michael D. Burk
Petra Burke
Betty Burnell
Jennifer A. Burns
Christine Burton
Joellen Burton
Shara Butterworth
Dot Byer
Margaret C. Caballero
Dawna L. Caldwell
Betsy Calkins
Silvia Camberos
Annabelle Cambier
Mary Campbell
Janna M. Campillo
Margie Cantwell
Dawn M. Capp
Helen Marie Capps
Verne M. Carlino
Kay Carlo
Susan Carnall
Bryton A. Carnes
Dalece Carson
Rachelle Carzino
Barbara Casciole
Anne K. Catterson
Rebecca Chambliss
Susan Chan, DVM
Laura M. Christiansen
Linda Chwistek
Karen Clanin
Alyson Cleal
Trish Cleary
Catherine Cline
Elissa Cline
Catherine R. Colley
Breanna Collins

Stephanie Colman
Martina C. Contreras
Karyn Convertini
Suni E. Cookson
Brent Cooper
Valerie J. Cornwell
Jan Costa
Paula F. Couturier
Victoria R. Cox
Karen Coyne
Shannon Coyner
Jennifer Craig
Laura M. Craig
Eugene Cunningham
Joella M. Cunnington
Melody Daggs
Kathleen Daly
Lynn Damme
Barbara Davis
MaryJoy Davis
Sherry Davis
Tracey Lee Davis
Stephanie Davis-Rae
Richard Dawson
Carolyn Day
Howard A. Day
Lynn Day
Catherine J. de la Cruz
Brittany Dearing
Dolly D. Dearth
Barbara DeGroodt
Nancy E. Delgado
Maryanne M. Dell
Thomas R. DeLuca III
Blair Diamond
Carlos Diaz
Patricia L. Dibsie
Nicole Dickens
Janet Diersen
Penny DiLoreto
Janis A. Dolphin
Ray Dominguez
Shirley N. Donovan
Uwe Doose
Aleita J. Downer
Cassandra L. Draxler
Christine A. Duane
Lauren B. Dube
Karen Duet
Ericka Duggan
Kathleen Dunn
Renee Dunstan
Jeannie Eagan

Debbie Eaglebarger
John David Earle
Laura J. Ecklin
Carol A. Edwards
Linda L. Elder
Kelly Elkins
Colette C. Emanuel
Krystal A. Emery
Michael Emmett
Patricia R. Emmett
Anastasia Emmons
Robert "Nobu" Endo
Jacquelyn England
Laura A. Enos
Tara Erickson
Terri L. Erickson
Robert K. Ernst
Carol Estades
Betty Estremo
Luther Evans
Elise Faber
Jim R. Faggiano
Laura Falteisek
Augusta P. Farley
Melodie Farrell
Glenn Farris
Nancy Feddeler
Rhonda M. Feinberg
Pamela Felgenhauer
Lisa Fey
Jack Daniel Fields
Tara Flaming
Salem Y. Flores
Dorothy H. Folley
Liz Force
Juanita R. Forrest
Patricia M. Forsberg
Shannon Foster
Valentina Foster
Janice J. Francis
Jan K. Frazee
Laurie Frazer
Carol M. Frazier
Tom Freeman
Yolanda A. Freeman
Jennifer M. Freilich
Nancy Frensley
Barbara L B Fuegner
Cortney D. Gacayan
Virginia A. Gagliano
Sherry Galka
Stuart Galka
Jennifer Gall

Anthony S. Gallegos
Susan Garcia
June E. Gardella
Jean Gauchat-Hargis
Bonnie Gebhardt
Cherie Gessford
Lana M. Getz
Anthony Gio
  Giammarco
Patrick Gibbons
Lynne D. Gifford
MaryLou Giles
Charlene Giller
Suzanne Golden
Anne Goldsmith
Carolyn Goodrich
Kim Goral
Karen A. Grangetto
Linda J. Grant
Camilla Gray-Nelson
Charlene Grayson
Gail S. Green
Jan Greenberg
Denise Greenstein
Zack Grey
Bill S. Griffiths
Carol R. Griggs
Bob Grosbeck
Melinda B. Grosch
Annette Groscup
Bret Gross
Gee Hahn
Jacquelyn R. Halford
Mary-Lou Halliday-
  Campbell
Carol R. Hamilton
Twyla L. Hammers-
  Seymour
Pamela R. Hammon
Michelle C. Handrop
Carroll Hansen
Leri M. Hanson
Masumi Hara
Kayla Hardin
Katie Harlow
Kathylea E. Harper
Robyn A. Harrel
Susan G. Harris
Beth Harrison
Allan Hart
Ruth Hartley
Teryn M. Hartnett
Richard C. Hawes

Gail M. Hawksworth
Rose Healey
Fred J. Helmbold
Jennifer Hernandez
Amy Herot
Eileen D. Heveron,
  PhD
Karen A. Hieger
Christy Hill
Michele A. Hill
Wendy Hilton
Kathleen Hoenow
Cindy Holloway
Jamie L. Holms
T. Mike Hooper
Stephanie Houfek
Sherry L. Howard
Sandy Carol Hoyt
Jamie Hulan
Alan L. Hummel
Annie Humphrey
Nicki Hutchison
Toni Hyland
Julie A. Iles
Michele R. Illes
Briana A. Isaac
Susan Isaacs
Katherine Jacobs
Cathleen M. Jahelka
Sandra J. James
Wendy L. Jeffries
Debra Jensen
Erin Jewell
Donna M. Johns
Christina Johnsen
Barbara Johnson
Kathleen A. Johnson,
  DVM
Pamela Johnson
Nancy J. Jones
Robert Jones
Donna K. Kading
Riney C. Kahler
Teri L. Kahn
Cathrine L. Kaiser
William S. Kasper
Lori F. Katz
Karen A. Kaua
Jennie Keifer
Jessica L. Keleshian
Carole D. Kelly
Sherry Kelly
Robyn Ann Kesnow

Bobbi Jo King
Beverly Kingsbury
Rick Kirichenko
Wendy S. Kirk
Sarah Kirschling
Jeanie Klemm
Ronald E. Knapel Jr.
Lisa A. Knight
Laura Kody
Trink Koenig
Nicholas J. Koep
Jimmy Koffel
Sheila A. Kolby
Julia Kopan
Susan M. Kopp
Charles Kramer
Erin Kramer
Wendy S. Krehbiel
Julie Kroonenburg
Kathy Kropp
Maria Kuss
Mary E. La Crosse
Denise P. Laberee
John E. Lacher
Patricia D. LaCour
Xaviera Ladd
Tina A. Lamey
Shelley Lampman
Caitlin Marie Lane
Debra D. Lane
Susan LaPierre
Galen L. Larson
Susan A. Latunski
Joann D. Lavis
Robin Lawton
Mike Lecuyer
Barbara K. Lee
Christine M. Lee
Ellen D. Lee
Margaret A. Lenoir
Addy Lerner
Robert Dwayne LeRoy
Jim Leske
Beverly Morgan Lewis
Ming Chin Lin
Anna Lindahl
Doreen K. Lindberg
Nancy E. Link
Nancy Lippman
Maheekens Little Wolf
Nickol Litwin
Ruby Liu
Karen Livell

Robert Livell
Amanda M. Livesay
Beth Lloyd
Irina Lockwood
Henry Losee
Marianne Lovejoy
Kathleen L. Lowmiller
Debby L. Lynn
Karl MacEachron
Meghan Madden
Cherie Maitland
Daniel Malinowski
Sandra A. Mannion
Patricia Manrique
Nicole M. Maples
Claudette Marco
Alexandra Mareschal
Francesca Marsh
Kim Marsh
Lee C. Martin
Sandra J. Martin
Susan K. Martin
Rita Martinez
Vickie L. Marx
Jetta Lynn Mascon
Valerie Masi
Valerie L. Masters
Gretchen
  Mavrovouniotis
Cristina M. Maxwell
Joan Hunter Mayer
Janis R. McAlister
Lori McCants
Penny McCausland
Marthina McClay
Jessica McCloskey
Patricia K. McDonnell
Marlene McFall
Sherry McGrath
Gwenn G. McKenzie
Chere McMillan
Sara McNutt
Amy C. McPherson
Lynn L. Medlin
Heather A. Mendoza
Ethel L. Mercer
Renee Meriaux
Linda J. Michaels
Chirleen A. Michelini
Alan G. Miller
Jill Kessler Miller
Renee E. Miller
Barbara P. Millman

Celeste Mills
Penelope M. Milne
Alina L. Mitchell
Laura Mitobe
Patricia Moffitt
Angie E. Monteleon
Darrin Moody
Sylvia Moody
Gordonna Catherine
  Moore
Anna Morey
Tricia Morgan
Kathy A. Morris
Sharon Morris
Lynn A. Mosher
Gina Moss
Amanda Mouisset
Carole Mukai-Rose
Judith A. Murdock
Darrell L. Murphy
Jennifer Murray
Nikki Myers
Sue E. Myles
Diane K. Mylymuk
Gail Naramore
Joanne Nash
Ashley Naylor
Chris Needles
Kou Nelson
Robert Newman, Esq.
Sha Newman
Roger A. Niccoli
Carolyn Niehaus
Sharon Novak
Fawn A. W. Nyvold
Priscilla A. O'Malley
Heather O'Neill
Lauren O'Neill
Vikki Ogden
Wendi A. Okabayashi
Karen A. Oliver
Amelia J. Olson
Michelle Onesky
Kimberly F. Pagones
Camie Palazzo
Kathryn H. Palese
Liz Palika
Lauren Palmer
Sallie R. Palmer
Dianne Panarella
Janice G. Pardue
Esther Parker
Diane L. Parness

Glenda Welch Pate
Marsha L. Pay
R. John Payne
Arthur W. Pearce
Diane Pearl
Patti Pearson
Wendy M. Pennington
Sandi Lea Pensinger
Barbara Peppin
Ann Pereira
Marsha Perloff
Neva Perrotta
Sharon Persey
Judith Peterson
Diane Pettersen-Blair
Janine Pierce
Nancy G. Pierson
Megan Pilarcik
Cathy Pitts
Josh Pitts
Julie A. Poimiroo
Valerie C. Pollard
Teresa (Terry) A.
  Popish
Gloria Post
Michele M. Potter
Lynn M. Potts
Kathleen Prendergast
Catherine Price
Connie S. Price
Tricia J. Prins
Bill Putnam
Silvano Radja
Linda M. Randall
Merl Rasmusson
Virginia Ann Ream
Rosemary Redditt
Cindy Reed
Dr. Pamela C. Regan
Sarah L. Richardson
Bobbi-Lynn Riley
Trevor Myles Riley
London A. Rivera
Penny J. Robinson
Karen J. Rochin
Robert John Rock
Lisa Lynn Rogers
Victoria M. Ronchette
Stephanie L. Ross
Karen Ross-Kennedy
JoAnne C. Rowles
Robin Roy
Nichole Royer

John M. Rubin
Leah A. Ruiz
Jeanna Ruppel
Vicky Rusconi
Patricia L. Rusko
Belinda Ryder-Loomis
Jennifer Sabo
Stephanie Salaz
Maria Cecilia Saleme
Erin S. Sanders
Terry R. Sandhoff
Kathy Sanguinet
Sue Sappok
Serena Saris
Karen Saunders
Beverly Sayman
Laurel Scarioni
Ann Schlobohm
Lynn W. Schmitt
Dr. Linda L. Schulte
Robert Schulte
Jeremy Schuster
Barbara E. Schwerdt
Cindy Scott
Penny Scott-Fox
Kathryn Segura
Rebecca A. Settergren
Wayne Shaffer
Donna Shawver
LouAnn Sherman
Richard Sherman
Kimberlee Shoopman
Joan M. Shugar
Phyllis Shurzinske
Marcia C. Siderow
Kristine Slane
Denelle Smalley
Chrystal Smart
Clarissa I. Smelser
Allen D. Smith
Christopher Smith
Lani Butcher Smith
Lynn J. Smithson
Donna D. Soderstrom
Susan E. Solari
Marlene A. Soldavini
Robert Sotelo
Melanie Sparks
Vivi Sparvoli
Suzie Spehling
Lu-Anne J. Spencer-
 Hartle
Richard Spindel

Jim Spiva
Alan St Andrew
Joanne R. Stacher
Bette Standerfer
Norman Stangler
Sheridan E. "Dan"
 Stanton
Lezle Stein
Julie Sterling
Larry L. Stewart
Charles B. Stockham
Kim Stofer
Carol Stone
Michelle Stone, PhD
Debbie Ann Stoner
Briana Stringer
Trina Strong
Tiffany Marie Stutzke
Lidia Svec
Kris Swanson
Alexandra Sweeney
Linda Sykes
James Taylor
Karen J. Taylor
Anne L. Terry, DVM
Roger G. Therriault
Danielle G. Theule
Cathy Thomas
Laura L. Thomas
Kay Thompson
Sandra Lea Thompson
Stacy Thompson
Paul Thurner
Ronen Tivony
Pamela E. Tobin
Kimberly J. Toepfer
Barbara Tonelli
Tia Maria Torres
Donna J. Tosh
Marjorie E. Trebino
Kathleen Tucker
Lydia Tucker-Clark
Mollie Harris Tunks
Amy N. Uecker
Gabriela L. Ugarte
Beverly J. Ulbrich
Ivy Underdahl
Jennifer L.
 Underwood
David A. Valantine
Valerie Vale
Lee Van Leeuwen
Cynde Van Vleet

Jaime Van Wye
Robert J. Vance
Deborah VanGelder
Julie K. Vanoni
Michelle Moore
 Vasquez
Lisa M. Vella
Donna N.
 Verbeckmoes
Jan Vincent
Mary L. Vincent
Sharon Vincuilla
Linda Voller
Marta Wade
Lori Wainio
Susan A. Walker
Donna Wallace
Debra Walters
Reena S. Walton
Trisha J. Wamsat
Stephen A. Ward
Kimberly Warner
Candie Wasson
Denyse M. Watkins
Peg T. Watson
Katheryn J. Weaver
Melinda Weaver
Caroline W. Weil
Larry S. Weiss
Nancy W. Weller
Dr. Lee Wells
Linda L. Wendorff
Geraldine (Jerry)
 Werk
Sarah Wharton
Lisa White
Marcia L. Wigdahl
Janet M. Wilhelm
Jyl Wilkinson
Chris Williams
Keith R. Williams
Susan J. Williams
Louise H. Wilson
Barbara Witzke
Claudia G. Wolff
Kelly Wolff-Arias
Cyndy Wood
Jo Woodison
Richard Wright
Patty J. Yocum
Margaret A. Young
Suzanne Logan Young
Elizabeth Yturralde

Anita J. Ziebe
Dana J. Zinn
Lesley Zoromski
Cat J. Zoyiopoulos

COLORADO

Amy Andrews
Jason T. Andrews
Laura Asbury
DeAwna Bailey
Sharyn L. Baker
Pat Bayne
Erica Beasley
Jim Beinlich
Susanne B. Bittner
Liz Blasio
Patricia J. Blocker
Randi Bolton
Joe J. Brakke
Jay C. Brigham
Marianne P. Brigham
Ann Brodie
Laura Brody
Megan Brooks
Susan M. Brown
Connie Brownson
Ronald Bruce
Vickie A. Byrne
Janele Caldwell
Barbara Calhoun
Megan Carpenter
Robin M. Carroll
Lydia Cayton-Holland
Jill Chalupsky
Marni E. Cherniss
Cathryn R. Clark
Linda Clark
Sarah Clusman
Ann Coffey
Jeanne Ann Cook
David Coop
Kristen Corbitt
Charleen M. Cordo
Lori H. Cruser
Tim A. Cruser
Kenneth E. Curby
Patti Davieau
Denise Dawson
Kirby DeMott
Robin P. DeSio
Barbara Deets Eaton
Johnnie M. Farmer

Fabienne Feutz
Michele Forto
Robert Forto
Janet R. French
Lynn R. Fruchey, DVM
Gail M. Gardner
Eric D. Gillaspy
Miguel A. Gonzalez
Sam Graeff
Glenna M. Grandbouche
Cara L. Guikema
Jill Haffley
Kathleen M. Haley
Carolyn L. Hazen
Jay Hemmingsen
Elaine S. Holt
Sarah Holton
Megan L. Honaker
Ronald V. Horn
Kathryn M. Howse
Robin A. Hug
Russell Ingram
John Isham
C. Renee Jarrett
Amber Johnson
Lynn Kaemmerer
Christine Kelly
Cathy Kennedy
Lisa Knowles
Cynthia A. Knox
Shannan B. Koucherik
Sandra L. Kruczek
Elizabeth Krupinski
Louise Kuipers
Karen F. Lamb
Pam Leisle
Pat Lester
Karen J. Lewis
Kara L. Lounsbury
Sally Lynn
Mary L. Majchrowski
Janice I. Mann
Dana March
Cheryl Ann Marino-Kresge
DruAnne R. Marshall
Kelley Martin
Patricia Maynard
Anita McAllister
Jo Ann McCoy
Ann M. McDonald
Sandra McFarland

Kasie McGee
Marion A. McKibben
Ana V. Melara
Charles E. Melvin
Fran L. Menley
Jill E. Messenger
Kate J. Mezney
Kelly Miller
Sandra J. Miller
Sean Miller
Kelly Misegadis
Krys Moquin
Leah A. Morse
Lyndsay Ann Morton
Whitney A. Mouton
Beverly B. Muhlenhaupt
Kelly Murphy
Linda Mutz
James Myers
Deborah L. Nabb
Maria Nardi
Nicole Newton
Carrie Nordlund
Patty Olney
Sonja J. Ostrom
Julie Parker
Alisha Parsons
Christena Pastoor
Melinda Peters
Cheryl Pettingell
Bernadette W. Pflug
Linda K. Phipps
Laura J. Pintane
Linda K. Port
M. Chartara Quinn
Jayna Rabke
Carl J. Reif
Laura Roach
Sr. MaryEllen Roach
Katherine Rodgers
Deborah Rogeness
Brant Rosten
Tana K. Rugg
Cherie A. Schnacker
Carole Schoenrock
Karen Scott
Marie Seelmeyer
Edward Shallufy
Cathy Shryock
Lisa L. Sickles
Shawn Smittie Smith-Murphy

John M. Sodia Jr.
Brenda Solomon
Sandi Sorley
Bridget A. Spangler
Marleila S. Springer
Hope A. Stanley
Dianna L. Stearns
Georgeann Steffens
Cindy Still
Rayna Stout
Sandra J. Stuerke
Ted Terroux
Tiffany Terroux
Kimberly Tesar
Terena Thomas
Teri Thomas
Kaleb Michael Tirrell
Jane Trude
Sandra E. Trzos
Judith Tudor
Laura Tyler
Laura Van Dyne
Erin Kelly Vannorsdel
Mark Villafane-Leon
Carol Volleberg
Shelley R. Voorhees
Rebecca J. Wacker
Laura Walker
Cynthia (Cindy) K. Wallace
Julie A. Warzecha
Rachel V. Watson
Maranda Weathermon
Barbara Weiss
Darla Welty
Cathi Wester
Lauren Whittemore
Ann Wichmann
Connie Palmer Williams
Dawn R. Winans
Julie Winkelman
Andrea L. Wojciechowski
Jamie Wolf
Jennifer M. Woodley
Betty Wright
Laura Wright-Smith
Julie M. Yamane

CONNECTICUT

Diane Abbott
Nancy Allen

Sarah Althen
Alice M. Anderson
Tammy A. Anderson
Kathleen Anton
Lisa Antonucci
Ashraf Awad
Linda Bacco
Penney Baker
Rita A. Balducci
Michael Bane
Scott Beebe
Arcelia M. Bettencourt
Valerie L. Bilodeau
Tina Binheimer
Joy S. Brewster
Jennifer M. Bridwell
Lynne Brouard
Gary Burdick
Dona Campbell
Britten Canida
L. Mae Charron
Linda Chernak
Dee Chuisano
Amanda C. Collins
Elizabeth A. Collins
Timothy P. Cook
Linda O. D'Ambrose
Josephine DeMenna
Gina M. DiNardo Lash
Carol J. Dobrozensky
Michelle L. Douglas
Mary-Jo Duffy
Lori J. Eliot
Christine Emt-Franklin
Laura Fass
Patricia Fernandes
Lauren M. Friedman
Susan M. Gagnon
Janice Martin Ganetsky
Jane E. Grauer
Susan Grey
Barbara Hayes
Bonnie A. Henderson
Kara Hickey
Abby Hill
Mary C. Horne
Richard L. Horowitz
Vicki K. Horowitz
Brian Kazlauskas
Barbara C. Keck
Kristina Kelley

Kristofer Kelso
Jodi R. Klim
Lori Kline
Joyce Kramer
Michelle S. Larson
CarolAnn LeBlanc
Marjorie A. Lineweber
Michele Longo
Tracy Longoria
Dawn Lowery
Kristen A. Ludwikow
Lea Lupinacci
Mandy J. Makein
Jessica Malone
Pamela Mannes
Marilyn Marks
Jane M. McLane
Paula S. Milnes
Susan Monroe
Lynda S. Moore
Lorraine Moule
Karen J. Moulton
Joyce O'Connell
Carla J. Onofrio
Jane Palinkas
Elizabeth A. Palmer
J. David Patenaude
Tracy L. Powell, DVM
Betsy Quitko
Margaret A. Reed
Dennis Reinholt
Mark T. Renick
Marilyn F. Rice
Sara Lynn Roy
Deborah Scanlon
Kathi Schapp
Robert Schneider
Nina E. Seturins
Wendy L. Shaw
Kathleen M. Shea
Dawn Shewchuk
Sally A. Sizer
Jeffrey W. Sochrin
Debra Sorosky
Suzanne H. St. Denis
Lesley Stone
Russell M. Strumskas
Lianne L. Sullivan
Matthew G. Svede
Cheryl A. Swarts
Christopher L.
  Sweetwood
Roberta (Robi) Tatkin

Janet Taylor
Grace Terwilliger
Heather Trocola
Karen Tuccitto
Audrey A. Tucker
MaryEllen Walsh
Jim Waltman
Margaret M. Warfield
Michelle Warner
Richard P.
  Weatherstone
Laurey C. Weiner
Lynn T. Whittaker
Danielle L. Wilson
Daniel W. Wilton

DELAWARE

Lesley Bowers
Kathy Braza
Donald P. Brown
Michael J. Brown
Luann D'Agostino
Charlotte T. Dowell
Alicia J. Fencer
Christine Gates
Allison Gil
Irena J. Kelso
Patricia A. Killalea
Jaime M. Lay
Mary M. Lukaszewski
Cynthia S. Martin
Susan I. McKain
Linda V. Miller
Joan Morse
Beth Ellen Peterson
Paul Peterson
Gwen Sherman
Karen Sullivan
Eugenia Thornton
Cyndi Turoczy
Susan P. Webb
Mary Woodward
Lynne J. Young

DISTRICT OF COLUMBIA

Joyce A. Dandridge
Hedda Garland
Kevin M. Simpson

FLORIDA

Frederick L. Abbey
Josh Abrams
James O. Ackermann
Janice Adams
Jean Albrecht-Murphy
Laura Alfano
Betty C. Allen
Delphine M.
  Anderson
Diane Anderson
Gabriele I. Anderson
Diann Andress
Jeffery A. Andrew
Katherine D. Ariens
Cecilia E. Armesto
Laura J. Ash
Veit Bachmann
Cathy Jean Backus
Jaira Baco
Sheila C. Baez
Carole Pergola Baikow
David Baikow
Bonnie C. Bailey
Donna Bainter
Mary D. Baker
Babette D. Barnes
Carla Barstow
Jeannie C. Bates
Bobbie Bauwin
Constance S. Beck
Heather Becker
Lisa M. Beckett
Marni Bellavia
Janet Billups
Marietta H. Birdsell
Deborah B.
  Birmingham
Pamela Blaco
Dorothy J. Blair
Holly E. Blakney
Marjorie Blomquist
Monica Body
Lynda Bogart
Tracy Boggs
Whitney Boles
Alfred A. Bollens
Andi M. Bower
Jeanine Brawn
Gordon Brennan
Carol-Ann Breton

Jeanne Brooks
Debra A. Brouillette
Belinda K. Brown
Brenda J. Brown
Cheryl Brown
Lynnie (Marilyn)
  Brown
Sheryl Jean Brown
Diane F. Browning
Dolores M. Bruno
Kayla M. Bryan
Kimberly Bryan
Dr. Mary R. Burch
Sharon L. Burch
Dayle Burger
Bethany D. Burke
Carol Burke
Dr. Tommy Caisango
Lynn Caisse
Crystal Callahan
Alicia Calogero
Kelly L. Campana
Shana Carranco
Linda S. Carter
Patricia Garey Caruso
Gina M. Chambers
Melanie R. Chan
Myndi Christie
Carol A.
  Christopherson
Susan Claire
Barbara Clark
Karla Clinch
Jane Collar
Dr. Terry S. Collett
Victoria J. Collins
Carol A. Comer
Lee P. Conger
Shirley M. Conley
Marie Conrad
Gail B. Cooper
Graham Coords
Scot D. Cornell
Edna Corney
Joan H. Costello
Frank Cowen
Mindy Cox
Lynne M. Crawford
Brenda J. Crim-Critelli
Brigitte Cruz
Terri L. Cummins
Kevin Curtin
Jennie L. Curtis

Terry Lynn Cuyler
Maria I. Cybyk
Mary Jo Czarny
Arlene A. Czech
Catherine Daugaard
Barbara Davis
Daniel De La Rosa
Paulina De Velasco
Margaret DeFore
Kailey Delisle
Peggy J. DeMinico
Marcia Deugan
Terry Devine
Carola Di Perna
Arlene Dickinson
Therese A. Dickinson
Kay C. Dinkla
Seymour Doctor
Dewey "Al" Dodds
Christine E. Donker
Jackie L. Dougall
Christina Douglas
Jeff Douglas
Donna L. Dowler
Susan M. Downes
Jeff M. Drier
Sandra L. Dunbar
Nancy Dunleavy
Lisa A. Durham
Maureen A. Earle
Richard Eckley
Bruce Edwards
Joan E. Edwards
Pete Eggers
Cynthia A. Elliott
Connie C. Ellis
Daniel Ellis
Germaine Eurich
Penny J. Evancic
McLane Evans
Sandra Fankhauser
Ann Farmer
Tracy B. Farmer
Tammy Farrington
George I. Felt Jr.
Elizabeth M.
  Ferayorni
Shelly Ferger
Kelley Ferguson
Linda Fishkind
Richard M. Flora,
  DVM
Laureen Ford

Valerie Ford
Kathy W. Fornes
Jackie Foster
Marni A. Fowler
May Frame-Inman
Carol Lee Fredman
Julie Freeman
Caleb Frisbee
Melissa E. Frye
Laurent Gabriel
Cori E. Gacusana
Anita Gard
Bonnie H. Geisen
Lorraine A. Gentile
Christine Geschwill
Cheryl L. Giebel-
  Petersen
Kim Gilchrist
Lauren J. Gilman
Teresa Gimbut
Helen Gleason
Laura R. Golden,
  DVM
Cynthia Gordon
Bobette M. Graves
Carolyn Gray
Mark Greathouse
Anne Maureen Greer
Monica Griffith
Ronald Guinta
Colby Gwyn-Williams
Jo Ann Haberl
Linda Haefke
Lisa Hamburg
Robert W.
  Hammesfahr
Paige H. Hanson
Karen E. Harper
Jennifer L. Harrison
John Hartman
Mary K. Hartney
Linda Hartshorn
Valerie Harville
Cassandra J.
  Haverkamp
Kelli Hayes
Maureen Henderson
Jordan Hennessey
Neil Hennessey
Raul Hernandez
V Sandy Herzon
Melissa E. Hess
Liz Hessel

Peggy L. Hickey
Kilmarie Himmelman
Mariah Hinds
Pamela M. Hinton
Marti Hohmann
Chris Hohn
Denisa Hoult
Patricia Hrovat
Cindy Hunt
Tiffanie Ivins
Melissa M. Jackson
Constance A. Jahr
Carolyn "Joyce"
  Jellison
Theresa A. Jennings
Heather A. Jensen
Maren Jensen
Renee W. Johnson
Susie M. Keel
Merilee Kelley
Sharit Melissa Kelley
Linda Kender
Pamela J. Kent
Sherrie B. Keshner
Lisa K. Kiefer
Aimee P. Kincaid
Kenneth Kincaid
Chris M. Kinstler
Carla Knapik
Shirley A. Knipe
Kerry Koppin
Leslie D. Kovacs
Victoria Kowalewski
Erika Kurtz
Jen Kurtz
Jacqueline P. Kurzban
Jeanneane M.
  Kutsukos
Nicholas Kutsukos
Susan Kynkor
Ryna C. La Valle
Tatiana M. Lago
Suzanne Lang
Pedro Luis Lanza
Terri Latronica
Stefani Lawrence
Kelly Legarreta
Marlene Lendrim
Rose Lesniak
Sunny S. Lichtenberg
Anne A. Lippert
Kathy E. Lirette
Nadine Litterman

Kristy D. Lockard
John L. Lockett
Patrick Logue
Judy A. Lucia
Deborah Lumley
Ilene Lynch
June Marie Lyness
Mary Maas
Kathleen C. Maino
Kelly D. Maliszewski
Jerome W. Manning
Alison L. Martz
Shirley L. Mason
Kerry Maxaner
Kim A.C. Mayes
Cindy Michelle
  McConnell
Johnna F. McGinnis
Lynda McGlynn
Kimberly A. McGrail
Jenn McGrane
John M. McGrath
Kathryn C. McKewen
Vivian McKinley
Elena M. McKnight
Candace C. McMahon
Jorge L. Mendiola
Linda D. Mills
Sandi Mirabito
Osa Mitchell
Joyce L. Moore
Virginia Morris
Sandra Moruzzi
Siobhan Reilly
  Mullally
Elizabeth F. Mulroney
Jacqueline Munera
Karen E. Murphy
Dr. Barbara A. Murray
Ileana M. Nadal
Janet S. Narushka
Deborah P. Neufeld
Maki Nieto-Menendez
Norine E. Noonan
Christine C. Norris
Amber Norton
Carl Nowell
Beth Nugent
Jennifer O'Brien
Kelli E. O'Donnell
Laurel A. O'Neil
Maria Oehler
Michelle Olandese

Denise M. Owens
Melody R. Owens
John Pacsay
Michele J. Panetta
Anne E. Pantall
Michael G. Pape
Albert Parayre
Linda S. Parsons
Lorena B. Patti
Patricia A. Paulding
Melisa A. Peacock
Richard H. Pearce
Suzie Peck
Jeanette L. Perkins
Kim Permann
Gale F. Perry
Tracy D. Perry
Francine Persan
Mary J. Peter
John H. Pfohler
Kathy Phebus
Angela L. Pietrantonio
Jennifer C. Pingleton
Celeste A. Platte
Gwen E. Podulka
Ann Meredith Polny
Jacqueline Powell
Rita Princivalli
Jacki C. Purdham
Yolanda Purvis
Claire Quilon
Larry Randolph
Hugh (Randy) R. Reed
Joe Retkowski
Rebecca Retkowski
Debbie J. Revell
Lyn J. Richards
Lisa M. Rieves
Jeannette Ringer
Rose Robinett
Jessica Robinson
Arlene Rodriguez
Brenda M. Rondinone
Allison Ross-Hofstetter
Walt R. Rubin
Birdena G. Russell
Lisa A. Russell
John C. Russo
Maureen Russo
Terry Ruthruff
Erin Saintil
Lisa Salapat
Brenda J. Saling

Michael J. Saling
Mary Ann Sanford
Cliff N. Santos
Linnea D. Saputo
Sally A. Saxton
Edith M. Scheurman
Wallace A. Scheurman
Jan Schmidt
Lucinda K. Schneller
Maureen Schooley
Susan Schrader
Silke E. Schroder
Sharron H.
  Schumacher
Charlotte Schwartz
William C. Schweizer
Tony F. Scitarelli
Diane Sedberry
Laura M. Segers
Mark J. Shambour
Kim Shanley
Brenda J. Sheldon
Betty Shorter
Carrie Silva
Sharon A. Simon
Clare Singer
Robert T. Skaggs
Janet Skinner
Roger Sklow
Judy A. Smeltzer
Lindsey Smith
Lorraine J. Smith
Marilynn Smith
Michael Smith
Debbi D. Snyder
Phil Snyder
Kathryn Souder
Karen A. Soukiasian
Dorie T. Sparkman
Heather M. Sparks
Jeffrey T. Speicher,
  DVM
Margaret Spence
Jeanne W. Spica
Dave Springs
Barbara Stebbins
Angelica E. Steinker
Linda L. Storts
Marc Street
Cecelia Sumner
Joyce A. Swegle
Charlotte Swindell
L. Dawn Tait

Arlene G. Tanel
Ellen Taylor
Pamala Taylor
Gene A. Teany
Chris Tejcek
Jana R. Thomas
Dawn M. Thomason
Diane S. Thompson
Lori L. Thorsby
Gwen Tomlinson
Patricia Totillo
Letty M. Towles
Suzanne M. Towne
Joan F. Trickett
Holly Trosino
Niki Tudge
Jillian Uhl
Betty Umberto-Wells
Linda M. Unger
Jose Valdes
Madelyn Valle
Marlen Valle
Laura M. Van Horn
Karen A. Vance
Pamela Vandenburgh
Sandra S. Vaughan
Paula E. Veibl
Melanie Villafana
Laurie Volpe
Erin L. Wagganer
Sandra E. Wagner
Susan C. Wallace
Barry Walsh
Lisa B. Walsh
Nellie D. Walter
Robin R. Walter
Victoria Warfel
Valerie Y. Warmuth
Rebecca A. Watford
Thomas Weaver
Quinn Webb
Tracey A. Wells
Lynne F. Wetherell
Lyndana Wethington
Colleen Whalen
Anthony J. White
Barbara White
Glen E. White
Simon White
Rebecca Whitney
Karen M. Williams
Edward K. Wilson
Rachel M. Wimmer

Joan Winchester
Barbara W. Winge
Martha Winters
Nell Wirtes
Jennifer Wise
Cindy L. Wold
Marilyn J. Wolf
Debra Wood
Kathy L. Worcester
Michelle Marie Worley
Mary A. Wright
Rebecca Young-
  Laplant
John M. Zakens
Marie Zaman
Marilyn J. Zappone
Candy Zimmerman
Isis L. Zometa

GEORGIA

Jessica Abney
Susie Aga
Alice R. Alford
Jennifer P. Bachelor
Charles Baranowski
Becky R. Barton
Bridgett Bass
Jenny P. Baum
Nicole Baylosis
Susan L. Benkiser
Georgie Blackburn
Susan Boekel
Ann Boles
Lynne A. Boring
Pat L. Bridges
Roycelyn Brownell
Cathy Bruce
Amber D. Burckhalter
Kate Carpenter
Claudia Clifton
Michael A. Clifton
Ashley Coleman
Kelli Collins
Judy Colvin
Amanda M. Conrad
Kellie R. Cosby
Ann Cranford
Carolyn Crockett
Mary Kay Crowell
Holly Crumley
Gloria Baughn Davis
Stephen A. Deal

Jessica Dean
Kristi A. Dement
Joan L. Dickerson
Bonnie DiCocco
Sandra D. Dixon
Heidy Drawdy
Doris Dressler
Fanna M. Easter
Tara B. Edwards
Christina Eichorst
Stefanie Elderkin
Tiffany A. England
Ruth Enlow
Sandra Fitterman
Cindy H. Flanary
Gloria Flippen
Jo Gahm
Leesa K. Gallo
Joseph L. Gavin
Vanessa Giddens
Deborah Gill
Wanda W. Goodson
Joyce Hagan
Vail D. Hanna
Lisa Harmon
Marty Harris
Suzanne Harris
Donna M. Hartnett
Franziska (Sissy)
  Haskell
Robert Lee Houshel Jr.
Robyn B. Huff
Jimmy W. Hunt
Patrick Ireland
Kate A. Jackson
Angelia Jennings
Channing Johnson
Anne M. Jones
Grant S. Juneau
Julie Kampling
Joyce Keeton
Mavis Kicklighter
Patty Anne King
Sherri Kwis
Xalina A. LaBarge
Darla D. Lacey
Robbie Lamping
Chris Laseter
Joan A. Lask
Mary E. Lawrence
Elaine B. LeRoy
Jennifer Lockwood
Pamela A. Long

CeCi J. Luongo
Jerry L. Lyda
Jan E. Mabry
Linda Maddox
B.D. Malone
Deborah A. Martin-
  Gerstle, PhD
Rebecca Matherly
Christine Mattucci
Virginia M. Mayhall
Tina M. McCain
Martha Woods
  McCloud
Julie McDaniel
Mailey McLaughlin
Cat Klass Meissner
Carolyn C. Meltzer
Amy S. Miller
Meredith Minkin
Kathleen Miracle
Pat B. Mitchell
Bob Monday
Jan Moore
Maryam Morrison
Marilu Novy
Justine Oakwood
Toni K. Ogden
Judy Padgett
Beatrice L. Page
Diane P. Pegram
Gretchen Penrose
Melony F. Phillips
Sheila Phillips
Patricia Ann Pierce
R. Darlene Pino
Stacey Pollio
Kathleen Predmore
Lisa G. Prince
Julianne C. Rask
Christy Redenbach
Jan Reid
Ginger Robertson
Jennifer Robinson
Lisa Rodier-Yun
Melissa M. Roton
Jason S. Samples
Jeffrey Santiago
Tracy S. Sargent
Patricia Schaeflern-
  Barnes, DVM
Holly W. Schmidt
Missy Schmidt
Tracey Schowalter

Eric L. Scott
Clara P. Seals
Jana T. Sellers
Ann Shaw
Janice Shields
Sheila Shreve
Lisa C. Sims
Michael D. Sinteff
Maryellen R. Slayton
Kenneth P. Slodowski
Georgia L. Smelser
Donna M. Smith
J. Rebecca Snider
Dawn Marie Snyder
Mark Spivak
Leslie M. Sprando
Marlene Keay
  Stachowiak
Lynn Stamegna
Andrea Stark
Karen Sumlin
Laura Summers
Edie Sutton
Kimberly Tank
Shannon Taylor
Donna Thompson
Mary J. Thompson
Minette Topham
Tina M. Van Why
Anne Marie Vaughan
Sherry A. Vernick
Gregory John Vickers
Tricia Vines
Carla Warren
Sandra Kay Watson
Jacob S. Weaver
Mara Whitacre
Luke Wilkins
Monique A. Williams
Naomi L. Williams
Sharon H. Willis
Mary Leslie Wilson,
  PhD
Elizabeth Wood
Candy Wright
Jamaul A. Wright
Sheila Yost
Thomas Zebrowitz
Christopher
  Zimmermann
Morrisa H. Zimmeth

Susan F. Ancheta
Margaret Blackmer
Betty W. Brask
Mary A. Buckley
Ellen M. Carscadden
Cheryl S. Chang
Mary E. Clarose
Joyce T. Clemens
Joanne N. Costa
Jeannette Crooke
Denise Davis
Jillian Davis
Anna Dorminy
Tobi S. Feves
Karen Furtado
Becky Gagnon
Teresa Gajate
Jenna Garrison
Lisa L. Giesick
Karen K. Hashimoto
Teri L. Hollowell
Gayle Igarashi
Deborah J. Kent
Ted Ketcham
Damien T.K. Kim
Tracy Laride
Cheri S. Larsen
Wendy L. Mah
Shari G. Masterson
Blossom M.L. Mau
Susan A. May
Carol A. Medeiros
Patrick E. Medeiros
Wendy Middleton
Frances M. Moniz
Dawn M. Patterson
Ricko Rask
Melissa M. Ronan
Marie Gabrielle
  Selarque
Charlene L. Shelton
Catherine M. Staege
Anthony Sur
Carole C. Sussel
F Lei Taft
Denise Van Ryzin
Chester Wakida
Elinor Yamauchi

IDAHO

Phil Arizola
Dorothea I. Barrett
Suzanne J. Belger
Karalee A. Blau
Kristi L. Bowers
Jill Bryson
Diana Cannon
Barb W. Carpita
Laurie A. Ceccarelli
James R. Closson
Brian A. Corcoran
Karen M. Culver
Sharon C. DeVita
Andrea J. Foley
Jane L. Guidinger
Virginia Hansen
Janet E. Hatfield
Dr. Jill Haunold
Eric Hess
Joyce A. Hughes
Elizabeth L. Kohl
Lorraine Kreider
Wendy S. Lowdermilk
Pamela Metts-Boyer
Christine Nelson
Alice A. Peterson
Sandra (Sandy) K. Peterson
Stacey M. Poler
Dyan L. Roessler
Lincea Ruth
Sandra A. Sartorius
Karen Schumacher
Connie J. Sharkey
Herman L. Shuping Jr.
T.J. Smith
Jim Sosler
Vicki Stephens
Cindie Swaim
Thora Thibaut
Josie Elaine Webster
Susan White
Andrea Williams
Richard Michael Yanez

ILLINOIS

Toni Aden
David Ahlgrim
Kerri Alexander
Tania Alich
Donna A. Angeleri
Marilyn Armstrong
Judit Arroyo
Carole Atkinson
Anne M. Baker
Deborah M. Baker
Mary C. Baque
Lisa M. Bataska
Brenda Baudler
Patricia A. Baur Crossin
Yolanda M. Belluso
Brenda Belmonte
Camille A. Belpedio
Bruce B. Berg
Lori Berg
Debbie Ann Bickford
Becky S. Blevins
Kimberly A. Bobka
Christy L. Boecker
JoDonna K. Boisvert
Lesa Bolt
Nick Booras
Pam Booras
Bobbi Borbely
Dawn Borg
Valeria C. Bourland
Shirley A. Bower
Kathy Brady
Jeffrey W. Branning
Joan Brehm
Vickie L. Brent
JoAnne Brettschneider
Kristi E. Brewer
Lynn Brezina
Dawn L. Bromley
Marcy Brooks
Diane K. Brown
Marlene Brzoska
Patricia Burgess
Susan Burrows
Judith C. Bush
Aimee Busse
Terri Byerly
Rebecca Cann
Jan A. Carlson
Danielle Carlton
Sally J. Carr
Cheryl Carter
Linda Case
Donna K. Cash
Brice Cavanaugh

Jason Chapman
Linda K. Chiaramonte
Linda Chmielewski-Larsen
Gregory A. Clark
Jane W. Clark
Randa Lyn Clark
Sherry Cole
Susan M. Cole
Lisa Collins
Diane M. Combs
Julie A. Condron
Jane Connors-Geddes
Lecia Conroy
Matt Covey
Rick Cox
Kay Creese, DVM
Ruth Anne Crisler
Michael Crounk
Michelle L. Cufr
Robert Czarnowski
Michael T. Dagley
Michael D. Daidone
Jamie L. Damato
Dennis H. Damon
Donna M. Darland
Sandy Davis
Shirley A. Davis
Wendy L. DeCarlo-Young
Behesha Doan
Alden A. Domrase
Connie J. Dorsett
Melissa Drost
Susan J. Duke
Lisa Dziedzina
James Earll
Elaine Edwards
Rich Ehrenberg
Lauren Evans
Mary Ann Even
Vincent Feltner
Patrick Ferland
Anne F. Feuerstein
Shari Finger
Charlene A. Finn
Julia Firlit
Karin Fischer
Sharon Fitzpatrick
Eva G. Fojudzki
Sue B. Folkerts
Nancy Gatza
Dorothy E. Gawne

Karen Gaydos
Gregory Geisen
Margaret H. Gibbs
Bonnie Glenn
Mary Jo Glenn
Nicolle M. Glenn
Linda E. Glynn
Judy Goodfellow
Anthony Gordon
Teresa Anne Gray
Wendy Greenfield
Mary E. Grueskin
Linda Guy
Jennifer Hack
Jeffrey J. Hakanson Sr.
Jessica Hamman
Elizabeth M. Hammond
Anna L. Hansen
Kathy Hansen
Rick H. Hartke
David Haskins
Kathie Hayes
Montana C. Hayes
Jeanne R. Heger
Jessica D. Heidrick-Cox
Susan K. Helmink
Cheryl A. Helsing, DVM
Connie K. Hillquist
Holly C. Hinton
Steve Hitz
Joseph R. Hodder Jr.
Christina M. Hoogervorst
Chari L. Hopper
Liz Huskey
Terry Irvin
Donna Jacobs
Heide Jakiel
Susan M. Jakobs
Kathy Janoski
Michael Jayko
Jeff Jenkins
Diane L. Jensen
Kathy Jensen
Paul Jensen
Judy L. Jurgens
Beverly Jurinek
Jennie Kang
Laura Karczewski
Kathy Karl

Michelle Karolicki
Sandi Keller
Lou Anne Kenwick
Michael G. Kestner
Joe N. Kidd
Bridget A.
  Kilcommons
Arlene G. King
Scott Klassen
Jen Knappenburger
Anna Kniaz
Georgene D. Knight
Irma Knoles
Philip J. Kocisko
Kimberly S. Koester
Gary Kong
Paul L. Kouski
Christina Kowalczyk
Sally Krostal
Julia Kamysz Lane
Anna M. Laue
Mary K. LeBreton
Lawrence W. Lentz
Barbara L. Lepke
Janet Lewellen
Janet Liesen
Sheila K. Lietz
Barbara Light
Richard Light
Lisa A. Lillie
Ramona Lilly
Richard Lilly
Nancy Lind
Anita Lindroth
Lynsi Long
Pamela M. Lowrey
Sherry Luckhaupt
Andrea P. Lynn-
  Goerke
Theresa Mariani
Marytherese Marosits
Kathryn I. Martens
Abe Mashal
Roy E. Mashaney
Robin B. Massey
Cindy Masterson
Jane M. Masterson
Holly May
Rhea Mays
Mary Mazzeri
Lisa R. McCluskey
Daniel McElroy
Maureen McNames

Deborah Mendez
Kent W. Meyer
Belinda M. Meyn
Jovita Miller
Matt J. Mirro
Marie K. Monaco
Laura Monaco Torelli
Annette K. Monge
Stephen L. Monyko
Arlene M. Moody
Leonardo Moody
A Moore
Jeanne E. Moore
Virginia Moore
Peggy C. Moran
Nichole Morrison
Hilary Moyle
Carol Mueller
Richard W. Murmann
Jason L. Murphy
Rodney Neel
Rosemary J. Nehls
Pat Nordenberg
Anne Hubbard
  Norton
Karen S. Okura
Nadine Onesti
Megan Ores-Uhrich
Lisa Pellum
Nancy Petersen
Amy J. Peterson
Sharon K. Peterson
Sheryl J. Phelps
Valerie A. Phillips
Morgan Pierce
Julie A. Pinn
Barbara Pische
Alice Piszczek
Melissa Plotner
Susan L. Poludniak
Laura Portee, DVM
Lisa A. Potts
Nina Pregont
Ami Prindiville
Marilyn G. Putz
Mary T. Ramsden
Tracy A. Regole
Dawn Rehus
Jaimie M. Rendall
Amanda Ressel
Mary Ann Riecke
Ellen Ritt
Jerri Rogers

Tammie L. Rogers
Carol A. Ronan
Allan Ross
Sarah Rothberger
Carrie Rzewnicki
Barbara A. Sanders
Jennifer Sanders
Kym Santos
Barbara Scalise
Dawn Schertz
Aimee M. Schilling
Trudi Schoening
Thomas G. Schukay
Annette M. Schultz
Connie L. Scott
Joan Seipp
Kennine D. Shinn
Mike Sides
Delphine Jayne Sieff
Mariellen Spiros
Julie C. Stahl
Cathy Stein
Sandra J. Stephenson
Emily Stoddard
Martin D. Sullivan
Jan Sund
Sara Swan
Teri D. Szarzak
Ronald R. Terven
Marie Thomas
Gary N. Tippett
Janice Lynn Triptow
Ashlee L. Trotter
Colleen A. Tsuji
Karen A. Turkowski
Deneice L. Van Hook,
  DVM
Lisa M. VanBogget
Dawn A. Vendegna
Mary Beth Wajda
Linda Wallenberg
Judith A. Warling
Dewayne L.
  Washington
Donna J. Webster
Donna Weisensel
Erik Weitz
M. Tommy Whang
Jeff White
Tina M. Widdows
Judy Williams
Diane Williams-Kidd
Eric Wilson

Lindsay Wirth
Michael Young
Jennifer Zychowski

INDIANA

Karen Marie Agli
Kim Anderson
Judy M. Archer-Dick
Cindy Atterberry
Kimberly Bachert
R. Theodore Baer
Craig Bale
Karen L. Bales
Hubert J. Ball
Carol Lynn Bamberger
Melissa Bannister-
  Selby
Tiffany Corrine Bartley
Mary J. Bastress
Brenda Bateman
Laura V. Baugh
Toni Bianchi
Alicia Bloomfield
Bobbi Jo Bottomley
Michael D. Braun
Cynthia M. Breiva
Mark Brooks
Becky Browning
Barbara F. Byer
Andrea Carlson, DVM
Julie Case
Gwen A. Chaney
Del Dean Cleek
Irene H. Clute
Delayne Corle
Sherry Cornwell
Charity Cron
Jeann Crowcroft
Barbara A. Croy
Rebecca J. Davis
Regan Dietz
Linda Dillbeck
Mercedes Dinkel
Deborah A. Dolak
Leslie Martin Dotson
Matthew P. Duffy
Laura A. English
Robert Fleming
Sheri Floyd
Madonna Gentry
Kathleen Gilbertson
Chelsea Gill

Robin C. Gindoy
Brenda K. Grice
Kerri Griffin
Deborah A. Gwaltney
Pamela Jo Hackstadt
Jan M. Harkner-Abbs
Ronald D. Harris
Melissa Heigl
Jennifer Hendricks
Brent C. Henschen
Gregory L. Hollen
Amy J. Hopper
Penny C. Hueston
Connie L. Jackson
Angela K. Jones
Mary Keifer
Shannon M. Kiley, DVM
Kelly Kosinski
Antoinette Krafcheck
Bonnie Krupa
DeAnna L. Lawyer
Robert A. Lewis
Kathryn Lovan
Sherry L. Massey
Carol A. Mayberry
Candice McKing
Bruce K. McNabb
Roderick G. Memering
Pamela J. Mendenhall
Richard L. Mintchell
Karen Moench
Nancy L. Moore
Beth A. Moreland
Michelle L. Mulligan
Lois Myers
Jan J. Nowicki
Stephany O'Dell
Vicki Lynn Palmore
Danielle A. Parker
Joann E. Peavler
Linda Pense
Sue Pfrank
Brad Phifer
Michelle Phillips
Cathy Price
Paula Price
Sabrina L. Prim
George E. Ramey
Carol L. Richardson
Laura Sprague Richardson

Shelly Rish
Julia A. Roberts
Jill M. Rodgers
Lina Rolland
Michael R. Rowland
Kristi Rush
Terri A. Sajdera
Patricia A. Sample
Nancy Schenck, DVM
Lucinda L. Schultz
Lynn M. Seering
Susan D. Sharpe
Donna Shaw
Patricia (Trish) A. Simon
Diana L. Skibinski
Kera Slowitsky
Laura Smart
Deborah L. Smith
Talva J. Smith
Jennifer K. Sneed
Shirley A. Spall
Margaret Stafford
Brenda K. Staley
Catherine Steinke
Cris Stevens
Judith Stevens
Sarah B. Stevens
Lori Tatum
Jennifer Thornton
Pamela A. Tibbs
Carrie Tichenor
Ailigh R. Vanderbush
Terry S. VanHook
Sharon A. Walter
Sarah A. Weiss
Bobbie Williams
Dawn Williams
Denise Wilusz
Jerilyn S. Wissler
Nick Wools
Nancy Wright
Makiko Yoshino

Charles Adams
Connie Adams
Deborah Anderson-Olgren
Connie V. Apling
Laura B. Brown
Randy Capsel

Cheryl L. Clark
Carol D. Clemens
Rhonda L. Crane
Gayle K. Curtis
Lisa Dohlman
Renee Dotzler
Ann M. Dresselhaus
Margaret Elliott
Darcy L. Emehiser
Tanja A. Frye
Paul D. Goldstein
Paul L. Grimm
Dave Hala Jr.
Mary Beth Haley
Lois V. Hall
Liz Hawkins
Ryan A. Heard
Nancy Hood
Michelle Huntting
Scott Hurley
Rev. Linda K. Jackson
Scott Joseph Jetter
Faith E. Jones
Carla G. Karr
Bev Klingensmith
Nancy Jane Levenhagen
Valerie J. Lillibridge
Jeanne A. Little
Susanne Lugrain
Susan Marshall-Herrick
Judy K. May
Cindy McDonald
Chris McGinnis
Robbie Meerdink
Monika Moeller
Frank A. Motto
Peter Murphy
Stephanie L. Neff
Lou Ann O'Malley
Debra L. Owens
Jim R. Reeves
Shirley Ann Richards
Sherry L. Rife
Doylene Roberts
Shannon T. Rodgers
Beth Rolle
Dawn Roth
Robert D. Salsbury
Patricia E. Saunders
Gloria Shipman
Marilynn A. Snook

Paula A. Sunday
Susan F. Swink
Helen A. Venneman
Sharon Wallway

Barbara Addison
Jocelyn M. Baker
Colleen Barricklow
Dennis Bastian
Rebecca Belanger
Beverly S. Benjes
Richard Benjes
Melody Boltz
Christi D. Bone
Kay Cassella
Terri Clarkson
Barbara L. Clauson
Nadine Conner
Jacqueline M. David
Rebecca A. Davis
Cynthia Debes
Cedric E. Devin
Liz Devin
Kim Downing
Marion V. Duer
Vicky E. Edwards
Kathryn L. Ewing
Maris Ewing
Kathy M. Farres
Rebecca L. Fouts
Janet L. Griggs
Liz Harold
Mose Hugghis
Kristine Jaramillo
Jerre Kay Karel
Corrinda L. Keezer
Susan A. Keller
Donna O. Lane
SueZanne M. Law
John Letcher
Gloria D. Logan
Mandy Masters
Cheryl May
Connie J. Mayes
Jeffrey J. Morck
Chuck Morris
Kay E. Nester
Russell L. Osburn
Barbara Retke
Perrin Riggs
Rick Riggs

Jeri A. Schupman
Lisa D. Smith
Pat Sorrels
Ron R. Sparkman
Kelly E. Spencer
Penny Stober
Denise S. Townsley
Laurie M. Vickery
Amber L. Wade
Patricia L. Wilson
Kathy Yager
Julie Yoder

KENTUCKY

Pamela C. Adams
Dr. Mary Belle
  Adelman
Johna Albritton
Jamie C. Baker
Sharon Ball
Cindy Barker
Peggy Bell
Heike Blessing-Purdon
Debbie Boaz
Linda Breck
Pamela D. Brown
Wanda Brown
Norma Campbell
Debbie R. Cavitt
Gabrielle L. Cecil
Linda S. Coates
David W. Cole
Tammy L. Cole
Terry Derting
Paul W. Dixon
Judy L. Donaldson
Marilyn R. Donlon
Kristin Ernst
Bonnie Faulkner
John L. Faulkner
Patricia Fendley
Tracy Frost
Lannis R. Garnett
Bella Gaudette
Jeff Gowen
Diana R. Grant
Sandra A. Gregory
Sharon S. Gretsinger
Stephanie Hagen
Nancy E. Hansen
Karin C. Hix
Ronnie Hogan

Lisa D. Hollander
Melissa M. Kampars
Christina M. Keller
Bunny D. Lanning
Terri L. Lattanzio
Jeff Lund
Jason Mann
Jill Marple
Ursa Major Marr
Tammy Marshall-
  Weldon
Barbara J. McCormack
Cindy M. McCouch
Debbie Menton
Chris Miara
Terry Moore
Ellen L. Murphy
Kay Murphy
Kristina F. Pattison
Belinda Perry
Molly A. Petrey
Dan Polo
Leigh Pridemore
Peter A. Purdon
Debbie B. Purdy
Carol Quarg
Beth A. Schofield
Connie Denise Sexton
Melody J. Southworth
Vicki Spencer
Robin L. Van Noy
Emma K. Wallace
Allen J. Watts
Allison Jamison
  Woosley
MaryAnn R.
  Zeigenfuse

LOUISIANA

Don J. Abney Jr.
Connie Back
Sue Ann Barnett
Paula P. Barras
Peter G.W. Betchley
Margaret R. Bird
Linda K. Booker
Patrick L. Booker
Patricia M. Boswell
Terri Rockvoan Breau
Jennie T. Carter
Patrice Edwards
Margo French

Linda D. Gagnon
Priscilla Gebauer
Alicia Holley
Ann M. Irwin
Maureen Kidd
Monika Kuss
Deborah Martin
Kenneth M. Martin,
  DVM
Terry F. Mayers
Susan McCormick
Sharon McDonald
Patricia Menard
Joan R. Morehead
Amber L. Nafe
James D. Nafe
Angela M. Portera
Mary Ann Richard
Marie-Alice Rousselle
Patti Savage
Elizabeth Scorzelli
James A. Seaman
Carmen Sereno
Sallie A. Shepherd
Catherine Stephens
Jeanne B. Stephens
Sally Stride
Jeanne R. Stulb
Diane Sylvester
James E. Thornhill

MAINE

Denyse M. Adams
Amy F. Allenwood
Patricia A. Beattie
Pamela Belcher
Debra Berthiaume
Lynn M. Boulier
Robert D. Boulier
Jody Buddemeyer
R. Wayde Carter
Penny J. Cary
June Cawood
Pamela J. Chandler
Kathy Charles
Diane Cunningham
Suzan J. Dexter
Glenda W. Drum
Liz Dudgeon
Cindy Dunham
Dale L. Dutill
Lane A. Fisher

Nancy J. Freedman-
  Smith
Marie L. Gagnon
Barbara Gibson
Renee Gordon
MaryJane Grant
Sumac Grant-Johnson
Shannan Hall-Nutting
Donald J. Hanson
Kathy Hartley
Rebecca Henderson
Naomi Kathleen
  Howe
Wanda K. Jesonis
Megan Kirkpatrick
Lynda X. Knowlton
Claire Marx
Linda May McKinnon
Judy Moore
Stephani Morancie
Irene M. T. Morey
Dawn Mulcahey
Gene L. Nardi
Betsy B. Newman
SaShell Nofsker
Karen Norteman
Rita L. Page
Elizabeth P. Parker
Becky Pelletier
Mary B. Peterson
Sherrylee D. Pierce
Adam J. Ricci
David J. Robichaud
Susan S. Robichaud
Julie Rodick
Carolyn Ross
Steven S. Seekins
Kim VanSickle
Donna R. Whitney
Lloyd D. Williams
Jenny Ruth Yasi

MARYLAND

Duffy Askin
Frederic B. Askin, MD
Lynda Bailey
Bonnie Jean Baker
Richard L. Begun
Wynard Maxwell
  Belton
Janet Bennett

Lynne Bettinger
Katherine I. Bleinberger
Jenna Bobetich
Barbara L. Bounds
Margaret A. Bradford
Debra J. Brannan
Marcia Bresson
Mary Ann Bruton
Joyce Burdette
Bernice Burroughs
Gale M. Campbell
Dianne Care
Susan A. Carlton
Mary E. Chrusciel
Linda A. Ciampo
Dennis Ciesla
Michele Clausen
Laurie F. Collins
Karen E. Connelly
Karen B. Cottingham
Brian Cox
Teresa Cox
Bevalee M. Crawley
Vicky B. Creamer
Lisa Marie Daniel
Robert L. DeLuca
Gina Downin
Eileen A. Edelblute
Peggy Faith
Leslie Fisher
Judy Franz
Andrew Fraser
Joy Freedman
Bonnie E. Garris
Diann Gastley
Deanna Gibby
Kathleen Bridget Gillen
Johanna C. Grove
Linda A. Grskovich
Jack Haesloop
Je'ree M. Hamlet
Timothy L. Hanavan
VerLynn Haneke
Aja Harris
Brenda P. Hasbargen
Karen M. Haynes
Carol A. Heisterhagen
Pamela S. Helmer
Sabine Hentrich
Susan H. Hertz
Thomas W. Hertz

Tecla Heuring
Cynthia L. Hill
Leslie L. Horton
Juliann M. Jacobus
Wesley L. Jenson Sr.
Amelia H. Johnson
Katrina S. Kardiasmenos, PhD
Edward W. Keyser
Kathleen L. Koebler
Carolyn D. Lathrop
Allie W. Lee
Charles A. Lerner
Kevin Lewis
Joyce L. Lilly
Roxanna Lowery
Laurie M. Luck
C. Liane Luini
Jennifer L. Lund
Elizabeth M. Lundell
Jennifer Lyons
Pamela Mackler
Brian Markowich
Jeanie G. Marshall
Odessa Yumi Maxwell
Judith A. Mayberry
Sara Meisinger
Diana M. Miller-Blandford
Patricia A. Mills
Ellen Moon
Linda F. Morris
Tracey Mullineaux
Leigh Murphy
Lindsey Nickerson
Katherine Novak
Jules L. Nye
Susan S. Osmansky
Diane G. Patrick
Merope Pavlides
Kristen L. Reimuller
Ann Riley
Elissette Rivera
Michele Rubadue
Judith M. Ruff
Diane Sammarco
Nancy S. Schultz
Claire J. Schwartz
Lissa N. Scott
Michael J. Soler
Richard C. Streett
Linda C. Surmacz
Dana Teague

Debby Tolstoi
Laura J. Totis
Tamara L. Tucker
Holly V. Wallace
Joy White
Alfhild M. Winder
David Winns
Denyse Winns
Margot Woods
Kim Yocklin
Albert L. Younger, IV

MASSACHUSETTS

Scott Abbott
Carol C. Ahearn
Marcia G. Albert
Dan J. Allman
Marjie Alonso
Katrin Andberg
Laura J. Aubrey-Cook
Luis L. Avery
Tracie Laliberte Bailey
Kimberly Bainbridge
Dorothy Baisly
Kimberly A. Balboni
M. Breslin Benyo
Joe Blancato
Donna Blews-Pappas
Michelle Borelli
Erin M. Brackett
Carol Bradford
Pauline Bragg
Janet K. Bramhall
Jacqueline M. Breault
Terri Bright
Rachel Brostrom
Jeanne Brouillette
Abbey Brown
Ginger A. Browne Johnson, DVM
Kathleen R. Buckley
Lauren E. Cannon
Donna Cansdale
John Cappellina
Debra Carlson
Sarah J. Carmichael
Michele B. Castonguay
Elizabeth Chase
Monique D. Chretien
Terry Christie
Joan M. Chrusciel
Lisa M. Ciampa

Madelyn L. Cirinna
Michael F. Citro
Robert E. Clark Jr.
Sandra E. Clark
Elizabeth Cleaves
Suzan Cluff
Deborah Cockrell-Duchemin
Jennifer Coes
Carin A. Cohen
Susan l. Cohen
Judith D. Cooney
Richard Cornwall
Jeanie Crosby
Anne M. Crouss
Donna M. Culbert
Paula J. Curran
Jadwiga (Yogi) Cutitta
Heidi D'Ascoli
Rolanda Dane
Bryna Davidow
Fred Davis
Jennifer Depiro
Bridget Desroches
Darleen P. Dimor
Harry J. Dowdall
Mary K. Dullinger
Richard Dumouchel Jr.
Joanne E. Duval
Marnina A. Edelhart
Ruth A. Ellis
Paul J. Emerson
Beth A. Ethier
Herbert A. Everett
Kathy A. Fardy
Mary E. Farren
Carleen E. Farrington
Barbara Ferguson
Karen B. Ferrante
Karen G. Fischer
Suzanne E. Flaherty
Marcia L. Flynn
Leea Foran
Gert Foster
Janice Fulton
Annie Galante
Doreen M. Garner
Heather T. Garre
Peter Gobel
Glenn E. Goldman
Elena M. Gravinese
Kathleen S. Grim

C. J. Grote
Janet E. Harris
Terrence M. Haskins
Brandon Hayes
Gina Lyn Hayes
Nora M. Hayes
Sue Ellen Healy
Jennifer Hearn
John Hines
Patrick Hogan
Linda V. Holway
Cory Hopkins
Kathleen Horgan-
  Burke
Peter Hunt
Liz Iacovino
Andria T. Iadonisi
Linda L. Ireland
Lisa Johnson
Cathy Johnston
Sheila Kamath
Stephanie Keesey
Kim Kezer
Melissa Kielbasa
Shawn Knoth
Dee Kohler
Teresia E. LaFleur
Karen T. Lanoue-
  Lambrecht
Edward H. Laraway
Kathleen A. Laraway
Jo-Ann M. Laughlin
Laurie J. LaValley
Stephen L. LaValley
Sharon Leahy
Kerry Lemerise
Heather Leonard
Leslie Lichtenstein
Arlyn Lightbody
Lori Ann Lodato
Romana M. Lovelock
Lori C. Lussier
Vicki Lynch
Frannie Lyons
Jennifer Machado
Roseann Mandell
Gail L. Martin
Ian Martin
Meg Massaro
Fran Z. Masters
Shawn Paul Masterson
Jean E. McCord
Dianne McCorry

Dianne A.
  McDonough
Cheryl L. McGraw
Elise McMahon
Jacqueline M.
  Medeiros
Kim Melanson
Kathy Menard
Katalin Judit Miller
Susan M. Miller
Amber S. Milliken
Alexandra Morgan
Alana RE Morlock
Pamela Murphy
Sean Patrick Murphy
Angela J. Nickerson
Dorothy M. O'Connor
William J. O'Hara
Karen Ogden
Tracy Powderly Owen
Lynne M. Panno
Haley-Dee Parlin-Gage
Catherine A. Paul
Michelle Payson
Beth Perron
Valentina Petrone
  Avery
Jennifer Pierce
Leslie M. Pirnie
Caryl-Rose Pofcher
Karen Priest
Alexandra
  Protopopova
Tracy Quinton
David Ranieri
Angela Reardon
Ashley Relyea
Tony M. Sala
Amanda M. Santos
Donna Savoie
Cathy Seale
Kathleen Segrin
Susan Davis Shaw
Spencer T. Shepard
Kaaren (Cotton)
  Silverman
Laurel Silvia
Jane Small
Ruth Smiler
Alison Dorothy Smith
Jasmine Smith
Leah G. Snow
Suzanne Spellman

Anne T. Springer
Karin M. Statkum
Robin R. Stewart
Cassie-Leigh Stock
Patricia A. Sullivan
Wendy Sylvia
Christina M. Taddei
Sue Thibedeau
Calli Towne
Debra Traugot
Rebecca Walsh
Mary Walter
Alyssa B. Ward
Heather E. Watson-
  Fournier
Ann Werner
Mary C. West
Carlene A. White
Robert White
Vera E. Wilkinson
Bette L. Yip
Ann-Marie Young
Jane M. Young
Melissa C. Zilembo

MICHIGAN

Maggie Adams
Randy Adams
Suzzette J. Allam
Kim Amatucci
Jeanine M. Asch
Kevin Bailey
Amanda Barber
Larry A. Barker
Diane Barrett
Cheryl Lynn Barton
Tammy J. Bartz
Lesa N. Bastow
Jamie Baumann
Jill A. Beaton
Colleen Belanger
Mary L. Belanger
Bonnie Bement
Venita Bentley
Jan Beregszaszy
Betsy Kaiser Bernock
Elizabeth Ann Bills
William E. Bills
Beth A. Bishop
Carol M. Bordua
Kathy Breedlove
Pam Brewington

LeeAnn Brinkel
Ann M. Bromley
Kimberly Brown
Nikki K. Brown
Robin Sue Brown
Leta A. Brownell
Tania Bruner
Elisabeth Buchheister
Michael P. Burkey
Kriss Dee Carter
Darleen Cattini
Karol C. Chase
Amanda M.
  Chrzanowski
Lisa H. Clark
Cheri K. Cline
Sue L. Clipper-
  Kotlarek
Lynn M. Collins
Christine L. Conklin
Gwen K. Coon
Lawren Coulam
Marianne Courey
Patty L. Crichton
Terese Crowe
Patrick R. Currey
Ken DeBoer
Diane Desrosiers
Susan Kim DeWulf
Jennifer E. DeZwarte
Monique Donette
  Diamond-Kilmer
Nick Dillman
Janet DiPirro
Sharon A. Drescosky
Nancy M. Duemling
Elisabeth J. Duman
Christine A. Elliott
Lori Elliott
Anita Ellis
Penni Elsesser
Jess C. Elson
Suzanne (Sue) M.
  Esper
Alexia Fallon
Lisa E. Farlin
Melissa Fenstermaker
Susan F. Fischer
Karen Dianne Fisher
Laura Fisher
Ali Flaig
Karen McGee Fletcher
Teresa Freese

Tami L. Frisbie
Carol W. Galvin
William Dean Gardner
Pennie R. Garwood
Mandy J. George
Kirk L. Gillette
Gwen Giznsky
Caroline Glasscock
Devene J. Godau
Lisa Gorczyca
Roz Granitz
Bobbie Green
Ellen M. Gruber
Marc F. Guerrieri
Sally Guritz
Gail A. Haba
Erinn E. Hadley
Jill Hadley
Barbara R. Hahn
Martha F. Hall
Michelle Halstead
Kassandra L. Hamaker
Dale M. Hamari
Sharon Hamilton
Jan Hamming
Amy S. Hansen
James L. Hansen
Jeffrey Head
Jenelle R. Hephner
Jean A. Herbrandson
Hector L. Hernandez
Gail A. Holfelder
Marie Hopfensperger
Eileen M. Hyde
Ed R. Jankowsky
Monica A. Joy
Shirley A. Julin
Susan D. Kapla, PhD
Mary C. Karakas
R. Douglas Karakas
Tammy L. Karakas
Barbara Kendall
Susan King
Christine Kloski
Sherry Knorr
Amber Koeller
Janelle Kowal
Carolyn Kuenz
Yolanda A. Lane
Kristine Larsen
Lee Ann Layman
Virginia A. Leis, DVM
Linda G. Lemmer

Sue Leon
Betty C. Lewis
Jeanne A. Lewis
Kaye A. Licata
Kelly Linke
Linda Lipford
Kristi A. Littleson
Sharon A. Long
Diane E. Loudon
Katherine K. Lucy
Julie A. Lyle
Irina Mackay
Deanna Malmstrom
Deborah L. Mapes
Michael E. Marshall
Dan Maurer
Keith W. Michael
Lynn Kay Montambo
Sarah Moon
Joan Morell
Christine L. Morgan
Marilyn L. Morgan
Michael G. Morgan
Dorothy Murmyluk
Kimberly L. Nelson
Candy Neusser
Linda K. Nichols
Kari Norton
Michelle Jacqueline
  O'Neill
Debra L. Orsburn
Namiko Ota-
  Noveskey
Sigrid Owen
Heidi L. Palmer
Karen K. Palmer
Lori Paradise-Grigg
Dianne Pennell
Shannan Perna
Amanda Phinney
Carol A. Pizzino
Jill S. Rankinen
Christie Reed
Laura J. Rescoe
Lewis Reynolds
Scott Reynolds
Julie E. Richards-
  Mostosky
Sally K. Richardson
Douglas W. Ritter
Deborah Sue Robbins
Shirley Robertson
Sarah Rodeheaver

Pamela Roehr
Meghan Rosenstengel
Sandy Roskey
Catherine Rospierski
Margaret Russell
Judy Sabo
Lorena Santek-
  Burggraaf
Lori Sargent
Lori M. Sauceda
Deb Scanzillo
William J. Schiffel
Annie Schiller
Suzan L. Scott
Karilyn K. Selinger
Lois A. Semple
Linda M. Shannon-
  Chaillet
Cheryl A. Shea
Robbin G. Shea
Kathleen B. Sherry
Pete Simakas
Karen E. Simchak
Melissa Simpson
Brent A. Smith
Janet A. Smith
Judy k. Smith
Virginia Smith
William F. Snyder
Patricia Gail Solomon
Beth Spanski
Donna J. Sparks
Dawn M. Staffen
Sherrie L. Start
Michelle M. Stemm
Grace L. Stevens
Ronald C. Stokes Jr.
Daphne A. Stover
Linda J. Sullivan
Kristie Swan
Terry Swanson
Wendy S. Swift
Maryann Szalka
Barbara J. Tahash
Jackie Takacs
Jeanne Cabot Telfare
Diane L. Thomas
Jeanne M. Thomas
Linda Thomas
Annette R. Tindall
Ronda Tkac
Vicki J. Tobler
Anna Tomacari

Kathleen Tourangeau
Carla Sue Town
Karen S. Toy
Richard L. Triemstra
Michael G. Turner
Kalin Turri
Mary Tuttle
Sandra A. Vaillancourt
Margaret (Peggy)
  Vennebush
Carol M. Visser
Laura Wagner
Bonny P. Wainz-
  Atkinson
Karen Waldrop
Joyce A. Ward
Cheryl Wassus
Kathryn A. Watters
Kelli Weber
Betty Welles
Elizabeth Wells
Richard Wells
Beverly A. Whitbeck
Dawn R. Wieck
Christine Grove
  Williams
Daniel J. Williams
Bruce E. Willoughby
Tracy B. Willoughby
Rhonda Wilson
Laura Wiltshire
Cheryl L. Witte-Haedt
Heather Lynn
  Woodard
Laurie Wright, DVM
Nancy Wright
Evy Lynn Wyman
Ronda L. Yarsevich
Brenda Young
Debra A. Young
Sharon Younger-
  Henderson
Donna J. Zaj
Max Zeidler

MINNESOTA

Dianna M. Anderson
Linda M. Anderson
Gwen Bader
Sara M. Bartlett
Maria A. Beaudin
Cindy Bender

Karen Beskau
Linda B. Blanchard
Linda J. Brodzik
Rebecca Brusven
Polly A. Callant
Sandra L. Cattanach
Elizabeth Chapman
Suzie Christenson
Gary G.
  Christopherson
Daryl Cooper, PhD
Diane Craig
Kathleen Riley Daniels
Lynn E. Davey
Lynn A. Davis
Andrea L. DelSignore
Annette J. DesLauriers
Natalie D. Faas-Gerber
Lisa Fabish
Diane Felicetta
Dawn Finch
Lisa Marie Fortier
Inga From
Barbara A. Gaffner
Karen Gaffney
A I. Gottsch
Janeen D. Grove
  McMurtrie
Laurie K. Haake
Tiffany Haltli
Libby Hargrove
Beth Harvey
Janice K. Heck
Mara E. Heck
Leona Hellesvig
Melissa Hennen
Susan (Sue) Herber
Rob-Lyn S. Hiltz
Timothy J. Hiltz
Andrew Hlusak
Brandon Holleran
Mary R. Holsen
Paul Howe
Tiffany A. Huebner
Julie E. Humiston
Jane L. Jacobson
Suzi Johnson
Shalise A. Keating
Karen Kelley
Sean M. Kelly
Pat K. Kinch
Cathy Kishel
Christiana E. Kjos

Carolyn R. Kraskey
Larry Kruft
Jodee Kulp
Julie M. Kustermann
Michol Langelett
Mary Leadbetter
Linda L. Legare
Lynnda Lenzen
Bob Levy
Daniel A. Lively
Pam Longville
Jody E. Ludden
Mary Malone
Carol A. Manley
Megan Martin
Reno Massimino, II
Debra Merritt
Mary N. Moore
Jolene E.R. Moran
Irene C. Mullauer
Linda L. Munson
Bernadette Murphy
Linda A. Murray
Nancy Murray
Lonna J. Nelson
Denise M. Nord
Linda O'Connor
Carin J. Offerman
Lois C. Ornat
William T. Panos
Laska Parrow
Pam Paulick
Mary Beth Percy
Tim L. Peterson
Brie Piller
Eloise Raymond
Larry Reese
Bridget H. Renlund
Cristopher J. Rhea
Sharon Rittenour
Claudia Roberto
Maureen J. Rodriguez
Kay Roe
Eileen Roston
Robin T. Sallie
Cheryl Sayger
Tory Schaefer
Debra L. Schneider
Jacob Aaron Schneider
Barbara W. Selton
Paul Severson
Susan L. Severson
Terresa M. Slusher

Catherine L. Solatycki
Mary E. Sonnen
Leanne Sprague
Ann Strickler
Leah Swift
Jodi Theis
Amanda Thorstad
Jessica Thovson
Connie J. Timmerman
Tracey Lee Torgersen
DeeAnn Trotta
Dolly Uhlig
Vicki Vail
Kathryn Varns
Mary Verness
Brigitte L. Vidas
Mary Lee Warnock
Denise J. Wedel
Dawn West
Nicole Wiebusch
Danielle C. Woodgate
Paula Kay Zukoff

MISSISSIPPI

Mary Ellen Borden
Jo Beth Britt
Dorothy Brooks
Betty Caldwell
Cecilia A. Charles
Sandy Conner
Clint Allen Earls
Mary Jo Elmore
Tiffany Greer
Kim Harrison
Megan M. Hill
Christi Kirby
Patricia Ann Lambert
Gwenda K. Murray
Lynn M. Rachkiss
Paige Rushing
Kathie G. Short
Teresa Sims
David J. Teta
Suzanne Vening
Jayne Wells
Jane B. Yeatman

MISSOURI

Sue Alkire
Karen S. Anderson
Lucy E. Bailey

Deborah A. Baker
Susan D. Bass
Kelly Batton
Karen M. Bazdresch
Kelly Benbow
Al G. Boeck
C. Jane Boeck
Linda S. Booth
Debbie Brakemeyer
Amy L. Braschler
Gayln J. Bratcher
Janice M. Brennan
Julie Briney
Tracy Buck
Sally E. Burgess
Linda M. Campbell
Angela Chamberlain
Steve Chastain
Susanne E. Chastain
Felicia A. Chesser
Merry L. Christiansen
K.L. Church
Barb A. Closser
Mona Cook-Guteriez
Janet E. Croy
Joann R. Curtin
Christine Curtis
Alan H. Dake
Laura L. Devine
Kathy R. Echols
Audrey E. Edwards
Linda A. Elliott
Linda F. Emmert
Diana Roberts
  Engeszer
Barbie L. Ernst
Fred Ernst
Patty Fiordimondo
J G. Flagg
Germaine French
Misti Fry
Lynsey Fuegner
Annabella Clark Gafke
Susan L. Giddens
Gayle Goedeke
Robert L. Good
Kimberly S. Gracner
Christi M. Green
Richard A. Green
Jeannie L. Greenlee
Trina Grubaugh
Joyce Guthrie
Roger Hampton

JoAnn E. Hankemeyer
Marie L. Harbers
Gretchen Hartman
Linda Mary Hayes
Valarie Hewett
Carol A. Hill
Leon L. Hill
Linda S. Hill
Teressa S. Hill
Patty Homer
Amy Horton
Darlene Hughson
Barbara L. Hurley
Virginia H. Huxley, PhD
Gail M. Jackson
Helen Jameson
Patricia Janovsky
Janet E. Jesky
Marion L. Johnson
Brad Jones
Michael V. Kaelin
Freda J. King
Stefanie Kitcher
Mary W. Kline
Kari Koch
Carolyn A. Krause
Kim M. Krohn
Russell B. Krohn
Christie Kucsik
Linda Kush
Gwen Lau
Heddie S. Leger
Victoria R. Leggitt
Judy L. Luther
Kim Lutz
Anne Mackey
Stasi L. Malloy
Lorraine Martinez
Richard A. Martinson
Amy Mathias
Rebekah McCormack
Debbie McHenry
Becky Meadows
Andrea Meinhart
Lynn M. Messer
Roberta L. Metter
Janice A. Miller
Jackie M. Mitchell
Marshia Lynn Morton
Melinda G. Murphy
Debra L. Murray
Peggy J. Nenninger

Toni L. Newcomer
Peggy Oertwig
Trish Olinghouse
Jessie Opperman
Peggy Pack
Diana L. Park
Leslee K. Pollina
Jeff Postle
Kama Preston
Barbara Pruitt
Jessica L. Queen
Wendy L. Ragan
Carole A. Ramsey
Sherry A. Rebel
Evelyn V. Redwine
Jo Reily
Doris Ridenhour
DiAnn Roberts
K. Ruiz
Nancy Jo Rutkowski
Leaha A. Ryon
Kellie Sadler
Diane Saltzman
Nancy Schanda
Marc Scher
Jan N. Schmitz
Susan M. Sczepanski
Mary Sellaro
Kevin Sharp
Lorri Sheets
Suzan Shipp
Jamie Jo Sieveking
Steven W. Sieveking
Elizabeth L. Simmons
Mat Sturm
Lotta Sydanmaa
Meghan M. Tallman
Chelsea Taylor
Jessie Teegarden
Kathleen S. Tharp
Nancy L. Thornton
Tracy Thurman
Joe Timmerberg
Kris K. Toft
Melanie Troby
Sandra Vaccaro
Cindy Vickers
John R. Vlasich
Rosmarie Von Fintel
Donna Welborn
Nadine Wenig
Sharon M. West
Cheryl L. Westhoff

Patty Wilcox
Cinder J. Wilkinson-Kenner
Paula Wilson
Amy Winston

MONTANA

Crystal A. Arnold
Eleanor L. Bell
Erin Bierwirth
Lynn Brown
Vicki Correia
Elizabeth S. Day
Barbara Delaney
Adele N. Delp
Anne Dixon
Margaret Shunick Duezabou
Karen Duty
Kimberly Gould
Tracy M. Graham
Holly R. Groff
Arial A. Harper
Caroline G. Hudnall
Darcy A. Jackson
Tom Kandt
Amy Killian
Merilee Lafond
Nancy M. Lane
Katherine (Kat) Lee
Vicki Lee
Nancy Loendorf
Sharon Lowry
Teresa M. Loya
Linda M. Lyon
Vicky MacLean
Cathy Mason
Jennifer McCandless
Jennifer Michaelis
Cherie A. Moldenhauer
Joni Kay Muir
Milt Munson
Rita Munson
Emily Petroff
Becky Roeder
Jackie Sampson
Albert E. Sepe
Sarah Shipman
Judith E. Strom
Anni Sutkus
Nancy Tanner

Susan Thomas
Helene K. Tiefenthaler
Ginny Traeger
Joni L. Wissinger

NEBRASKA

Julie Allbery
Steph R. Anderson
Dawn M. Antoniak-Mitchell, Esq.
Marcia A. Becker
Camtrice Bexten
DeAnn Blakeman
Jamee J. Bockerman
Marla K. Bouton
Donna Bundy
Pamela J. Burgess
Pam Burr, DVM
Nicole A. Busey
Tiffany Byrkit
Nancy Carver
Donna M. Casey
Maggie Colwell
Pamela K. Eby
Barbara L. Flick
Maxine M. Fox
Catherine A. Guinane
Patricia Guticz
Nikki Harris
Kendra K. Holman
Darla D. Hook
Mary Hostetter
Mako M. Jacobs
Lucy M. Kerby
Michael P. Kerby
Ann Kleimola
Michelle Kohlhof
Dianne M. Krantz
Stephanie L. Larson
Gale Lothrop
Bridgett M. Miller
Sharon K. Miller
Sandy Nekuda
Diane Newman
Diane L. Nitz
Kim Ostermann
Jerry L. Petersen
Patricia Pratt
Dian Quist-Sulek
Shawna Stecher
Tammy Taylor
Dawn Thrapp

Stephanie Tornquist
Eileen M. VanLent
Judith Ann (Judy)
  Vitamvas
Jeannie M. Warnke
Cheryl Wilson
Erika Wilson

NEVADA

Sarah K. Anderson
  Shamel
Michelle Armstrong
Robin L. Baizel
Stephanie Beetsch
Lynn A. Bjorklund
Leland Brannum
Sandy Brannum
Sandra L. Burns
Geralynn Cada
Eyvonne Carter-Riley
Gregory Conner
Noelle L. Cota
Cynthia Danielson
Renee Davis
Carrie E. Dempsey
Alissa Edmands
Edward Fizer
Donna Foreman
Carol Frisby
Philip R. Gang
Rebecca A. Gang
Stephanie Gerken
Greg J. Gibbs
MaryKay Grahn
Leanne Hall
Karen Hanna
Sonya Hersh
Francee M. Heun
Courtney D. Hoffman
Maria T. Hosmer
Erin E. Josephs
Rosalie Lansdowne
Amber Lee Martin
Kathy McCarty
Richard McCarty
Stewart Miller
Joanna Moritz
Lisa M. Myers
Moriah Ochoa
Brenda L. Paul
Donna Porria
Dana K. Provost

Mari Purvis
Laurie Robinson
Eric Saunders
Debbie Smith
Sheldon Smith
Linda Solheim
LaDonna J. Sprinkle
Valerie A. Stanert
Pamela J. Wangsness
Jana Lea Williamson
Cheryl Wise
Cynthia M. Yurek

NEW HAMPSHIRE

Rachel W. Anderson
Joanne F. Baker
Carolyn M. Bancroft
Jennifer Barg
Karen G. Betournay
Renee Blouin
Lisa M. Borst
Cheryn R. Breeling
Helen L. Bridges-
  Hamlin
Eileen Brouck
Leisl Bryant
Kelly A. Bryer
Barbara A. Burri
Gail Cappadona
Susan T. Carney
Laura Chapman
Mary-Jo Chiklis
Cynthia Cinq-Mars
Robin Crocker
Holly L. David
Annette J. Delaney
Kathy A. Duffy
Dorothy A. Ernst
Diana W. Ganley
Gail Gorrow
Lola Grab
Dale P. Green
Pamela Griffeth
Debra Harmon
Linda L. Heath
Jessica B. Hebert
Cheryl Hodgdon
Shirley Hutchins
Dorothy Hyde-
  Williams
Jessica Marie Janowski
Valerie Ann Jesson

Theresa A. Kelley
Lynn A. King
Wendy A. Kropac
Arthur R. Landry
Carol M. Landry
Maribeth Lazich
Kathy Lorenz
Meredith Lunn
Diane Ellis Manocchia
Denise Rockwood
  Mazzola
Lori McGibbon
Lynn M. Millette
Ramon Miranda
Lynda D. Nelson
Helen Nicholls
Anne Nichols
Melanie S. Nichols
Britney Teague
  Normandin
Anna O'Sullivan
Keryl K. Olson
Karen Pellegrino
L. Mark Pilant
Mike P. Robertson
Maureen M. Ross
Erin Sargent
Sarah E. Short
Karen M. Smith
Kelly Sullivan
Charlene M.
  Swainamer
Maribeth Swift
MaryBeth Tessier
Ann K. Tremblay
Carolyn Vanderhorst
Gwen Weisgarber
Rowena C. Wilks
Sharon Wirant

NEW JERSEY

Kathleen L. Agolio
Patricia Ali
Dottie L. Allen
Susan Amisson
Victoria Ann Babcock
Dee Bailey
Michael C. Bakert
Jeffrey David Ball
Donna G. Ballotta
Janice Barlow
Elaine Barone

Jennifer W. Basile
Amanda Berk
Claire D. Bower
Kim Bowers
Beth Bradley
Robert H. Brandau
Roberta Dawn
  Brandau
Sarah Breace Brandau
Vivian Bregman
Bonnie E. Brown
Donna Buccellato
Maryan F. Burton
Peter J. Campione
Paige Carey-Buono
Barbara E. Carlson
Valerie A. Casperite
Trish Castelluccio
Elisabeth Catalano
Ana M. Cilursu
Shelley Clawson
April Lynn Cloutier
Marie Colasanti
Diana Coles
Kristan Conner
Kristine A. Conway
Brooke Adair Corson
Kathleen Costaney
Debra D'Elia
Gina DeAlmeida
Marie DeRosa
Jennifer J. Dilmore
Michael J. Divito
Ami A. Dobelle
Regina A. Dougherty
Donna A. Downs
Susan D. Drastal
Earl Dunn
Vicky Durnye
Lora Durr
Walden F. Dury III
Cheryl L. Eliason
Joseph Phillip
  Eppolito
James Erven
Frederick J. Ezell
Louis A. Fallon
Bonnie L. Fletcher
Barbarann Ford
Peg Forte
Leslie A. Fried
Madeline S. Friedman
Sharon Gaboff

Priscilla A. Gabosch
Natalie A. Galdi
  Weissman
Eleasha Gall
Laura Garber
Dan Gentile
Florence R. Gerst
Ron Gewirtzman
Jean-Marie Glaser
Lynne Godshall
Eric Goebelbecker
June Golden
Madelyn Graffia
Liz Gruen
Phil Guida
Alice Harris
Mary L. Harwelik
Ruth Henningsen
Linda E. Hobson
Terry Hooretz
Joanne G. Horton
Carol-Lynne Inman
Katrene Johnson
Pat E. Johnston
R. Thomas K'Burg
Debra A. Kaikaka
Sp./Ofc. M. B. Kanis
Jodi Kellar-Jackson
Andrea C. Kelly
Carolyn J. King
Betty Kish
Greg Kleva
Kim E. Kosko
Alice C. Kovacs
Dory M. Kowal
Diane E. Kramer
Gail Kulur
Pam Davies Kundro
Stacey La Forge
Francine La Marr
RoseMary Laubach
Teryl L. Lebkuecher
Christian Lehmann
Anna M. Liccardi
Barbara Lidke
Henrietta C.
  Lindeboom
Anne E. Macaulay
Diane MacEwan
Jill R. Makoujy
Loren M. Marino
Lisa Mattson
Lori Mauger

Jennifer Mauro
Barbara McClew
Michael L. McMahon
John C. McWilliams
Margaret Melse
Ronald J. Meyer
Vyolet Michaels
Shelly S. Middlecoop
Patrick G. Miller
Lori Minardi
Nancy K. Minarik
Janet Mines-Krings
Sharleen Mompalao
Joseph F. Mosner
Barbara Nagy
Terri O'Brien
Joanne A. O'Donnell
Sean O'Donnell
Corianna O'Leary
Cara O'Reilly
David Pappalardo
Lisa M. Parsley
Oscar Pelaez
Lynne M. Petermann
Renee K. Premaza
Joni Primas
Beverly A. Pronovost
Shelley Raskin
Patricia L. Raymond
Carol M. Reina
Ruby M. Reuter
Donna Riley-Sweet
Angelika M. Robinson
Lynn Robinson
Oscar A. Rojas
Michele Rossbach
William R. Rylee Jr.
Kathy L. Santo
Terry A. Sarro
Patricia Scagliotti
Karen R. Scheiner
Giselle M. Scull-
  Monroe
Ann Marie Shaw
Elaine Shoe
Renee Shriver
Joanne C. Silver
Norma A. Simpson
Elizabeth E.
  Soderlund
Alice M. Sposa
Dorice Terry Stancher
Sara J. Steele

Melanie Steffens
Molly Sumner
Maryellen Swiatek
Susan Tapp
Norine Twaddell
Melissa A. Van Note
Christopher Velez
Mary Ann Verdinelli-
  Burg
Tammy L. Vreeland
Laura Waddell
Ms. Teresa E. Walker
Lisa Wance
Judith L. Ware
Joana Watsky
Ann B. Watson
Dawn Watson
Charles F. Webber Jr.
Leslie Wiesner
Samuel Wike
Janet Williams
Laura J. Williams
Tracie Williams
Laura J. Wilson
Martha Windisch
Walter T. Wojtaszek
Wendy J. Wojtaszek
Jill Wright
Kira Ann Wright
Diane Zdrodowski
Susan Zietara

Leonore H. Abordo
Denis J. Arseneault
Patricia E. Audibert
Jacqueline C. Barron
Amanda Bean
Lisa Berry
Karen Blisard
Marsha Boggs
Sarah Brinegar
Mary A. Carson
Susan Coffey
Donna Crary-Johnson
Charlene M. Curry
Nancy A. DaCosta
Stephanie DuBois
Diana M. Durland
Evelyne H. Fox
Lisa Frankland
Suzanne Fuqua

Ron George
Shelley M. Green
Joyce Grimm
Marissa Hallett
JoAnn D. Hise
Allen R. Jackson
Cathy Jacobs
Vicki Keener
Mary Leatherberry
Vicki Loucks
Wendi C. Luce
Marilyn Melin
Estelle Metz
Janet E. Miller
Jacque L. Obermeyer
Marta Ortiz
Hannah Padilla
Elizabeth M. Pearson
Terri L. Robinson
Ellen Rowe
Susan Ann Shields
Gail Skee
Diane D. Sullivan
Marcia S. Sullivan
Ronna M. Torrisi
Lois J. Whitmire
Dawn J. Woodring

Patricia Adamo
Kathy Adams
Lee J. Alger
Carol J. Allen
Maria J. Allio
Samantha Almeida
Dorothy Anderson
Virginia Anziani
Andrea J. Arden
E. Chris Argento
Madelyn P. Ashman
Carol Aufmuth
Tara Baggerman
Debra A. Bain
Flora Baird
Jodi Ball
Deanne Balutis
Donald A. Bambrick
Michelle Barlak
Kathleen C. Barton
Danielle Basciano
Toni Belmonte
Helen A. Bemis

Christopher M. Bennett
Ken Berenson
George Berger
Bobbie Bhambree
Diane M. Blackman
Kerry A. Boisvert
Tamra M. Bojarski
Bill Bokowski
Diana Bonelli
Patricia Bonino
Heidi N. Bonorato
Charles R. Bostick
Mary A. Bourgeois
Mara Bovsun
Jennifer L. Boyce
Alyssa Boyea
Vicky K. Brachfeld
Deborah A. Bram
Lillian Browne-Burdick
Beverly M. Bulson
Suzanne M. Bunney
Karen Buttenschon
Frank Cahill
Elisa M. Calabrese
Adrienne Caldwell
Lisa Carl
Brian Cauthers
Nelson Chan
Emma J. Channing
Jamie L. Christman
Jenny K. Chun
Maxine Clark
Rebecca L. Clark
Bernice N. Clifford
Laura A. Clute
LeeAnne Cogdill
Patricia Coglianese
Kelly H. Conn
Sarah W. Connaughton
Marilyn Conner
Kate Connick
Eileen Cosentino
Janice Costa
Valerie Coté
Kimberly S. Courtney
Joanne M. Cowulich
Stephanie A. Crawford
Catherine J. Crawmer
Deirdre H. Crofton
Donald L. Crumb Jr.

Terri Cude
Candice Cunningham
Lynn A. Currie
Frank C. D'Andrea
Roxanne T. D'Onofrio
Deanna L. Dalton
Christine Danker
Dana Davis
Jeanne Day
Marylyn DeGregorio
Dianne DelPozzo
Rena L. Dershowitz
Val DeSantis
Darlene Devlin
Amanda J. Diefenbach
Andrea L. DiMaio
Kathryn E. Dingledy
John J. Dolan Jr.
Lezlie Dono
Janelle Dorsey
Michelle R. Dunn
Laura Dutton
Ellen N. Dwyer
Patricia Dwyer
Lisa j. Edwards
Jean E.R. Ellsworth
Suzanne Etherington
Tami L. Evans
Susann Everett
Lishelle Fazzone
Joseph R. Feeney
Caryn Fellows
Joan P. Fingar
Sally S. Fionte
Peggy Florian
Bonnie Folz
Erin R. Franco
Barbara K. Frey
Christine O'Leary Fuller
Gail K. Furst
Debra S. Gaeta
Ritsa Galitsis
Dr. Karen R. Garelick
Laurie K. Garland
Kimberly A. Gerosa
Kathleen L. Giacherio
Anne M. Gibson
Barbara Giella, PhD
Linda Giordano
Bonnie Glazier
Glenna Godown
Carvel Gold

Alisson H. Goldberg
P. J. Goldsmith
Michelle Gorta
Joan L. Greenwald
Philip Greis
Elena Gretch
Sylvia A. Grimes
Jeanne P. Gurnis
Debi Hachler
Babette H. Haggerty
Kimberly A. Hahn
Anna Hall
Susan Hamlin
Melissa K. Hammond
Karlene L. Hanley
Bonny Harris
Carol Harty
Sandra C. Hawkins
Robbin L. Heim
Dusty Sue Hellman
Lori A. Hicks
Patricia A. Hicks
Linda R. Higby
Kathy Hildreth
Colleen A. Hitchcock
Michael Hoesterey
Virginia Hoffmann
Helen Hollander
Diana Holtzman
Diane Houck
Travis Houser
Joanne M. Hurst
Kristen Hurwitz
Rebecca Hutchins
Elly Hyde
Rebecca M. Iannone
Marta J. Illing
Geraldine Jaitin
Anthony Jerone
Joseph Jimenez
Linda M. Jobson
Sonja Johanson
Suzanne Johnson
Kendell Jones
William L. Jones
Carin Jordan
Toni Kaste
Linda S. Kellogg
Jane M. Keroack
Colleen E. Kimble
Ann King
Beth Ann Klein
Tracie Klusek

Michelle LaMarca Knapp
Debora A. Knatz
Chelsea Koslow
Darlene Koza
Kristen Kranjc
Deborah L. Kreider
Katrina Krings
Justin Lamb
Linda D. LaPier
Stephen G. Laton
Vanessa Lee
Mira M. Leibstein
Barbara L. Lenahan
Michele Lennon
Larry G. Leogrande
Timothy G. Leto, II
Rebecca Letson
Ann Lettis
Leslie A. Levine
Jeannette K. Levinsohn
Teresa M. Levy
Susan G. Limeri
Casey Lomonaco
Lisa Long
Harry Lozada
Rosie N. Lucitt
Toni Lund
Toni F. Mapes
Charlene Marchand
John Marinos
Cheryl E. Marks
Kenneth W. Marks
Margaret J. Marrano
Kay Martin
Neil A. Martinez
Jason C. Matson
Virginia M. McCauley
Lorie McCrone
Kevin McGill
Jamie McKay
Judith A. McManus
Michael Mei
Saundra Mercado
Kimberly Mercy-Wagner
Kay Meyers
Jason Mickalauskas
Alexandra Miles
Karen Miller
Shelly Miller
Gail Miller Bisher

Robert P. Minchella
Lisa Mitchell
George F. Molloy
Lizbeth K. Molloy
Alexandra Monroe
John Alfred
  Monteleone
Catherine H. Munnier
Patricia A. Murphy
Erica Nance
Susan K. Nastasi
Martin J. Neely
Janet M. Newcomer
John Nidweski
Jeannette R. O'Hanlon
Michael Oberman
Daisy Okas
Lyn V. Ory
Linda M. Pacioretty
Christopher Padden
Renee P. Payne
Lila J. Peacock
Beth Ann Pedersen
John Peltier
Linda H. Penney
William Peralta
Lisa Peterson
Jodi Piacelli
Debra Pica
Jenn Pinsof
Lois Jean Piva
Amanda Pontarella
Marlene M. Porzio
Margaret B. Pough
Judith M. Questel
Diane Ranaldo
Laurie Reagan
Rosemary C. Redick
Melissa Reed
Sarah Reed
Karen Reilly
Susan Reising
Pamela F. Renock
Cynthia A. Rickey
Margaret A. Rivers
Victor Robinson
Edith G. Rodegerdts
Peggy Rogan
Deborah Roth
Debbie L. Routhier
Cheryl Runyan
Amy Russell
Rose C. Russo

Susan P. Ryan
Jennifer Jo Sahrle
Stacey Samela
P. Leigh Sansone
Holly Santana
Dani Santanella
Eden H. Sargent
Melissa S. Sartori
Kim M. Sauer
Susan L. Scelzi
Dorothy Schroeder
Alan Schultz
Jacque L. Schultz
Deborah Scotto
Linda Seipp
June A. Selby
Emily Shako
Mona M. Shaw
Christine M. Sheffer
Laurie J. Shepard
Calise A. Shoemaker
Elizabeth Shulman
Christina M.
  Shusterich
Nick Siebert
Donna I. Sims
Clarissa V. Skawski
Christine Sleurs
Denise C. Smalt
Cindy D. Smith
Kathy Snowden
Tammy L. Snyder
Wendy Anderson
Regina M. Sourwine
Gordon Stockman
Suzanne S. Stone
Daphna Straus
Elizabeth Lyons
  Stroter
Nancy W. Strouss
Pat Sullivan
Marian Szebenyi
Rebecca L. Tehon
Barbara M. Teplesky
Jennifer Towers
Sheryl Townsend
Nancy J. Tucker
Lori Tyler-Ochsner
Karen R. Van Slyke
Cynthia M.
  Vandawalker
Stormi Vasta
Lisa A. Vathy
Michael C. Velapoldi

Douglas Vohnoutka
Marlene Wagner
MaryEileen D. Walter
Jacqueline M. Walters
Deb Watrous
David P. Watson
Traci A. Weaver
Marion Weiner
Wendy Weisberg
Karen E. Wells
Virginia M. Westfield-
  Slowik
Alison Wheeler
Pamela J. Whittles
Jennifer C. Wilhelm
Marilyn Wilson
Nanette Winter
Amy Wonderly
Nikki Wood
Miranda K. Workman
Karen Wrey
Laura Yaghy
Tang Hiu Yeung
Dorothy Zaris
Mariann Zelinski

NORTH CAROLINA

Cindy Abate
Rudolph D. Abate
Teresa Alexander
Elaine H. Allman
Wendy Anderson
Elizabeth Arellano
Sharon Ashe
Mandy Baker
George E. Beglane
Elizabeth W. Bernstein
Kristine Berry
Laura L. Blanz
Maggie A. Blutreich
Delores Gaye Bougie
Gail S. Boyd
Hannah Branigan
Marsha Bridges
Maureen M. Bridges
Brette Brooks
Elizabeth A. Brown
Hutsien H. Brown
Victoria A. Brown
Lyn Buck
Laura Bullock
Andy Bunn

Adam Bush
Phyllis E. Campbell
Steven L. Canady
Christie Canfield
Iris L. Cannon
Ellen Carey
Leslie J. Carpenter
Amy Clear
Matthew Cochran
Shannon Coleman
Sioux Cook
Heide Catherina
  Coppotelli
Tam H. Cordingley
Betty P. Dampier
Nancy F. Davis
Jasey H. Day
Lynn N. Deuterman
Amy Dunphy
Melissa A. Duran
Roel C. Escamilla Jr.
Jewel L. Fader
Teresa Faucette
Suzi Faulkner
Jane P. Finneran
Joan M. Florentine
Mario Fonseca
Emily B. Foster
Lynne Frady
Kirsten Frisch
Kady Gantt
Michele Godlevski
Jeani S. Gray
Margaret J. Hager
Rick Hairston
Debra Hallock
Suzanne Hefner
Christine Helm
Wanda Sue Hepler
Tonya B. Hess
Sherry R. Hickman
Jennie Hill
Nancy R. Hook
Carol Hoyle
Vicki P. Hughes
Suzanne J. Hunter
Timmy B. Hunter
Mary C. Isenhour-
  Long
Susan P. Jackson
Bob M. Jones Jr.
Shannon Jones
Joyce Christine Judah

Rebecca E. Justice
Patrice Kaizar
Suzanne C. Kalafian
Natalie Kauftheil
Shawn E. Kearsey
Geralyn Kelly
Linda Kerr
Nicole Kesler
Hayley Marie Keyes
Jeff Klein
Deborah L. Knowles
Karl Knowles
Gabriela Baluskova Knox
Sue Kocher
Susan Kreig
Crystal Landreth
Laura Lankford
Monique Laracuente
Kara L. Lashley
Will Lashley
Janelle M. Lavoie
Lyell E. LeBron
Penny Leigh
Michelle Lennon
Sylvia Lesniak
Barbara A. Long
Jenni L. Lough
Kimberly Lovingood-Owens
Pamela Manaton
Ashley Manning
Dona Maria Marcham-Baker
Ellen Weinel Marshburne
Pamela L. Martin
Denise D. McDonald
Shirley McKee
Sue McKinney
Barbara L. McNinch
Jennifer Merritt
Debra Miller
John Mitchell III
Carolyn Molder
Linda Monico
Daniel M. Morgan
Pat Muhammad
Brian P. Mulligan
Terry Murphy
Joetta Newman
Mari-Beth O'Neill
Barbara Ohmann

Julie Orellano
Jodi S. Oscar
Karen Owens
Marcia G. Owens
Angela H. Parker
Nancy L. Parrott
Kathy Pashby
Melissa D. Pate
Angela J. Patterson
Margaretta V. Patton
Karen E. Payne
Jane H. Peck
Elaine Pendell
Kristi J. Perman
Debra H. Peterson
Sylvie H. Pleasant
Mary L. Pollard
Erin Purgason
Jason Purgason
Lorretta Pyeatt
John A. Quy
Barbara J. Raab
Judy Raiford
Barbara L. Randall
Laura M. Reed
Karen Reuter
Kirk Ridge
Tamara Roberts
Katherine M. Robertson
Katharine R. Rodgers
Donna B. Rogers
Marty D. Rooney
Dorothea A. Rosencrans
Patricia Rotella
Linda M. Sample
Jan M. Santel
James H. Saxon
Olyn (Skip) J. Schnibben
Samantha Seal
Ray Sgambati
Elizabeth E. Shepherd
Kellie S. Siers
Nanci L. Slane
Jessica A. Smith
Larry L. Sorenson
Ginny Spencer
Cindy Stansell
Robin L. Stansell
Deborah Steely
Thomas Steinbacher

Gretchen Chapman Stephenson
Jennifer Sterka
Jaime Stuart
Sydney Suwannarat
Elizabeth R. Taylor
Florence Taylor
Linda Taylor
Gabrielle L. Tesarz
Ally J. Thomas
Paula M. Thomason
Judy Thorne, PhD
Terrie Cathleen Tobin
Patty K. Van Sicklen
Carol E. Vaseleski
Frank Verni
Denine Vooris-Shenise
Brad Waggoner
Lisa Waggoner
R. V. Wakefield III
Thomas M. Wallace
Dee Wallis
Heather L. Walters
Celia B. Waterman
Randy Eugene Webb
Christine Weisse
Barbara "BJ" Welker
Renee Westich
Tina M. Whisnant
George S. White
Jeanne L. White
Sandra Whiteside
Traci Whiteside
Jamie L. Whitt
Henry T. Williams
Jan Wilson
Adam Witherspoon
Jerry Wojenski
Shelley A. Wood
Paula M. Zaro
Angel Zebraski

NORTH DAKOTA

Linda R. Berg
Candi Brown-Fredriksen
Sharon L. Buethner
Helen L. Corlew
Theresa Flagstad
Lori Fritel
Betsy A. Hamkens
Donna M. Johnson

Ann L. Jussero
Sandy Martens
M Lavonne Marubbio
Stevie L. Mathre
Daria A. Miller
Shelley Olson
Cyndy Raeshke

OHIO

Kathleen Adamle
Charlene A. Akenhead
William Alan
Elizabeth Allen
Kenneth L. Alrick
Christopher M. Altier
John D. Armstrong
Dana Ash
Karen S. Ausprunk
Jane E. Babinsky
Steven R. Bader
C. Diane Balint
Ellen Ball
Peggy Baluch
Jay Barman
Kristi S. Baum
Mary M. Beam
Kristin M. Bliss
Shana Bockelman
Barbara A. Booher
Jeffery A. Bowling
Nancy L. Bradley
Alicia K. Brand
Mary Ellen Branick
Jonathan Brinkley
Betty J. Brown
Joanne Buehner Brown, DVM
Kenneth L. Buchele
Lisa T. Burke
Gail K. Burket
Bonnie Burman
Wendy Bush
Melissa A. Bussey
Donald F. Butts
Tina M. Caldwell
Dr. Lawrence Michael Cameron
Rebecca J. Campbell
William Corky Campbell
Julianne Carlson
Chris Carroll

Ramona Cartwright
Joyce Cates
Tara R. Centea
Alex Chodakowski
Norma J. Christopher
Janelle Cline
Melissa C. Cochran
Donna C. Collier
Barbara A. Collins
Sandra Combs
Leslie R. Conley
Charles Cook
Candy Cooke
Richard Copley Jr.
Bill Cosgrove
William L. Cox
Joan L. Currey
Mary Jo DeBrosse
Ruth DeFranco
Debra DeHoff
Norene A. Demaline
Ed Dickson
Cris D. Doss
Dolly F. Doyle
Susan Dunay
Mack W. Duplaga
Margie Duplaga
Dani Edgerton
Karen L. Elliott
Laura J. Evans
Vickie R. Fairchild
David Faller
Peggy Farrell-Kidd
Mindy Faulkner
Sheila H. Ferguson
Connie S. Fields
Heather Michelle
  Finch
Beth Fink
Jeri Finley
Stacy Forchione-Allen
Virginia Francis
Maria E. Frank-Allen
Kathe Friedlander
Raechal Friess
Farrah Fry
Judy Gaetje
Karia A. Gali
Vicky L. Galle
Leslie L. Garofalo
Susan Geers-Meiners
Suzanne Geisler
Jo Ellen Gellart

Lori L. Genaw
Amanda George
Amy P. Gibel
Perri L. Graf
Peg A. Gross
Amy Gutmann
Julia A. Hagedorn
Christopher Hall
Mary Beth Hall
Shari Hall
Barbara Hammer
Sherrie L. Hart
Marsha L. Hatfield
Beverly E. Heindl
Ernest Heintz
Diana Henderson
Carissa N. Hensley
Rebekah Hodous
Leeann L. Holloway
Kelly Hopkins
Lorie A. Hopp
Cynthia Hoppes
Randall A. Howard
Brie Huddleston
Jane C. Hufstader
Joann M. Hughes
June E. Hulit
Carol S. Humberger
Pamela J. Huson-
  Douglas
Judith Iaconianni
Beth Iler
Heather L. Jackson
Kymberlee D. Jarvis
Leslie A. Jeandrevin
Susan L. Jenkins
C. Terrence Kapp
Sharon A. Karns
Bonnie Kasik
Diana Kenne
David C. Kessel
Carolyn A. Kinley
Anne Kiser
Donna Klinger
Carol A. Knock
Bernita Lynn Koepfer
Sandra L. Kordis-
  Rubin
Kimberly L. Krause
Cheryl Kubista
Roberta Kublin
Katelyn Lance
Diane M. Laratta

Susan R. Lautner
Tiffany Leckrone
Bonnie Leinberger
Carole J. Lenehan
Debbie Leonard
Sally J. Lines
James J. Ling
Sandra W. Ling
Michael F. Loesche
Laurie A. Long
Lesa Long
Karen M. Lutz
Linda M. MacDonald
Victoria Machor
Katie E. Maess
Patricia Maistros
Barbara Malicki
Natasha Mallery
Bevala Manning
Pete Mansell
Sal Mansell
Edith Markoff
Sharon K. Masica
Jennifer L. Mauger
Elaine Mayher
Lydia M. McCarthy
Therese McClain
Phyllis McDonald
Crystal McElroy
Kristina L. McIntosh
Belinda A. McKinney
Carl P. McNair
Lisa J. McWilliams
Raul Mendoza
Mary A. Mignogna
Lucinda B. Miller
Melissa Miller
Tara Miller
Dorothy M. Miner
Glenna J. Mockbee
Kathleen A. Moore
Randall N. Moore
Mary Kay Morel
Lori Morrell
Anne Morrison
Tiffany Murphy
Wendy B. Nelson
M. Christine
  Nickerson
Erica Noneman
Marijo J. Nootz
Denise A. Norris
Delores N. Norsic

Susan Novotny
John Nugent, II
Vilma T. O'Neill
Elissa B. O'Sullivan
Eric Ogletree
Carrie Ohlinger
William R. Oliver
Anne Oviatt
Laura Pakis
Nicole R. Palsgrove
Michael P. Palumbo
Rebecca Park
Karen K. Parrill
Garry T. Paul
Christy Paxton
Karen Phillips
Peg L. Phillips
Judy Picklesimer
Karen Pilis
Frederick A. Pisani
Jessica Porter
Sharon Porter
Rebecca Potkay
Steven M. Proehl
Nikki Puccini
Constance Crumley
  Pugh
Angie Pullano
Darlene E. Rak
Jennifer Ray-Swope
Joy Reese
John J. Reilly
Sue Rhodes
Elizabeth M. Richards
Diane J. Riley
Tracey A. Rithaler
Ann M. Rogers
Karen E. Romine
Amy Rowen
Rebecca Rupert
Diana Salla
Karen D. Sanders
Trish Sansbury
A.C. Kelly Saunders
Marie-Josee Savignac
Terri Schaar
Beverly A. Schill
Caryn J. Schill
Gene Schill
Linda M. Seifert
Deanna K. Seitner
Annette M. Severance
Laverne Shapley

Jerry Shields
Pat Shields
Martha Skilton
Lisa D. Slama
Vickie L. Slis
Kelly-Jean G. Smick
Julie F. Smith
Kathy Ellen Smith
Kim S. Smith
Linda J. Smith
Patricia A. Smith
Sharon Kaye Smith
Linda Smithberger
Amy L. Snyder
Marlys J. Staley
Kathryn L. Stapel
Terrie Stephens
Dr. Carol Stephenson
Rena Stevens
Patricia J. Stover
Sandra J. Stover
Stacey L. Sucky
Kathleen Sutliff
Gary Swaninger
Mary A. Swingle
Pamela K. Tansek
Bridget Telencio
Kathy K. Teller
Belinda D. Tharp
Dru Therrian
Christy Thomas
Charmagne
 Thompson
Karlene Fuller
 Thompson
Susan Trudeau
Marlene Turner
Pamelia B. Utso
Scott J. Van DenHaute
Laurance Van Tuyl
Patricia A. Vesalo
Michelle S. Wallace
Marty Warchola
Renee Waring
Linda J. Warner
Mary A. Watcher
Mark Weber
Cathy A. Weil
Megan C. Wesney
Jillian West
Scott Weston
Gloria J. White
Lois M. Whitman

Tonya A. Wilhelm
Jennifer Will
Sandra L. Williams
Alice A. Williamson
William F. Wittrock
Carol L. Wolfe
Kathleen A. Yontz
Karen L. Young
Regina Young
Lori E. Zakel
Andrew A. Zoll
Jenny R. Zoll
Rebecca S. Zoll
Kathi Jo Zornes

OKLAHOMA

Patricia L. Adams
Winford L. Adams
Lori L. Baer
Antoinette J. Bailey
Jim F. Bowles
Vicki T. Boyer
Sherri Brittan
Vicki N. Bronson
Amy A. Brown
Laura Sobel Brown
Stephanie Burnside
Kris J. Butler
Lisa M. Bycroft
Stephanie A. Carroll
Cynthia Jones Clark
Thomas G. Comstock
Annabelle Conner
Victoria Courtney
Vickie Cupps
Billy M. Davison
Sandy Davison
Merit Day
Angela M. Dayton
Karen deCordova
Don R. Duerksen
Shelley Erdman
Nina S. Flannigan
Robbie Gilbert
Sammy Jo Golemon
Mary B. Green
Kaylan Head
Pam Hixson
Katherine R. Huggins
Brenda Hughes
Brandi L. Jakola
Maureen A. Kelly

Kacy Parker Kinsey
Gisella Klindera
Holly Kruse
Debbie Lang
Audrey Lewis
Jan Logan
Jerry H. Mabry
Scott Malone
Joyce A. McIntyre
Billye J. McNeil
Maryanne Morehead
B. Diane Myers
Mary J. Nevin
Donna L. Newville
Penny L. Nichols
Karen K. Ohde
Susan Parker
Jill Perry
Kathy Rasmussen
Misti Reynolds
Brandon M. Ross
Dovie A. Ryan
Carol Ryther
Gayla Sesher
Edna C. Shade
Susanne Shelton
Louis Sider
Larry K. Simpson
Dorothy M. Smith
Lawanna Smith
Terri Lynn Smith
Dev Snider
Angel Soriano
Dan Stahl
Monty Steele
Dave Strickland
Christine Lee
 Summers
Kimberly A. Sykes
Travis H. Taylor
Mike Thomasson
Cynthia Tidmore
Karen Titterington
Jamie M. Weaver
Patricia E. White
Henry V. Williams Jr.
Mary F. Williams
Kathryne Williford
Sandie L. Wyman
Cindy Rowe Zelbst

OREGON

Lorain M. Abel, DVM
Lynette Alfano
Jeanne Allen
Bethany Andrews
Sunny Arruda
Debra Lee August
Constance Joy Bacak
Laura Beck
Patty Bensene
Jessica Blake
Janene H. Bradfeldt
Lorna M. Brandt
Cynthia Bruckart
Andrew D. Bynum
Bryan Castleberry
Mark Chryssanthis
Christina Coberly
Stephanie
 Collingsworth
Mary Lou Cook
Jason W. Coutts
Jane V. Devlin
Phyllis Dinsmore
Doug Duncan
Michelle Dunn
Virginia M. Dunn
Marjorie A. Ediger
Melody E. Fair
Jessica Farnes
Christine Feldman-
 Bartnick
Susan Fletcher
Randy J. Freeman
Rebecca French
Bonnie Fuesser
Meredith Gage
Gerri Galer
Krista Gately
Stacey A. Gehrman
Floyd Gerstenfeld
Sharon W. Gotcher
Katrin Greim
Barbara Griffin
Ann Griffith-Morris
Sue Hanna
Kim Harney
Cynthia Hauser
Carol Hibner
Shirley Hill
Hilary Hines

Lynn Hobbs
Theresa L. Iverson
Kathy Jacobsen
Constance E. Johnson
Laurie Beth Johnson, DVM
Kathleen Kane
Kristin Kerner
Lori Kirby
Kathryn J. Knowles
Janice Koler-Matznick
Christine Kuhlman
Alexandra Lantis
Krista Llewellyn
Jenni Lott
Bruce MacNeill
Maura A. Mallory
Claudia L. Marbury
Lynda Martin
Mary Lou Mathis
Lynn McAward
Nannette McCloud-Evans
Terry L. McCullough
Jonna McGinnis
Deena McIver
Dawn Mellon
Patricia E. Mills
Dana Mitchell
Alethea Mohr
Terri Jo Morgan
Casey E. Newton
Lori Nickeson
Nicole Noland
Marlene E. Palmer
Laurin Parker
Robert E. Pendergast
Lucille Perry
Ramona K. Pessa
Skye Poitras
Wendy Pool
Joanna Rand
Nancy G. Rand
Scott Raymond
Jennifer Reid
Holly Reynolds
Quinn Richardson
Tanya Roberts
Lesa A. Rose-Smith
Mary H. Rosenblum
Rebecca Rossi
Kerry Ryan
Kirsten A. Salvito

Lynn M. Schilling
Susan M. Shearer
Danielle Shultz
Amy Smith
Anne-Marie Smith
Shannon Smith
Sheila K. Smith
Wendy J. Snyder
Caroline Spark
Brenna Spencer
Janice F. Sproul
Teresa St. Hilaire
Joy H. St. Peter
Barbara S. Stewart
Dana Stillinger
Patricia (Patty) K. Storkel
Sioux Strong
Donald C. Stuart
Esther Anne Underkofler
Irene J. Valenzuela
Stella S. Van Cleave
Paulena E.C. Verzeano
Chris Wallen
Carol Webster
Patricia (Trisch) Wentz
Rachel Westlund
Carol Wilder
Sharon R. Wilder
Sue Wiley
Mara Windstar
Deborah J. Wood
Kathleen Woodbury
Darryl Wrisley
Nancy Yamin
Lynda D. Ziegenhagel

PENNSYLVANIA

Barbara A. Adams
Janet Agresti-Norman
Barbara L. Anderson
Donna M. Anderson
Calvin J. Arter
Valerie M. Attrill
Debra L. Bach
Robert L. Bachrach
David E. Balmat
Donna K. Barnett
April L. Barr
Diane M. Battis
Linda A. Beard

Barbara R. Bekker
Patricia A. Bentz
Melinda M. Berger
Lisa T. Berkenstock
Carol L. Berman
Petra Betterton
John Bickel
Maryanne Block
Tina Bloom
Andrea D. Boyd
Sandy Boyko
Alison K. Brown
Regiene E. Brown
Deannda Bryant
Jane Brydon
Kathryn A. Bullock
Linda Burley
Joanne Burns
Shelley J. Caldwell
Samantha Canuso
Stephanie Capkovic
Mary Jo Carabello
Jeanne Carbone
Michelle Lee Carroll
Frances W. Cashdollar
Frank J. Catanzaro, II
Roberta M. Cerra
Debra Chaar
Lyne R. Charlsen
Christine J. Civil
Tammy M. Clapper
James A. Clark
Patrick Coleman
Rachel Converse
Cynthia A. Cook
Donna Cooper
Linda Cors
Kathleen M. Croft
Robin L. Crum
Carol Culp
Ronde J. Dalton
Joan E. Dandy
Crystal A. Davis
Jeanne K. Davis
Crystal DeEsch
Rachael Demeter
Jason L. Demko
Debra M. DeSantis
JoAnn Dhanse
Sonia Dieter
Maggie DiLullo
Denise M. Dissinger
Jeffrey L. Dissinger

John Docherty
Kathy Dolan
Carol A. Dotts
Eileen M. Drummond
Barbara Dubinett
Todd Dunlap
Judy C. Ebersole
Sandra M. Ebersole
Lisa N. Edwards
Elizabeth Elvidge
Judy Endo
Denise A. English
Deborah M. Examitas
Suzanne Falatko
Ms. Pat Fallon
Valerie M. Faris
Caryln Fasnacht
Marcy Fenell
Alan Finn
Joan B. Fiser
Terri L. Florentino
Judith A. Fox
Gloria J. Frick
Michael Friend
Susan Frisch
Shaun Froshour
Michelle L. Frumento
Michael Fry
Sara J. Fry
Scott Fry
Debra Galan
Michele Gardner
Lisa Gebhardt
Ann Gehrlein
Sheri K. Gintner
L. Debbie Greusel
Michaeline Grill
Christopher W. Grim
Dorothy M. Grocott
Thomas M. Gross Jr.
Sally Grottini
Cathy Guyer
Felice C. Haggerty
Charmaine W. Hall
Evelyn M. Hall
Renee M. Hall
Arlene Halloran
Faith Harrop
Janice F. Harvey
Lynn Haughwout
Anne M. Havey
Jude Hercules
Bonnie Hess

Faye Hilborn
Cathy Hivner
Elizabeth M. Hoffman
Anne R. Holiday
Linda S. Honsperger
James L. Hornberger
Betsy Howell
Lindsey Jackson
Bonnie J. James
Colleen M. Jansen
Linda D. Johnson
Amanda Jones
Debby M. Kallaher
Renae Kelly
Nancy A. Kieffer
JoAnn Kirk
Valerie L. Klein
Toni E. Klemko
Joan M. Klingler
Roberta A. Knauf
Cynthia C. Knowlton
Palma A. Kokowski
Emil J. Kolick
H. Frederick Koons
Nadia Kopinski
Christina Kovacs
Phyllis R. Kraft
Annmarie Kramer
Derry Krause
Marjean Krech
Mary D. Kutulakis
Diane Kwiatkowski
Joyce Lazell
Lisa A. Leipold
Barbara Levenson
Pamela Lewis
Lisa M. Lightner
Rebecca S. Lindeman
Lee Livingood
Jackie Lockard
Bruno Lombardo
Sharon W. Long
Tammy Lee Lorince
Carolyn F. Lundvall
Kathryn W. Lupinacci
Marci Lynne
Debbie Shoener
  MacDonald
Richard D.
  Mackintosh
Jill K. MacPherson
Michele M. Manion
Stacey Manzo

Cecilia C. Margani
Sarah Marino
Elizabeth Maslow
Barbara Mattes
Linda A. Maugle
Elaine K. Mayowski
Nicole McBride
Paulette McBride
Lisa McDonald
Marie S. McDonough
Jennifer Lynne McElya
Wendy McKelvy
Stacey K. McLaughlin
Debby McMullen
Kathleen P.
  Meccariello
Mary Merrell
Eileen Mesi
Cheryl Metzel
Rachel Michak
Patricia Mickowski
Mychaelann L. Miller
Sharon M. Miller
Carol Millinghausen
Marissa Mitcheli
Patricia J. Mock
Carrie Mogel
Michaela Mohr
Johanna M. Molitano
Linda Moore
Kathy Moran
Marie C. Morris
Barbara A. Morrison
Crystal Morton
Annette Murphy-
  Wales
Donna S. Musico
Helen Natelli
Sharon Naylor
Elizabeth Neely
Carol Prines Newbury
Barbara E. Newman
Diane Nikander
Jacqueline M. O'Neill
Susan M. Oakes
Susan M. Onraet
Betty L. Padgett
Missy Palumbo
Rebecca A. Panzak
J. Douglas Parson
Amy Parsons
Maxine A. Pellis
Mary F. Perrego

Harry Peterson
Anna Pettit
Cindy Pfister
Kathy Z. Poole-Price
Barbara J. Powischill
Karen A. Price
Paul M. Price
Lois M. Prilla
Lillian M. Puchalski
Kenneth W. Radle
Michele Rafferty
Dawn Reed
Mary Remer
Arlene L. Renninger
Dawn Rexrode
LuAnn Rittenhouse
Marsha R. Robbins
Camille M. Robinson
Tracy Robinson
Sharon Roble
Dawn B. Romanczak
Michael Romberger
Jim Rosasco
Susan Rosetti
Donald Ross
Rhonda Mateer Ross
Valli Rovenolt
Jayme R. Rutter
Marylou Ryan
Thomas J. Ryan
Karen Sage
Olivia A. Sailus
Ann M. Sanders
Susan Sanders
Deborah E. Sangrey
Richard C. Sangrey
Pat Santi
Betty M. Scarnato
Tammy L. Schaas
Nancy Schilling
Linda Scopa
Darlene Seibel
Peggy Seiler
Eugene P. Selner
Holly J. Sensenig
J Scott Sensenig
Lisa M. Serad
Patricia A. Shaeffer
Deb Sheasley
Susan M. Sheldon
Loretta Sherwood
Sally Shilling
Melanie M. Shufran

Carol A. Siegrist
Kay Sivel
Helene Skopek
Michael A. Small
Helen Smith
Kacey Smith
Marjorie A. Smith
Terri C. Smith
Kelli Sorg
Marjorie W. Sovec
Diana Squicciarini
Julie K. Stack
Evelyn I. Stackhouse
Kristine Stellato
Carol A. Stewart
Harry R. Stiller
Charlene Stone
Diane E. Stout
Cynthia Strada
Elizabeth Strecker
Julie Swanger
Linda Swenson
Nanci E. Takash
Vivien G. Terzaghi
Robert Thompson
Susan F. Thompson
Beverly L. Tomei
Becky Toner
William P. Townsend
Shari Trythall
Ruth Ann Van Dyke
Nancy Vanderslice
Rise VanFleet, PhD
Brian Vaughan
Annamaria Ventresca
Bernadette M.
  Verhoski
Dayna Villa
Summer R. Voth
Ann Walker
Susan E. Walsh
Alice R. Ward
Katie Watterson
Susan M. Watts
Michele Kay
  Weatherly
Neil O. Werner
Linda White
Wendy J. Whitelam
Laura L. Whitman
Karen Wiley
Danielle M. Wilson
Sandy Wishnick

Ann Withun
Silke Wittig
Victor J. Wojciak
Robert Wolf
Colby Woodring
Vicki Wooters
Angelina M. Worman
Patricia Wotring
Geraldine A. Wray
Dean Wylie
Kodey Young
Antoinette Yurkovic

PUERTO RICO

Eleanor S. Abarca
Cristina Sousa Eden
Alma J. Febus
Sheyla E. Gutierrez
Raul Martinez
Beatriz Ramirez
  Abarca

RHODE ISLAND

Michelle Alexandre
Kristin Barney
James A. Barry
Alice M. Boucher
Stephen Croteau
Byron C. Davies
Lynn B. DePrizio
Jenny Dickinson
Kevin P. England
Megen Gifford
Sara Grenier
Linda Hilliard
Barbara J. Hockhausen
Kristin L. Hogan
Christina L. Johnson
Kerri Kershaw
Cristin Larson
Betty Laurin
Marlene Lendrim
Karen M. Mancini
Peter J. Manning
Nadine McCaffrey
Cailin Monahan
Kendra Nault
Brian J. Nicastro
James W. O'Neill
Heidi Palmer
Susan Parker

Victoria Patridge
Kathleen McKenna
  Perkins
Karen Perusek
Kathryn A. Sayles
Christine A. Seibert
Diana F. Sheehan
Susan Sullivan
Lisa F. Sylvester
Tara Valletta
Judy A. Vess

SOUTH CAROLINA

Sherry Ahlers
Allison L. Allen
Rebecca Wendy Bass
Phyllis A. Beasley
Kirsten M. Beeker
Julie Bentley
Abby Bird
Patricia A. Carter
Patrick Cheatham
Susan T. Colflesh
Connie B. Compton
Susan F. Conklin
Stella M. Cooper
Peggy M. Crawford
Gina Crist
Patricia A. Czaikowski
Lori Duncan
Elizabeth C. Dunn
Martha Sue Eckles
Debe Edwards
Leon M. Ember
Faye Erickson
Kathy M. Evans
Lois C. Fair
Jane A. Fink
Nora "Cheryl" Finks
Montese S. Fishel
Katie Fleming
J. Hilary Gamble
Linda C. Garrett
Christine Geisel
R. Wanda Gipp
Joan L. Gormley
Tommy Grammer
Sylvia G. Hammett
Sarah R. Hawkins
Denise M. Healy
Barbara Q. Hefner
Monica Henderson

Jamie A. Hinson
Matina Hollis
Anna Howe
Caroline C. Hunt
Erin James
Melissa Jarriel
Mira Jones
Crystal D. Jordan
Cynthia B. King
Linda E. Kolb
Michael D. Lauer
Grace Lichtenwald
Roxann MacKinnon
Susan A. Marett
Elizabeth L. Mitchum
Eleanor F. Moore
Kittie Kay Moore
Margi Baldwin Moore
Catherine M. Morton
Harold D. Page Jr.
Danielle Pellicci
Tiffany R. Pitkin
Jerri Rector
Teri Ribley
Edward Rockwell
Norma Rockwell
David Ryan
Patricia Rose
  Schwietert
Robert Smith
Ann M. Stauffer
Thurmon Lee Stogner
Christina R. Stoner
Marleina Ra'Nae
  Storey
Jon A. Tholkes
Ms. Susan Vickery
Jillian Walker
Kathaleen F. Welborn
Jessica Young
Patricia A. Zeigler

SOUTH DAKOTA

Pam D. Bethke
Mary Bohn
Karen Bos-Carey
Susan Busk
Karen Cameron-
  Howell
Tana Clark
Amy Frink
June Greenwood

Michele Hanten
Debra J. Hohn
Mary Jo Jaqua
Joanne M. Johnson
Linda Kelly
Jenny Martens
Deborah Munger
Sally Peoples
Barb Rosane
Lois J. Schmoll
Heather Schuller
Sandra L.
  Shaughnessy
Monica L. Trabing

TENNESSEE

Cindi A. Anderson
Audra Argo
Grady V. Barefield
Aviceen Barlatier
Nathan Bass
Patricia Belt
Wayne Booth
Robin R. Bowen
Barbara Burns
Nancy Cambron
Ann Campbell
Jane Carrasco
Janet P. Casey
Sherie Catledge
Cindy Choate
Beth Clark
Linda F. Cockburn
Bridget Corrigan
Christopher Crews
Holly Deeds
Sue DiCero
Margaret L. DiCorleto
Daniel Dobkins
Jamie Dunn
Lisa Dyer
Donna Eddins
Mary Ehrhart
Bev Eitner
Meghann Esters
Matthew Faccinto
Dorothy E. Fletcher
Linda R. Frei
David J. Frensley Sr.
JoAnne Fusco
Pamela Gentry
Laura Cass George

Dominique A. Gower
Julia M. Gregory
Katie Griffiths
Jennifer Hale
Julie Halsted
Leah A. Hans
Melanie Harriman
Peg D. Harrington
Ali Hemyari
Bonnie Herrell
Cynthia Hollis
Jill C. Hootman
Linda Hurst
Abigail Hyndman
Laurie E. Johnston
Andrea G. Jones
Jennie R. Jones
Irving Kaplan
Pamela Kinser
JoLene Lee
Charles N. Leggett
Keith Lowe
Ellen J. Mahurin
Richard Mann
Deborah Y. Martin
Kat Martin
Jill Mats
Terri L. McCarthy
Christie L. Meyer
Kriste L. Meyer
Anne Morrison
Carrie O'Brien
Stephanie M. Paulter
Karen S. Pilkay
Sandy A. Pope
Jaime Ramseier
Xan Rawls
Sandra W. Rene
Cherryl-Ann Ricard
Breezy Roach
Bonita G. Rodgers
Katherine Rollins
Ruth A. Romillo
Cynthia Anne
  Routledge
Shelby Salestrom
Shannon Shepherd
Sharon Sheppard
Dorothy K. Sherer
Peggi A. Stahr
Carolyn A. Steed
Larry Stogner
Jon Stolzer

Carol L. Stone
Shanna L. Summers
Mark A. Sumonka
Gabor Szilasi
Debb Taylor
Fay C. Taylor
Kathy A. Temple
Ashli Thomas
Christine Thomas
Marina Thorne
Rita R. Tinsley, DVM
Cheryl Tisdale
Elizabeth A. Tolley
Sheri Trudrung
Rita S. VanBebber
Melissa R. Victor
James L. Watson
Heather J. Wilkerson
Gary W. Williamson
Kathleen C. Wilson
Justin T. Wiseman
Elta Woodliff
Rebecca Wysock
Mary B. Zopfi

TEXAS

Nancy Adams, DVM
Mim Aiken
Rebecca G. Andrews
Pedro Araujo Jr.
Teresa M. Arnett
Mary F. Arnold
Robin Ashman-Terrell
Tracy Atkins
Jorge Ayala
Stephanie J. Ayers
Patty Bacher
Brandy Baker
Barbara A. Barclay
Linda Barnett
Charlotte Bascom
Susan Lauer Bass
Sue Beaver
Stephanie Bennett
Irma M. Bice
Patricia S. Bidwell
Cinda Bishop
Deanna L. Blackwell
Gayla Blades
Jennifer D. Blanton
Amanda Bloodworth
Jackie Bloomer

George Anna Bobo
Robert Bolander
Melissa Ann Bonar
LeAnn Bonnett
Regan Bonnett
Jeff Bornman
Robert A. Boudreau
Ann Bridges
Annette R. Brooks
Karen L. Brooks
Robert Broussard
Judy A. Brown
Debra Bruce
Kimberly Brucksch
Matthew J. Bryant
Valerie M. Bryant
Paul Bunker
Laura Burdett
Kimberly Lynn Burgan
Dee Ann Burgess
Terri L. Burrows
Cristopher L. Burton
Melissa A. Cano
Kathy A. Carlson
Diane V. Carpenter
Terri Carver
Shannon B. Casto
Lisa Caughlin
Amanda Chaffin
Moriah S. Champagne
Nancy Chaney
Jennie Y. Chen
Gail S. Clark
Linore Cleveland
Paul Coffman
Barbara Cole
Bill Coleman
Olivia R. Colvin
Kathie Compton
Timothy A. Cook
Carolyn Cooper
Dana Cooper
Kelli Corcoran
Patricia A. Crawford
Sherry L. Creighton
Michele L. Crouse
Jill Cruz
Kevin A. Curran
Shari A. Curran
James Dalton
Walter L. Darr Jr.
Vicky David
Jane Davidson

Dan Davis
Kimberlee S. Davis
MaryAnn Davis
Tamara L. Davis
Barbara M. Day
Stephanie M.
  DeGesero
Jane Del Re
Tammy F. Dennis
Angie G. Dickinson
Kayla Dohmen
Joanne P. Doucet
Donna Doyle
Steven F. Drake
Claudia L. Duffield
Deborah S. Dunbar
Carol S. Duncan
Colleen Dunlap
Charlene R. Dunn
Courtney D. Dunn
Terry Dyck
Susanna Ebest
Janet L. Echavarry
Aleta J. Eldridge
Sharie Elkins
B. Ellis
Bart Emken
Heather Emswiler
Sandra M. England
Judy Estes
Cheryl G. Etheridge
Don Etheridge
Ronda N. Evans
Juan Faura
Crystal Fetting
Erica Feuerbacher
Marianne Filemyr
Lana K. Forman
Kelly Frankie
Margery A. Furbish
Holly Furgason
Kat Gamble
Al Garza
Francine Gaynor
Benjamin L. Geeslin
Susan C. Geib
LeAnn George
Kerri Georghiou
Amanda Gerdes
Angela Michelle
  Giangrossi
Nicole A. Giles
Monica Gilliland

Lynn Godbee
Carlos A. Gomez
Jan M. Gordon
Elise Gouge
Evelyn B. Greenberg
Stacy A. Greer
Judy Lee Gregg
Kim Grieff
Melissa Griffin
Sharlotte Griffis
Adrianna Grimes
Karen S. Guenther
Tia L. Guest
Sherell A. Guichard-
  Thomas
Miriam L. Gustavson
Eleonora Guzman
Richard W. Harbin
Rita A. Harris
Abby Harrison
Jessica Harrison
Jeremie Harvey
Christine Hastings
Jamie L. Hastings
Patricia G. Hawkins
Stephen Haynes
Anne L. Healy
Donna M. Heavner
Sheryl Edna Hebert
Sylvia Ann Hebert
Tamara S. Heggie
Katie Hiett
Perry L.
  Higginbotham Jr.
Dean O. Hildreth
Michael Alan Hill
Shirley Hilscher
Hepzibah E. Hoffman-
  Rogers
Debra S. Holmes
Brenda Howard
Annette L. Janis
Ashley Jeanes
Carlos Jech
Sumee Mikkelsen Jech
Cat Jensen
James Johnson
Margaret A. Johnson
Sally L. Johnson
Steven K. Johnson
Malinda M. Julien
Gayle F. Justice
Aloana Keaton

Mary R. Kegarise
Brenda K. Keller
Merritt Kennedy
Susan A. King
Michelle D.
  Knevelbaard
Linda Knowles
Melissa S. Knox
Tracie Kolnsberg
Eileen M. Kosakowski
Debi Krakar
Mark D. Kuykendall
Bonnie M. Lacombe
Casandra Dee Lambert
Elise Lavin
Miranda Lawrence
Bobbi Leverich
Sue Loessberg
Marcia Ann Long
Clinton M. Lovelace
Jennifer M. Loyless
Trellis Q. Lucas
Gregory D. Lummus
Linda Lundgren
Lisa A. Lynady
Eileen M. Mahoney
Deborah Maicach
Kathrine Mancuso
Paul Mann
Mark A. Marek
Tracy L. Marek
Sandra Marr
Pat Marshall
Norma J. Materne
Marcia Maxner
Brenda J. McCray
Kathleen A.
  McCullough
Cynthia McFadden
Kay McGuire
Tina McIlveene
Sandra B. McKinley
Debbie McKnight
Natalie McMahon
Tod McVicker
Cassandra Merryman-
  Scifres
Kathleen K. Milford
Joan S. Miller
Joyce L. Miller
Dr. Ronna Miller
Tammy L. Mills
Karen Minson

Katrena A. Mitchell
LaDonna Moment
Jimmeye S. Moore
Stella M.R. Moore
Altha Morgan
Angie Morgan
Kristy L. Muir
Traci A. Murdock
Brenda I. Mygrant
Katrina Nicholl-Basye
Cheryl D. Nichols
Cathy Niles
Marion G. Nixon
Sheri Nunez
Jan Nuzzo
Sylvie M. Nuzzolilo
Mona E. O'Gorman
Rosemarie A. O'Hara
Anne M. O'Neill
Laura A. Ocheltree
Jennifer L. Ochoa
Walta Ocker
Monika Olbrisch
Gary A. Oswalt
Kim M. Paetzel
Wendy Palmer
Maureen Patin
Elizabeth A. Patschke
Victoria Paul
Patricia R. Pearce
Carol J. Pearson
Kimberley Elmore
  Petross
Donna D. Pettit
Joan M. Pfeifer
Sherri Pharo
Leann Anne Phenix
Sharon L. Poppenger
Donald S. Praeger Jr.
Lisa A. Praeger
Danielle Prince
Paula Baker Prince
Marne Pringle
Janice D. Pryor-Regier
Marilyn Pryor
Amy Pyeatt
Emily Pyle
Debby Ann Quigley
Cathryn L. Ratzloff
Brandon Ray
Lydia Rayner
Sandra M. Reid
Judy Rentrop

Andrya Rhodes
Cmdr. Pamela J.
  Rhyner-Hirko,
  USNR
Annasheril H.
  Richards
Jack Richards
Eamon P. Riley
Marlene K. Ring
Misty Roachelle
Cindy Robertson
Michelle V. Robinet
Tina Rosado
Jana Rossorelli
Sharon L. Roy
Natalia Sabrina Rozas
  de O'Laughlin
Steve Rum
JoAnn R. Russell
Jeffrey S. Ryan
Frank W. Saling
Rebecca M. Saltwick
Adam Sanders
Susen Santoro
Tom F. Sawyer
Chuck Schifferling
Karen S. Schuller
Aaron Seligman
Alyssa Shade
Gregory Sharp
W. Brett Shayler
Linda Sikes
Amanda Simmons
Michael Simpson
Patricia J. Simpson
Jasmine Skala
Kristine Skowbo
Ana Marcella
  Slaughter
Bobbye Joyce Smith
Diana Ney Smith
Elizabeth Smith
Jan Smith
Laura Smith
Shannon M. Smith
Sharon Smith
Troy L. Smith
Kellie Snider
Nic St. Clair
Liz Stamey
Judeen Stauffer
Lori Stevens
Mary Stevens

Jocelyn E. Stout
Ellen Stovall
Russell A. Stovall
Paul Sulinski
Debbie Sullivan
Mary Waugh Swindell
Susan A. Tackett
Deborah J. Taliaferro
Stacey Talley
Laurie Telfair
Shelia Tenison
Jacqueline Konold
  Teuschl
Novalene I. Thurston
Vivian Siuve Tjeng
Lynn C. Trafton
Pat A. Turnage
Cara Vacchiano
Juan Vasquez
Linda Veldman
Mary T. Vigil-Covert
Shelby Brogdon
  Walden
Nancy E. Ward
Susan Warren
Mary L. Weigandt
Paula Weir
Angie R. Welch
Pamela S. Welch
Judy C. Weldgen
Tonia Whilden
Harry D. White
Dina Whitehouse
Elizabeth Widmer
Vickey L. Willard
Glenn D. Williams
Dawn Willsher
Jean Witt
JoAnn F. Wolf
Rebecca L. Wolfe, PhD
Cindy R. Wolfshohl
Inka Wolter
Wanda J. Woodworth
Dana E. Wray
Aki Yamaguchi
Karen K. Yates
Laura J. Young
Caroline G.
  Youngblood
J.P. Yousha
Loralei A. Zwitt

UTAH

Ann R. Allums
Stacie Bailey
Linda L. Benton
Judy Campbell
Maloree Campbell
Judith E. Clark-Upton
Karen E. Davis
Susan Lindsey
  Fletcher
Jaime Gardner
Jessica H. Goodliffe
Heather N. Hampsten
Kyle R. Hennefer
Katrina M. Henrie
Cindy A. Herl
Lisa R. Higley
Joe Holm
Synethia M. Kinsman
Michelle M. Larsen
Dorinda I. Lauer
Mary Lehman
Jeremy A. Mathews
Wendy Sue McCleery
Greg McCoy
Lorraine Milner
Penny L. Morrison
Kathleen Murray
Donald A. Pawlak
Jan E. Perkins
Eric Peterson
Christina Preziosi
Stephanie Ramirez
Alice R. Reis
Michelle Rizzi
Linda Robinson
Tania Rogers
Betty Ruffini
Martine Savageau
Jennifer K. Severud
Dianne E. Sipe
Astrid Smith
Dave Smith
Donna G. Smith
Julie Stacey
Shelley T. Stanley
Nancy Thornley
Jan Vincent
Patrick Whitacre
Gail Workman
Jeanette Worsencroft

VERMONT

Lorie Abair
Alice Ayres
Deanna Baker
Lori A. Bielawa
Candice Bourque
Laura Bowles
Deborah L. Brown
Pat Clark
Elaine J. Clarkson
Peg Cobb
Erica Ferland
Catherine A. Fisher
Carolyn Fuhrer
Ann P. Gavett
Maria J. Germano
Darlene S. Gould
Amy Haskell
Michele A. Hemenway
Lalita M. Karoli
Kasandra Kenney
Susan Kenney
Sharon C. Kroker
Cassandra Lamothe
Jacquelyn McLaughlin
Lorene McLaughlin
Joan Neely
Megan O'Brien
Pamela S. Parkinson
Amanda J. Poquette
Claire Silver
Joyce M. Smith
Margaret Pierce
  Teitelbaum
Barbara Van Raden
Dale West
Nathan Whitehorne
Christina M.
  Williamson
Alysia M. Wolf

VIRGINIA

Patricia L. Abel
Tonya M. Adamson
Patricia A. Allen
Amy Fay Alliston
Martha B. Anderson
Annie L. Andrews
Yvonne Ansick-
  Bleistein

Bryant A. Arrington
Elizabeth Atkins
Debra Barrows
Claudia N. Bates
Kathy Benner
Robin Bennett
Melanie Benware
Isabelle J. Bertrand
Michelle Blackwood
Katherine K. Blair
Edmond J. Blausten
Toshiko I. Blausten
Bonnie Boger
Dee Bogetti
Kim Bolster
Julie Bowles
Susan Scott Brafford
Elizabeth F. Breyer
David J. Brobst
Virginia Broitman
Corally Burmaster
Anne-Marye S. Byrd
Julio Cesar Cabrera
Michelle L. Carter
Scott Casino
Tracey S. Cassidy
Carol L. Chapin
Jamin Chenault
Clinton B. Cochran
Dawne W. Coleman
Susanne F. Coleman
Lisa Colon
Stephanie Conrad
Krispin Cranwell
Nancy Cronce
Eleanor M. Crout
Erin L. Culhane
Barbara Currier
Deanne Davenport
Anne W. Davis
Ashley Davis
Marie D. Davis
Jennifer M. DeGarmo
Cheryl Dellinger
Peggy J. Dobbins
Lynne Dunham
Noreen C. Dunlap
Deborah H.
  Duttenhofer
Lauren Early
Carol M. Ellia
Kimberly Elliott
Lynda H. Fairchild

Cheryl Falkenburry
Beth P. Falwell
Sarah A. Ferrell
Michele Fisher
Lesa Fork
Jeff Franklin
Daniel L. Freye
Deven D. Gaston
Sandra L. Getz
Barbara Gipson
Cameron Glahe
Patricia A. Goettler
Teresa P. Greer
Laura S. Gregory
Jennifer Grimes
Mark Hackathorn
Rickey N. Hall, II
Teresa Hanula
Richard T. Hardin
Barbara Z. Harding
Victoria Harter
Bruce A. Hartsell
Jodi Haveles
Donna M. Henley
Laura Rosie Higdon
Maureen E. Hill-
  Hauch
Jemi S. Hodge
Ann E. Hogg
Mark Francis Hoggard
Karen R. Hough
Paula K. House
Mary Hovey
Betty Ann Howell
Abbie Hubbard
Mary Marcella Iannelli
Melissa Jennings
Christine N. Johnson
Pamela H. Johnson
Ruth Ann Johnson
Robert Jordan
Sean Julian
Linda Ann Kauffman
Wendy G. Keene
Lenora Keener
Jacy H. Kelley
Anke King
Barbara S. Klotz
Connie M. Kniseley
Karen (Kari)
  Koulmentas
Sandra S. Kowalski
Jennifer L. Kyzer

Patricia M. Lacy
Dara Lambert
Lynne Lambert
Renee Lamoureux
Nicole Larson
Judi E. Lefebvre
Patricia A. Leininger
Amy Lewett
Rachel M. Lewis
Nancy Liebhaus
Andrea S. Lindamood
Donna K. Lindsey
David Linnemeyer
Debbie S. Lipcsey
Katie Locks
Margaret Lockwood
Pam Lucas
Victoria M. Lyman
Joan MacKenzie
Carole A. Marshall
Teresa F. Mathern
Natalie Maticka
Rhonda May
Elsie M. Maylott
Lee Anne McAdam
Joanne McCleary
Kathy McCoubrey
Cher G. McCoy
Cheryl McKee
Patricia L. McKeown
Karen E. McKnight
Tara G. McLaughlin
Donna Meade
Christiane Merk
Mick A. Merlin
Rosemary S. Miller
Lisa J. Millican
Linda Montgomery
Ismail Moore
Sherry D. Moore
Janice C. Morton
Theresa A. Myers
Ann Nadjar
Pamela Nashman
Carroll O. Neuner
Linnea J. Nicely-Dix
Jean G. Nohle
Helen G. Noles
Marti E. Nottingham
Debra O'Boyle
Mary Alice Owen
Kelly L. Palmer

Alexandra M.
  Palmquist
Judy A. Paris
Kelsey Parker
Ann Parris
Melanie Parrish
Sara J. Parsons
Teresa A. Patton
Maynard Pease
Marvin W. Peck III
Carole Peeler
Sue Peetoom
Colleen Pelar
Patricia Persinger
Sally L. Petty
Arlene D. Pilcer
Amanda Pitsenberger
Paige M. Port
C. Ann Priddy
Hazelanne Prokop
Erica Pytlovany
Jagannathan
  Rangarajan
Desiray Rice
Thomas Rivers
Vicki M. Rizzo
Joan N. Robinson
Nicole Roccograndi
Dorothea Romano
Pamela J.
  Rommelmeyer
Cindy A. Rose
Tammy Rosen
Natasha L. Royal
Kathy Ryznar
Veronica G. Sanchez
Marilyn Sanders
Silke Satzinger
Jackson Savage
Robin L. Savage
Melanie T.
  Schlaginhaufen
Jayne Secor
Judy S. Sexton
Pauline S. Shatswell
Aleta Shelton
Cynthia Shope
Paula Shupe
Janice M. Simmons
Janie Simmons
Christina L. Sims
K. G. Skerl
Colleen A. Smith

Katherine Smith
Ron C. Smith
Jim Smotrel
Judy Smotrel
Joyce C. Sobey
Butch Spangler
Pat Speas
Hallie Stanley
Jan Stice
Chelsey Stimson
Marianne Sutherland
Jenny Swiggart
Vanessa Talbert
Wawashkashi Tashi
Elizabeth S. Thomas
Paula Czech Thomas
Summer Thomas
William S. Thomas
Donna H. Thompson
Elizabeth Thomson
Cristy Trevino
Nora C. Trodden
Susan C. Tucker
Jill B. Vaden
Wendy R. Velasquez
Janet W. Velenovsky
Nancy G. Vest
John C. Voorhees
Joyce S. Walters
Dale Ward
Jodi Watts
Katherine M. Wells
Leslie Wemhoff
Amanda Wentzel
Linda M. Westerhoff
Laurie C. Williams
Richard L. Wilmoth Jr.
Marie M. Wilson
Kasha A. Winston
Kimberly D.
  Woodring
Shelley Woodside
Patty A. Worthington
Mary Zoller

WASHINGTON

Rachel Agent
Judith Anderson-
  Wright
Carol Jean Andrew
Suzanne Baird
Blynn Baker

Sarah J. Baker
Judy Bandlow
Lora J. Bannan
Mireille Baumoel
Sally R. Bazzell
Judith Bell
Laura Berger
Florence Bernhard
Valerie Berry
James Bogart
Cynthia A.M. Boone
Juanita "Jo" C. Bott
Cheryl Bowers
Alison A. Brendel,
  DVM
Sarah Kelly Broderick
Karry Brooks
Amanda Brothers
Deborah Brower
Michelle Brown
Heather Brush
Jane M. Bumgardner
Christina J. Bunn
Jane E. Burkey
Andrea Busby
Ripp Campbell
Karen Cannard
Coleen Case
Cynthia Hanlon
  Caterson
Claudia Celano
Joe Cera
Liz Ciancio
Margie B. Clark
Jacqueline M.
  Clemens
Tony Cloud
Julene A. Cooper
Chris S. Cornell
Laurie Cottier
Dan Couch
Lezlie Couch
Joan Crane
Patricia A. Crisp
Leslie Csoknsy
Kimberly J. Dailey
Sandra Dain
Gaye E. Davies
Angel Davis
Heather Dawson
Becky Dickerson
Jennifer H. Dix
Leysa Dole

Alison Eberhard
Karyn M. Eby
Cynthia Elkins
Krystal R. Ellingson
Paula J. Ercoli
Cassandra Erickson
Carolyn Joy Evele
Greg Fishback
Sharon R. Fisk
Pamela Fitzgerald
Julie Forbes
Cathy A. Fox
Marcia K. Franz
Dolores French
Chrisy Fry
Carol J. Gannaway
Susan Garka
Bonnie P. Giles
Joeri Goedertier
Rebecca Graham
Melissa Grant
Jim Grasley
Susan J. Grill
Colleen W. Hackett
Karin Haderly
Mary Hager
Deborah Hall
Karen B. Hall
Christine A. Hamer
Jeanne T. Hampl
Theresa Hampl
Karen L. Hanka
Laurie Hardman
Cheryl L. Hass
Melanie Helms
Yvonna J. Hoffman
Joann Honcoop
Cindi Howell
Allan E. Immerman
Kathy Jackson
Jill Jensen
Dr. Noreen Jeremiah
Ali Johnson
Danette L. Johnston
Stephanie C. Jones
Tracey Jones
Ann Jorgensen
Terri Kaluza
Sarah Keck
Marilyn Petrie Keech
Emily A. Keegans
Janyce M. Keogh
Toni M. Kincaid

Lauren Kliewer
Scott Kruse
Lana S. Kuivikko
Brooke A. Lanigan
Jennifer A. Lauridsen
Savana Leffew
Jennifer Lewis
Linda Lohdefinck
Nick N. Lungu
Charlotte Mace
Katerina Machackova
Jan Magnuson
Sharon A. Majewski
Caren Malgesini
Dana L. Malone
Jan M. Manning
Laura L. Mansmith
Cindy Manson
Pat Marlow
Cindy McBride
Shannon McClure
Victoria McCracken
Colleen K. McDaniel
Heidi L. McDonald
Susan B. McGregor
Carol Medrzycki
Dale Michaelson
Eileen Michals
Jill A. Miller
Machelle R. Miller
Lisa Miller-Selthofer
Kerry C. Mitchell
Dana Mongillo
Elizabeth A. Moon
Kelly Mooney
September B. Morn
Lori J. Morrison
Cynthia (Cindy) A.
  Mozingo
Sandra A. Munson
Dennis A. Nay
Amanda Obeng
Kathi Ogawa
Sharon M. Olsen
Regina Osborne
Betty N. Pace
Gay Parrish
Donna S. Parsons
Celeste Patten
Heather Paul
Monica Payson
Phyliss A. Pederson
Daisy Peel

Val Perry
Becky S. Petrinovich
Carol Phillips
Glenda J. Phillips
Valerie Ann Piltz
Latricia (Trisha) Porter
Tracy L. Preston-
  Cassatt
Janine A. Prindle
Edward D. Putman
Pat A. Putman
Cara Putnam
Jean D. Rassbach
Jessica Ray
Terre Reeson
Diane Rich
Betty B. Richardson
Noel J. Ritter
Kathleen B. Robbins
Deborah J. Rosen
Tracy Ross
Terry D. Ryan
D. Cheryl Sackmann
Linda I. Scherer
Jennifer Schneider
Debra Schneiderman
Michelle C. Schraeder
Katherine O. Seaman
Julie Sharp
Susan Shearer
Mary K. Sheeran
Jean P. Sheffield
Susan Signor
Connie R. Skinner
Cheryl S. Smith
Faye Smith
Norma Snelling
Kerry S. Southern
Sarah Steiner
Grisha L. Stewart
Maria Stopforth
Denise C. Stringfellow
Glory Taggart
Larry Tanner
Barbara A. Taylor
Carie Taylor
Jesse G. Taylor
Ellena M. Thomas
Linda M. Thompson
Richelle Tilzer
Georgia Towle
Dorothy Turley
Stacie Ventura

Lori Vicari
Amy Wagner
Denise K. Waiting
Tamara (Tammy) Walker
Kathie L. Wamsley
Janet E. Warner
Elliot Weiner
Pat A. Wells
Julie Ann Westcoat
Alan White
Rae Wickersham
Julie Wilcoxson
Carmen K. Williams
Deborah D. Wing
Tony Wolfe
Sheryl Womble
Carol Woodward
Shari C. Wright
Cheri Yates
Dianna Young

VIRGIN ISLANDS

Laurie Keefe
Judith Kovach

WEST VIRGINIA

Laura W. Anderson
Amy Bailey
Tammy L. Barker
Kimberly Blackwell
Nancy Jean Bowman
Kathleen Brunner
Julie Angela Cantrell
Angie Cooper
Susan Cummings
Bruce A. Felton
Ann Khiel Fern
Judy A. Grumbling
Laura M. Huggins
Lisa K. Lepsch
Cindy Luster
Karen McBee
Robert "Gene" E. McDonald
Cari Messick
Donald A. Miller
Joan Mituniewicz
Patricia L. Mulkerrin
Marilyn Noah
Diane Nuzum

Karry A. Pettitt
Sidney Pond
Debra Lynn Queen
Tonya R. Ray
Rita E. Richard
Melissa Richards
Timothy A. Richmond
Shawnda Robertson
Angela Sellards
Connie L. Smith
Marta Sue Spry
Rebecca S. Stanevich
Tracey White
Kimberly Wiacek-Richards
James D. Wilmoth

WISCONSIN

Sheila C. Allen
Heather D. Alvstad
Michelle Ambrose
Johanna Ammentorp
Linda S. Anderson
Valerie Anderson
Alice D. Applin
Patricia Arnold-Mora
Julie A. Asmus
Robin Baake
Betty Badem
Richard Bahr
Lisa M. Bailey
Dona K. Barsul
Terese M. Barta
Renee Basye
Nicole Bearman
Jean J.P. Beauchesne
Joby Becker
Nicole S. Belmore
Meredith Biehl
Jan L. Blue
Elizabeth Bobbe
Linda M. Bobot
Melissa A. Borde
Karen Brauch
Joanne Brault
Annette M. Braun
Alicia Buckingham
Cindy A. Bundy
David J. Burns
Lynn D. Busse
Jennifer G. Callewaert
Ernest Champion

Deborah Chvilicek
Cheryl L. Cieslinski
Melinda S. Clark
Carla Coleman
Karen Combs
Karen J. Conell
Kathleen E. Cuff
Mary A. Curran
Renea L. Dahms
Lisa A. Dake-Jones
Polly A. Dake-Jones
Cindy C. Dasbach
Joy M. Delwiche
Robert A. Desotelle
Cory Dittmann
Nancy Doherty
Mary E. Domes
Judy Donmoyer
Christine M. DuBois
Claire Lynn Earhart
Janeen Eide
Jeri El Dissi
Mary D. Ellis-Stigler
Kristin Elmquist
Lauri A. Engness
Christine Esposito
Laura Everson
Jacquelyn R. Filipiak
Erina D. Fitzgerald
Linda S. Fodor
Sara L. Fraker
Pamela A. Frankowski
Carol J. Fryar
Sarah Garfunkel, DVM
Linda L. Gensch
Lise Gijsen
Margaret A. Gloudeman
Jodi L. Goocher
Christina Gremo
Jacob L. Guell
Tiffany L. Gutman
Val Gutteter
Susan I. Hager
Cynthia L. Halberg
Deborah J. Hamele
Andrew Han
Mary Hanneman
Jill A. Hart
Rita Hasel
Jennifer B. Hatten
Julie C. Hauck

Ann Heinrich
Ann Helm
Doris A. Herber
Michael W. Hermann
Teresa A. Hestekin
Rebekah Hintzman
Catherine Hubert-Markos
Angela M. Iannone
Karen F. Iding
Jean M. Jahnke
Deborah Jelich
Cathy Ulfers Johnson
Jolene M. Johnson
Molly Johnson
Rita M. Johnston
Stacey Jorgenson
Michelle Kahl
Debra M. Karnes
Mary S. Kasten
Cheri A. Katzung
Mitchell Keating
Roger D. Keepers
Anna Kelton
Donna L. Koehn
Melissa Kraner
Patricia R. Krause
Breinne Krueger
Heidi M. LaCosse
Sue Lienau
Carol Lofquist
Catharine I. Los
Deborah A. Lukasik
Aimee Mabie
Robin M. MacFarlane
Marylou Mader
Christopher Madson
Beth A. Madunic
Judith A. Maloney
Virginia S. Marchel
Kelly Marean
Jamie Marmes
Patricia J. Maye
Jacquelyn A. McCurdy
Dave G. McGuire
Nila McKendry
Timothy S. McLarty
Andrea Meadows
John C. Mecca
Lynette Bartelt Meissner
Michelle Metzner
Lisa Milbrandt

Amy B. Miller
Jill A. Miller
Laura Minette
Mickey Mueller
Angie Muma
Edward S.
  Muraczewski
Patti Muraczewski
Jan C. Nyland
Katie M. Oilschlager
Justina M. Olp
Randi R. Olsen
Barbara M. Olson
Christine L. Olson
Betty Jane Parrott
Alecia Pass
Shar D. Patnoe
Christin Peto
Kathleen S. Platt
Maureen Pogorzelski
Mary Ellen Pongracic
Judith Proell
Melodie Quall
Holly F. Rahn-Heim
Arleen K. Ravanelli
Fawn Richards
Joy Richardson
Pamela A. Richardson
Susan L. Robinson

Tracy Robinson
Cheryl A. Robotka
Bethann Marie Rogan
Lori K. Ross
Robert Roszak
Karen J. Rude
Cheryl M. Sargeant
Christine C. Schachter
Lisa K. Schmick
Donna L. Schmitt
Kay M. Scholl
Melanie Schroeder
Kathleen Schuessler
Kathy L. Schuh
Joan L. Simon
Cynthia Simonsen
Ginny Singleton
Cindy L. Skarda
Barbara L. Stanek
Brianne Statz
Cynthia A. Steinke
Laurale Stern
Cheryl A. Sulewski
Corinne Swatzina
Robyn L. Templin
Jayme Thomas
Ginny Thompson
Mary E. Thompson
Todd R. Thurber

Jennifer S. Tollefson
Deanna Trampe
Mary Jane Trate
Anne Vaini
Rita Van Den Heuvel
Dianne M. Walker
Kimberly J. Waugus
Melanie Weber
Patt H. Wegmann
Brittany Weiss
Julie Westphal
Kelly J. White
Sharron Lee Ann
  White
Kim Whitemore
Lori A. Whitney
Giene L. Wicker-Keyes
Peter J. Williams
April Wilson
Kathy Wirka
Barbara J. Wojs
Barbara A. Wolf
Jodi Wolfram
Nita Woulf
Jody Yehle
Laura Yurchak
Natalie Zielinski
Patti Zimmer

WYOMING

Catherine Anderson
Lisa M. Anderson
Athena R. Brown
Scott Card
Cathi Carr-Lundfelt
Rebecca Hale
Melissa Hardy
Kate L. Huver
Anne K. Iske
Angela Jensen
Harline A. Larkey
Andrea R. Linn
Molly Myers
Sandy Myers
Clara Ortiz
Nora J. Pridham
Ericka Rossman
Leslie M. Schwartz
Sonya Smiley
Annique Alice Smith
Kathy F. Spahr
Joyce A. Trainer